Foreign Travelers in America
1810–1935

Foreign Travelers in America
1810–1935

Advisory Editors:

Arthur M. Schlesinger, Jr.
Eugene P. Moehring

AMERICA,

AND

THE AMERICANS

[James Boardman]

ARNO PRESS
A New York Times Company
New York—1974

Reprint Edition 1974 by Arno Press Inc.

Reprinted from a copy in the State Historical
 Society of Wisconsin Library

FOREIGN TRAVELERS IN AMERICA, 1810-1935
ISBN for complete set: 0-405-05440-8
See last pages of this volume for titles.

Manufactured in the United States of America

∾∿⌣∾∿

Library of Congress Cataloging in Publication Data
Boardman, James.
 America, and the Americans.

 (Foreign travelers in America, 1810-1935)
 Reprint of the 1833 ed. published by Longman, Rees,
Orme, Brown, Green, & Longman, London.
 1. United States--Description and travel--1783-1848.
2. Canada--Description and travel--1763-1867.
I. Title. II. Series.
E165.B69 1974   917.4'04'3   73-13120
ISBN 0-405-05443-2

AMERICA,

AND

THE AMERICANS.

"AUDI ALTERAM PARTEM."

BY

A CITIZEN OF THE WORLD.

LONDON:

PRINTED FOR

LONGMAN, REES, ORME, BROWN, GREEN, & LONGMAN,

PATERNOSTER-ROW.

1833.

London :
Printed by A. & R. Spottiswoode,
New-Street-Square.

TO

LAFAYETTE,

THE COMPANION OF WASHINGTON,

AND

THE FRIEND OF MANKIND,

THE FOLLOWING PAGES

ARE MOST RESPECTFULLY INSCRIBED,

BY

THE AUTHOR.

PREFACE.

" WHEN a writer," says the excellent Paley,
" offers a book to the public, upon a subject
on which the public are already in possession
of many others, he is bound by a kind of literary justice to inform his readers, distinctly
and specifically, what it is he professes to
supply, and what he expects to improve."

In compliance with this injunction, I shall
proceed to state the causes which induced me
to incur the responsibilities of an author.

In the course of my travels and residence
in the United States of America, which
country I visited solely with commercial
views, and unprovided with any direct demands for what are termed civilities, notwithstanding the plague spot, slavery, in one
district, I saw so much to cheer the philanthropist, so much to delight the lover of liberty,

so much to interest even the money-spending, as well as the money-getting class; in short, I saw a nation so much further advanced in all the useful arts, as well as the elegancies of life, than I, in common with the great majority of Englishmen, were willing to believe; that my impressions upon the whole were decidedly favourable, and were freely communicated to all with whom I conversed.

The praise of Englishmen is esteemed by the Americans, perhaps somewhat more highly, on account of its being so rarely bestowed; but although it was evident my observations were often such as the latter might desire to appear in print, no such wish ever fell from their lips; nor could a single native, with whom I came in contact, even suppose from any thing which fell from mine, that in tendering civilities, or in performing any other act, his conduct or manner might, perchance, contribute to the aggregate estimate of national character in the note-book of a traveller.

On my return to England, I found, even among the population of the great emporium of American commerce, Liverpool, such gross ignorance as to the actual state of society among our trans-atlantic descendants, that I felt a strong desire to assist in removing the feeling generated during the long reign of Toryism.

Accidentally taking up a periodical, in which was inserted an article, containing an allusion to America, I read therein, with disgust, the following libellous tirade : —

" America, where there is nothing to steal but grass or water, where the spade is the only thing of value, and the land the only thing out of which a man can live ; America, where every man must be his own tailor, carpenter, lawyer, and rearer of cabbages ; where, if a man devises the stealing of a pair of breeches, he must first slay and strip the wearer, inasmuch, as no man, from the president downwards, has a second pair ; where the arts of life consist in planting maize and potatoes, and the luxuries of life consist in boiling them into puddings ; where there are more acres of land than knives and forks, — a looking-glass is a show that congregates the population of a province. A picture has never

been seen, a salt-spoon is a phenomenon,
which no American traveller, who values his
reputation for veracity in the States, has ever
ventured to announce; and it is notorious,
that a tea-service of French plate, accumu-
lated the unpopularity of the Adams to such
a degree, that it overthrew that ancient dynasty, and federalism along with it for ever."
Waxing warm, I screwed my courage to the
sticking place, and resolved to give to the
world the result of the observations of an independent "business man," to write a book which
should not only contain the truth, but the whole
truth, which should render the Americans
justice, and which should inform my countrymen, that on landing in the United States, in
the older ones at least, they neither fall among
Chocktaws nor Chickasaws, nor have they to
fear the tomahawk and scalping-knife; but
that they land in a country in a high state of
civilisation, — a country in which " every village contains legislators, where the obligations
of society are universally understood, and a
degree of information on the nature of law and
civil subordination is diffused, such as history

affords no example of*;" further, that they land among a people who, although they eat with their knives, as all Englishmen were wont to eat, before rare roast beef was superseded by beef *à la daube,* and as ninety and nine out of every hundred of those who have anything to eat still do; — a people who, because their political institutions are the most perfect in the world, would fain have every one believe that nothing American can be faulty, are, despite of these peccadillos, polite without being affected, liberal without being ostentatious, and whose test of their fellow men is neither the unphilosophical doctrine of *caste,* the fruit of barbarism, nor the possession of " the damned earth that places thieves, and gives them title, knee, and approbation with senators on the bench;" but moral worth, and the cultivation of the natural gifts of God, the only true touchstone of his creatures.

---

* Lord Wycombe's opinions of the Americans, as expressed to the late Dr. Currie, and communicated by that celebrated character in a letter to Dr. Percival. *Vide* Memoirs of Dr. Currie, by William Wallace Currie, a work of great interest, and highly creditable to the talented son of so talented a father.

During the progress of my task, which has
been protracted by circumstances beyond my
control, several works upon the subject of
America have made their appearance; and I
might have hesitated upon the very eve of
committing it to the press, had not some extracts from the most extensively circulated of
the volumes alluded to, for I have not yet perused the works themselves, led me to believe
that an unprejudiced account of America, one
free from that bane of English authorship
when treating of other countries, *John Bull-
ism,* was even yet a desideratum.

How far I have succeeded in the attempt
the public will judge: that I have done my
best may be supposed, but that I should
escape the lash of criticism is more than I
have a right to expect. And although the
elegant biographer of the Medici has observed, that the disadvantages under which an
author labours are no excuse for the imper-
fections of his work, it may, perhaps, be some
slight extenuation for such, in my case, to say,
with the great and learned Johnson, whose
language, as applied to my nothings, I use

with all humility, that my book has been
written amid inconvenience and distraction;
and, however defective, I deliver it to the
world with the spirit of a man that has endeavoured well.

If the perusal tends, in the smallest degree,
to disabuse the British public of their prejudices as regards America, and to teach them
to respect a people, from any individual of
whom the immortal Byron was proud to confess, he valued a nod more highly than the
gift of a snuff-box from an emperor, I shall
feel abundantly recompensed for my midnight
oil.

AMERICA,

AND

THE AMERICANS.

CHAPTER I.

After a dozen years, wishing to visit the land of promise, as the United States of America have been called, and having eagerly devoured whatever the press sent forth relative to that country,—whether in quarto, octavo, duodecimo or infra, presidents' messages, and all,—the time at length arrived for the gratification of my transatlantic *penchant*.

" Know thyself," and " Husband thy resources," were phrases with which I had been familiarised at school; but it is in maturer years, in the school of the world, that the value of these, as well as other golden maxims, are duly appreciated; and not being *fortunæ filius*, I was obliged to open my travelling ledger with the word " Economy " upon every page, as our mercantile forefathers were wont to inscribe " *Laus Deo.*"

The fame of the American packets is spread far and wide ; for who has not heard at least of the beauty of the ships, the politeness of their commanders, and the luxurious accommodation afforded in these marine hotels, where the inmates, wind and weather permitting, — a necessary proviso, — may enjoy their " champagne and chat," in a style not unworthy of the first public establishment in London ?   Limiting my views to a sound and fast-sailing vessel, with a sober and attentive captain, all which I found in the M—— H—— of New York, I embarked with my better half at Liverpool, on the 9th of May, 1829, on board the said good ship, bound to the former port.   Being fairly under weigh, and having waved our last adieu, I took a survey of things as they were in our noble argosy, which, like the ark of old, held both the clean and the unclean.   The cargo consisted of coals, slates, iron, salt, and manufactures of woollen, cotton, and earthenware.   Of animated beings the muster roll presented both number and variety ; to wit, five cabin and seventy-five steerage passengers, twenty-five sailors besides

the usual officers, twenty rams, ewes, and lambs
of various breeds, Yorkshire and Norfolk, two
shepherd's dogs, two brace of pheasants, a
Shetland poney, and a cat; in all, bipeds and
quadrupeds, one hundred and thirty-six, besides a quantity of ducks, geese, and fowls,
destined to be roasted, boiled, spoiled, or
washed overboard, as the case might be.

" The sails were fill'd, and fair the light winds blew;"

so that, in spite of our morning dreams of
plough boys whistling o'er the lea, of farm
yards, and woodbined cottages, all which rustic imagery was naturally associated with the
bleating of the sheep, the barking of the dogs,
crowing of cocks, and the cackling of geese,
we were soon on the bosom of the dark blue
main.

To those who have made a voyage it would
be superfluous to say any thing; but those
who have not, cannot conceive the degree of
ennui created by such an artificial situation as
that of being cooped up in a vessel for any
length of time; to be in fact prisoners, with
the chance of being drowned. Like Byron,
we found a beef-steak the best remedy against
sea-sickness; and the perusal of that poet's

writings, together with those of the immortal
Shakspeare, among the best antidotes against
dulness : albeit, a rubber at whist had its attractions ; and followed up, as it was wont to
be, by a tale or anecdote, oft-times formed an
agreeable finale to a monotonous day.

It is probably known to most persons that
the quarter deck of a ship is a kind of sanctum
sanctorum, over the threshold of which none
but the privileged may pass ; and of course
what are denominated steerage passengers are
not among the favoured few. As there is no
barrier in reversing the affair, I sometimes
took occasion to spend an hour or two in conversation with the various characters among the
emigrant crowd. I found them to be principally
farming labourers with their families, some of
whom had been sent out at the expense of the
public, not being able to subsist upon the scanty
pittance termed wages. Others were of a higher
grade, being mechanics who had nothing to
complain of either on the score of work or pay,
but who wished to visit this wonderful America,
or El Dorado of the age ; and a few seemed to
be men of all work, as one individual informed
me he was by profession a gardener, but could
undertake plain sewing, which was fully proved
by his being engaged in making a set of Irish

linen shirts, which he intended to pass as his own, free of duty, and afterwards dispose of in New York to a considerable profit. Passengers of this description find their own provisions, which they cook at a fire place specially provided for them. The niceties of the culinary art, as displayed in our grandmothers' days, by that good housewife Mrs. Raffald, to say nothing of the dainty dishes of the eel-torturing Ude, were not in requisition on the deck of our vessel; for, alas! potatoes and coarse biscuit seemed to be the standing dishes; and as to beverage, whatever might have been the habits of these emigrants at home, they were rigid disciples of the Darwin school at sea. That the majority were not members of the temperance society from choice, however, may be inferred from what follows. The captain having been applied to by a loving husband for a bottle of brandy to comfort his *cara sposa*, who complained of fever and ague, and the request being liberally granted, a score of similar applicants soon appeared, either proving the contagious nature of the malady, or the agreeable quality of the remedy; and it was found expedient to put a speedy stop to the supplies. The measuring of the brandy happening to give rise to some remarks concerning weights and measures, the curious fact was elicited, that only one Englishman on board the vessel knew how many gills formed a pint, while all the Americans answered the question correctly. How the prevailing error that two gills make a pint has become so general, is somewhat extraordinary; and although it is rectified in the tables of measures in that useful and excellent publication, the Companion to the British Almanack, where it is rightly stated that four gills constitute the pint, the insertion of this fact in all arithmetical school books should appear without delay.

After ringing the changes of calm, moderate weather, and gale, the monotony of the scene being occasionally relieved by exchanging salutes with the ships of Monsieur, Signore, or John Bull; a how do ye do, or a where bound to, with perchance Brother Jonathan; after witnessing the gambols of great whales, of porpoises, and at night enjoying the sight of magnificent auroræ boreales, on the twentieth day from our departure we found ourselves on the banks of Newfoundland. Escaping from the fogs of this stormy region, twelve days more sailing brought us to the sought-for coast, and the welcome sounds of

Land — land! were soon followed by a clear view of the hills of Never Sink near the bay of New York. Although I had previously made a European voyage, and had felt the peculiar excitement on the first sight of strange lands, yet this of the western or other world gave rise to feelings of a nature essentially different from any I had before experienced. In lieu of an old country, whose annals teemed with associations through its iron, its golden, and its silver ages, I was about to set foot in one, the discovery as it were of these latter days, and one which, from circumstances, had sprung into powerful existence with scarcely a period of infancy; moreover, one in which the great problem, Can man be free? has been triumphantly solved.

As our gallant vessel approached the coast, the interest of the scene as rapidly increased. Differing from the iron-bound rocky shores of Great Britain, the hills and country, as far as the eye could reach, seemed covered with woods, which, fringing the bold irregular outlines of the former, produced a beautiful effect.

Vessels of all descriptions, from the richly freighted China ship, to the deeply laden coasting sloops with their cargoes of fire-wood, were approaching the port, and all were distinguished by a gaiety of appearance not observable among the shipping of northern Europe.

At this time a melancholy accident took place at no great distance from our vessel, but of which we were not aware until after our landing. A sailor having fallen overboard from a ship which we had just passed, was unfortunately torn to pieces by sharks, before a boat could be got out to his assistance, the poor fellow perishing in sight of his shipmates. Near Sandy Hook, the entrance of the outer bay of New York, and from which place information is conveyed by telegraph, we were boarded by a pilot, who, from his appearance, however, might have been mistaken for a knight of the thimble fresh from the bench, so unseamanlike was this American Palinurus. Immediately after the arrival of this important personage, an emissary from the newspaper offices stepped on board, eager to receive the very latest particulars of the struggle between the Russ and Turk, as well as of the state of the Liverpool markets; for, although we only brought one day later, as the phrase is, than the other vessels from

England, yet twenty-four hours in the commercial as well as in the political world, may be

" Big with the fate of Cato and of Rome."

The inner bay of New York is approached
by a short strait, called the Narrows, which at
this season (June) exhibited the most luxuriant
vegetation, even to the water's edge, the weeping willows, in some instances, almost dipping
their graceful branches into the very tide.
In grim contrast to the beautiful scene is the
insulated fort Lafayette, with its three tiers of
fiery mouths, and, on the heights, are also
a series of works and formidable batteries
bidding defiance to the boldest invader.

Steering for the quarantine ground on the
shore of Staten Island, where are situated the
hospitals of that establishment, we soon beheld
the city of New York, with its spires and
cupolas a few miles distant, rising like a new
Venice from the waves.

On this station we were visited by a medical
officer, who proceeded to examine the list of
passengers, marching the steerage class in
review past the quarter deck. As one case
of sickness in a vessel may sometimes cause
the whole of the passengers and crew to be
kept in durance vile, every one at these me-

dical inspections is anxious to appear to the best advantage ; and it was somewhat laughable to witness the sudden restorations to health, and the assumed elasticity and vigour of limb amongst poor emigrants, who had almost lain dormant the whole of the passage.

By the time this necessary overhauling, as the sailors termed it, was completed, the pilot, who, from his arrival on board had been upon the most intimate footing with the steward and the brandy bottle, had become completely intoxicated. In spite of the rubbing which he gave his leaden eyes, and the rapid transfers of his quid from one side of his mouth to the other, he still saw double ; two New Yorks stared him in the face; and it was only by the seasonable interference of the captain that we reached the anchorage abreast of the city without accident.

An officer from the custom-house here took charge of the vessel, but in mentioning this personage it must not be understood that he was one of the grade of those who execute similar duties in the ports of Great Britain; on the contrary, the New York officer was a gentleman both in manners and appearance, and, as I afterwards learnt, he was, like all the officers of his rank, in the receipt of a salary

sufficiently large to render him independent,
and to ensure a faithful discharge of his trust,
at least as far as legislative enactments can
secure the same.

The shades of evening had now set in ; and
as twilight exists but for a short period in this
latitude, we determined to remain on board
until the following day.

The extreme clearness of the atmosphere,
which displayed the great concave of the heavens in all its brilliancy, together with the
balmy softness of the " stilly night," strongly
reminded me, as I lay reclining on the deck
of the vessel, of the same season in the harbours of the lovely Mediterranean ; and, had
it not been for the absence of the guitar and
mandoline, imagination would have readily
transported me to those voluptuous scenes.
Early the next morning, after submitting our
baggage and effects to the somewhat rigid ordeal of the searchers deputed by the one who
had remained in charge during the night, we
set foot on terra firma, and located ourselves,
as the phrase is, at a boarding-house which had
been recommended to us.

My first impressions, on landing in New
York, — and they were subsequently confirmed, —were the high character and appear-

ance of the working classes; for, excepting a few of the black porters, or *niggers*, as they are vulgarly called, the remnants of slavery, there was a total absence, not only of mendicants in rags and filth, but likewise of the class we designate mob or rabble.

The carters, workmen, and others, who earn their bread by the sweat of their brow, appeared extremely well clothed; were intelligent; and, if addressed civilly, were civil in return; yet without any doffing, or even touching the hat, or making the slightest approaches to servility to those who, according to English phraseology, would be styled their betters.

All exhibited an independence of feeling not observable in the same classes of society in England; and yet nothing like insolent vulgarity was apparent. In short, they looked like men who knew that they were free; but who knew also how to enjoy freedom.

That even more than the comforts of life were within the reach of those who toil, may be inferred from the following circumstances, which occurred soon after our landing, and which exhibit the prosperity of the working classes in a striking manner.

Having had occasion to hire a cart for the

conveyance of some merchandise, I addressed a young man who was standing by his horse, and enquired whether he would take the package in question to a certain part of the city. The young carter replied that he could not, just at that time, having a previous engagement ; and on my asking whether he would be at liberty in half an hour, he raised his white frock, and referred to an elegant gold watch !

Shortly after, an elderly man of the same profession, supposing me to be the owner of the Shetland pony which a fellow-passenger had brought from England, freely asked me what I would take for it, as he should like to purchase it for his little girls to ride upon after school hours.

In regard to those who, in common parlance, would be styled the richer or elevated classes, there appeared more gaiety of costume amongst the softer sex than is seen in the same ranks even in London.

The females, who, while young, are often beautiful and extremely sylph-like, although not sufficiently *embonpoint* to European tastes, were ultra Parisian in their dress ; for the gratification of which partiality their fine climate is well adapted.

The àttire of the gentlemen, also, savoured

rather more of Paris than London; but no
male of any class had whiskers, which peculiarity was striking.

Amidst the crowd of vehicles which throng
the Regent-street of the city, I looked in vain
for any thing like state : no bedizened livery
servants or powdered menials, receiving their
mistresses' commands, with one hand raised to
an enormous cocked hat, whilst the other
grasps a gold-headed cane, large enough for a
drum-major's staff.

Every thing here, on the contrary, was
simply for convenience; from the omnibus
with its dozen passengers, to the one-horse
chaise or sulky.

The private carriages are neat and light in
their construction, and are generally driven by
black coachmen, dressed in plain clothes. No
rampant lions, or mantled shields, as large as
the panels themselves, are blazoned on the
American vehicles; and although now and
then a heraldic device may be seen, such may
oftener be attributed to the whim of the
painter than to any indulgence in the pride of
ancestry, or to aristocratic feeling on the part
of the owner ; for I observed the same subject
on perhaps a dozen different equipages, as well
as on hackney coaches, gigs, and waggons.

As an Englishman, I felt somewhat disappointed in finding so little to remind me of the mother country. A few of the older streets are still allowed to retain their original names, as Thames, Greenwich, Whitehall, Chatham, — mementos of colonial times; although Crown-street, and some others equally obnoxious, were metamorphosed at an early period of the revolution. The name of Crown was exchanged for that of Liberty. The style of building, although in many respects similar to that of England, is still in others essentially different, to say nothing of the wooden-frame houses, which are scattered all over the city.

The majority of the names over the shops and places of business present a compound of those of all nations, although Dutch and English prevail ; but as the settlers were from every part of those countries, there is even in the latter of these languages a greater variety than is observable in most towns in England. The names of Arcularius, Doremus, Bang, Storm, Sy, See, and Van Pelt, were all new to us, as would have been that of Van Winkle, had it not become familiar through the pages of that most agreeable and elegant writer, the incomparable Irving. The following inscription, which I copied from the sign-board of a feed store, alias a corn and flour warehouse, may serve as a specimen of the various notices which attracted our attention : — " Dyspepsia flour. Bakers' wheat. Rye flour. Rye corn. Wheat. Bolted and sifted white and yellow Indian meal. Coarse and fine homony. Buckwheat. Cracked corn. Oats, ship stuff, and shorts. Genessee and Rochester family flour."

It may be requisite to inform my readers, that dyspepsia flour is considered to possess peculiar digestive properties ; that homony is a preparation of maize ; cracked corn is broken maize ; ship stuff is meal ; and, if I recollect rightly, shorts are what we call bran.

Over one blacksmith's shop, I saw the word " smithery ; " over that of another, the old English word " stithy ; " over a bookbinder's, " bindery ; " on the door of a dealer in poor Jopson's materials, " finding ; " and, I may add, that places appropriated to the sale of mixed articles bore the titles of " fancy and variety stores."

It is not, however, the novelty of these and a hundred other terms differing from those used for the same things in England, that alone surprised us. The free use of new verbs, the

varied usages of epithets, together with the peculiar pronunciation of certain words, amount
to an obstacle to conversation on the part of
the stranger nearly equal to that experienced
in speaking a foreign tongue, of which one is
not the master. The universal aspiration of
the letter H, which is heard as forcibly in the
word Birmingham as in that of house, is not
less disagreeable to the ear than its total sup-
pression by the illiterate cockney.

To say nothing about the use of the word
guess, upon which the Americans are so ridiculed, but which is perhaps not more commonly used than the phrase you know is in
England,· we heard of individuals being clever
but possessing no talent, the former epithet
only being applied to manner or kindness of
disposition; others, who in England would be
styled really clever, were designated as smart
men. I was told of matters progressing, of
pictures being fixed, of money having been
loaned, of persons having located themselves
in such or such a street; and in one instance
my attention was directed to a sooty chimney
sweeper who was, as a friend termed it, located
on the top of a chimney. Elegant weather,
elegant hogs, handsome music, handsome

c

lightning, were familiar as household words ;
and if a relative or friend was unwell or ill,
they were invariably termed sick.   In speaking of time the word fortnight was never used,
but two weeks ; the term semi, however, occurred often in combination with the words
weekly, monthly, annually ; as semi-weekly,
semi-monthly, semi-annually.

To these examples of Americanisms I may
add, that I was more than once asked where I
kept, when the enquirer was desirous of knowing where I resided; and sometimes I was
accosted by workmen, coal dealers, woodmen,
and others, by the title of boss, that being the
term substituted for master, which with these
sons of freedom is quite obsolete.   The variations from the present usages of the mother-
country in respect to many words and expressions really English can only be accounted
for by supposing the language now used in
America to be the same imported by the pil-
grim fathers and others to the period of the
separation of the governments, since which the
Americans have ceased to look to England as
their model.

This idea is favoured by the almost total alien-
ation of attachment, to use the mildest term,

to the parent country which distinguishes the bulk of the inhabitants of the States in the present day, and which disinclines them to study the customs of their progenitors.

We found chests of drawers still called bureaus, dress-makers manteau-makers, sofas sittees, cups of tea dishes of tea; and a number of other things designated by names long out of fashion in genteel society in England.

That the Americans have shown judgment in the coining of many new words will be readily allowed, as well as that they have abundant authority in the best English writers for their present uses and significations of old ones.

The subject of their present language and orthography is interesting; and those who are curious to investigate it will find much valuable information in the recently published dictionary of the learned and indefatigable Dr. Noah Webster, which able work will, in all probability, ere long supersede that of the great English lexicographer in the United States.

To our further surprise we did not find the habits of the Americans differ less widely from those of modern England than does their language. The very early rising, the system of boarding, the hours for business and meals, the mode of cookery, the viands themselves, and the rapidity with which the meals are despatched, so different from the English idea of enjoyment, all combined to convince us that we were indeed in a foreign land.

CHAP. II.

The gay emporium of the west, the city of
New York, which already contains above two
hundred thousand inhabitants, is situated at
the south end of an island of about fourteen
miles in length, by one and a half in breadth.
It is bounded on the west by the Hudson or
north river, which is here above a mile in width,
and on the east by the river of that name,
which separates it from the populous town of
Brooklyn, on Long Island. The point opposite the bay at the junction of the rivers,
and called the Battery, from its being the site
of the old Dutch fortifications, is laid out
with taste as a park or mall; the verdant
foliage of which affords a most agreeable
shelter from the scorching rays of the sun,
and renders it a delightful and favourite
promenade.

In a pretty railed and planted enclosure in
the immediate vicinity, still called the Bowl-
ing Green, and which forms a beautiful termination to Broadway, formerly stood a gilt lead

statue of George the Third. This loyal memorial had been erected but a short time previous to the breaking out of the revolutionary war; and on the commencement of the struggle it was melted into bullets by his majesty's rebellious subjects, to be used against the royal army.

The iron balls which surmounted the railing at intervals were broken off for the same purpose; and the mutilated rails remain to this day, unnoticed by thousands who are ignorant of the circumstance.

The main street, called Broadway, is two miles and a half long, in a straight line, and proportionably wide, with broad flagged trottoirs or side-walks, some parts of which are shaded by poplars and other lofty trees; but in the quarter devoted to business, canvass blinds are stretched from the shops to permanent wooden rails of a convenient height and neatly finished. The architecture of the buildings, however, does not at all correspond with the magnificent scale of the street, the greatest irregularity prevailing; handsome edifices of brick, and even marble, of four and five stories, being side by side with those of two or three, and in some parts actually intermixed with miserable wooden cottages.

Four of the largest episcopal churches, as well
as the principal hotels and boarding houses,
are situated in this great thoroughfare ; and it
is also the Regent Street for shops, or stores,
as all depositaries of merchandise, whether
large or small, are called. They are mostly of
mean exterior, although furnished with every
variety of goods from all parts of the world.
In these establishments may be found concentrated the productions of the infant work-
shops of America, together with those of the
maturer ones of England, France, Italy, and
Germany, as well as of the more distant and
ingenious Chinese.

Broadway is likewise the focus of the lot-
tery offices; which species of gambling, to the
injury of the morals and impoverishment of
its votaries, is carried on to a ruinous extent.
The present plan of the American lotteries
was introduced by an ingenious Florentine,
who, having realised a fortune by the sale of
his patent, has returned to enjoy his *otium
cum dignitate* in his own lovely Val d'Arno.
The other great streets are Greenwich, Washington, Hudson, Canal, and Bowery, almost
all devoted to retail concerns, and Pearl;
which last contains the wholesale depots,
where the valuable cargoes of manufactures

are received, the greater part of which are sold by auction on arrival; the duty on these sales forming a considerable item in the revenue of the state.

The streets in the old part of the city are somewhat irregular, from the want of a good plan to act upon in its infancy; but this defect is remedied, as respects its extension, in the present day; the new avenues and streets being all equidistant, crossing each other at right angles, and in lieu of their being named, as is the custom in Europe, they are regularly numbered, to the great convenience of the stranger. A farther peculiarity and facility is observable in the numbering of houses, the numbers being alternate on each side of the street. Many of the streets exhibit a want of attention to cleanliness and neatness. Swine innumerable roam at large. Ashes, rubbish, and other matters, are regularly thrown into the middle; and packages, as casks and boxes, full or empty, with obstructions of various kinds, are allowed to remain on the side walks. Some of the hotels are very large establishments, and are well conducted, but upon quite a different system to those of the old country, as England is often termed. Private apartments can be had when ladies are in the case ; but gentlemen take their meals in the great public room, where from fifty to one hundred persons regularly sit down at the same table.

Numbers who do not sleep in the hotels eat at such places, and assemble a few minutes before the appointed hours, in either the bar or coffee-room. The moment the bell is rung, and the dining-room doors are thrown open, there is a simultaneous rush to the chairs, and in an instant all the knives and forks are in full operation. The tables display a profusion of viands ; and although the mode of cookery is not more in accordance with the palate of the Englishman than it is with that of the Frenchman, yet both can always find some dishes, which even those most wedded to national habits may relish.

The despatch at meals, particularly among the mercantile classes, is almost incredible to those who have not witnessed it, — five to ten minutes sufficing for breakfast, not much more than twice that time for dinner, and tea, or supper, as it is styled, is taken with equal, nay, sometimes with greater, celerity. This last is not the simple bread and butter or toast meal of England, but is accompanied by dried beef sliced, cheese, radishes if in season, fruits, sweetmeats, cakes, and other items, more or less agreeable.

Each person leaves the table as soon as the business of eating is finished, without regard to his neighbour's proceedings. Englishmen are always the last, do what they will; for however little I ate I always found myself quite unable to keep pace at meals with the Americans.

As may be supposed, with all this haste, there is little room for conversation or social chat, nevertheless the courtesies of society are not neglected; and I may observe, that we found the waiters performed their duties with all the expertness of the best of that useful class in England, without the slightest stimulant in the shape of douceur or reward from the guests.

The *pensions*, or boarding-houses, are very agreeable places of residence; although private parlours, at present rare and expensive lux-uries in America, would add much to their comfort.

All the various inmates meet at table as at the English watering places; and a well-fur-nished drawing-room, with its French time-piece, candelabra, and vases, is open to all during the day, as well as for the re-unions in the evening; where music and dancing for the young, and conversation for those who have passed the heyday of life, contribute to the enjoyment of these mixed but polite and agreeable circles.

To the credit of the proprietors of the most respectable boarding-houses, gambling is not permitted in any form.

The expense of living in the best hotels and boarding establishments is, from a guinea and a half to two guineas per week, exclusive of wines and private fire.

The boarding-houses of those numerous classes, the smaller shopkeepers and merchants' clerks, are in general miserably furnished, and the provisions and cookery too often in strict keeping with the poverty of those concerns.

It is by no means uncommon to see four, or even five or six beds in the same room, and these are of the meanest description, without furniture even in the depth of winter : a chest of drawers is, indeed, a rara avis ; each boarder making a general depository of his trunk or portmanteau, as poor Jack does of his chest in the forecastle of a ship.

The whole economy of houses of this grade in New York has been so humorously, and, making allowance for a little high colouring, upon the whole, so faithfully described by the pen of an anonymous writer, through the medium of one of the journals of that city, that I cannot resist transferring the communication to my pages.

It is entitled, " Picture of a New York Boarding-house, by one who knows," and appeared during the autumn of 1830.

That it is the production of an American pen is evident, from two or three circumstances which will readily strike the English reader. The writer thus proceeds : —

" Mr. Editor,

" Do you hire your board ? This may seem to you an impertinent question, but I have a particular reason for asking it. If you answer ay, I need say no more on the subject ; but if you say nay, I beg leave to send you a sketch which I have drawn of a New York boarding-house.

" It is not intended for any particular one, but may serve as a general portrait, — at least I can answer for its resemblance to the hundred and seventeen at which it has been my misfortune to board, and at which I have paid from four to six dollars a week. I do not here include hotels, which are well kept.

" If the picture should seem to you extra-

vagant, you will recollect it is the colouring
of one who has felt deeply what he undertakes
to depict; and I appeal to the testimony of
my fellow-sufferers that it is no caricature.
In the first place, I will conduct you to the
breakfast-table.

" There you will feast your eyes on at least
two dishes; a salt shad or a mackrel, and a
lean beef-steak, which has been dried, not
broiled, over the coals. Perhaps one or other
of these may be alternated with a fresh fish,
sausages, or a pork-chop. No fowls ever
make their way to the breakfast-table.

" Along with the fish or flesh may be seen a
plate or two of bread, sometimes of rye, sometimes of wheat, but no admittance is allowed to
toast or hot rolls. There is usually plenty of
butter, but it is of colours nearly as various as
the rainbow; and after being doubly salted at
home to make it weigh the more, it is salted
again by the mistress of the boarding-house,
to make it go further.

" So much for the eatables.

" At the head of the table sits madam,
drawing from a coffee urn, and distributing—
oh, heavens!—I have not yet found a name
for it. The basis, however, is water, which
in its purest state is scarcely drinkable. Added

to this is a small quantity of damaged coffee,
burnt crust, or roasted rye, well pulverised;
which, having boiled a while, is pretty well
incorporated with the water, and thus drawn
with it into the cups, exhibiting the appearance of black broth or dark puddle-water. As
for the taste of this queer mixture, I leave it,
Mr. Editor, to your imagination. The lady
presidentess never asks you, ' Is your coffee
agreeable, sir?' — ' Do I make the coffee to
suit you, madam?'—lest some one should have
the impudence to ask for more sugar or milk,
and she should be a loser by her ill-judged
politeness.

" I will next conduct you to the dinner-
table. The prospect here, it must be confessed, is a shade or two brighter, but the
meat having been bought at a reduced price
in the market, does not, of course, consist of
the prime pieces, and, what is worse still, is
spoilt in the cooking. If roasted, it has never
felt the softening and savoury influence of the
basting spoon, but is as dry as a chip, and
totally destitute of any inviting qualities; add
to which, it is not accompanied by gravy, or
any thing deserving of that title, the contents
of the butter-boat being neither more nor less
than unmingled grease at the top, a watery

mixture in the middle, and a variously com-
pounded sediment at the bottom. Such is
the character of the roast, whether it be
beef, mutton, veal, or fowls. A boiled leg or
shoulder of mutton is rarely seen ; and when
seen, usually makes its appearance without its
legitimate attendant, drawn butter and parsley;
but roasted mutton, reeking in its own grease,
is seldom wanted to grace the table.

" For vegetables you will find potatoes, such
as they are, sliced beets, corn and beans mixed,
alias succutash, but for celery — crisp, well
blanched, delicious, appetite-inspiring celery —
you have none of it. Wait a minute, and you
shall see the dessert, which is nearly as barren
of attraction as the deserts of Arabia. An
apple-dumpling, with the crust so tough, that it
needs not, like old King George's, to be sewed
to keep it together, but rather requires an axe
or cleaver to cut it apart, enclosing an apple
so sour, that if you eat it your teeth will be
set on edge.

" A pudding made of rice and water, in
which the latter ingredient most plentifully
abounds, or boiled rice to be eaten with
West India molasses; apple-pie, with crust like
sole leather, and the apples as tart as the woman
that made it; or, if sweetened at all, it is merely

with the same West India molasses; or perchance the dessert may consist of fruit, which
is purchased the cheaper for having been
thoroughly picked over previous to the purchase. But all this is princely compared with
the tea-table, which, in the first place, is
nothing but a suite of bare boards, mahogany,
and, may be, well polished; but no table can be
considered decent without a cloth. However,
it is not so much the table itself I would depict, as the articles upon it, and the mistress
at the upper end of it. As at the breakfast,
so at the tea-table, there is never any toast to
be seen. Dry bread and extra-salted butter
are the main articles; but the tea, or the
liquid so called, is the object most deserving
of your particular attention.

" How so large a quantity of the beverage
could be made with so small a quantity of the
Chinese herb would be matter of marvel to
any one not acquainted with the economy
of a New York boarding-house. Some might
suppose it was owing to a peculiar virtue in
the inside of the teapot, but I can assure
you this is not the case; and no person who
has once tasted the decoction will have any
doubt as to the mode of its preparation.

" One thimble-full of tea is put into a quart,

or gallon, or any assignable quantity of water, and the leaves of the herbs may be seen like the wrecked Trojans, *rari nantes in gurgite vasto.*

" The mistress of the house always measures her tea in a thimble. At first the teapot is filled with water, and after a thorough decoction of the thimble-full it is brought upon the table. As soon as it begins to run low, it is again filled with water. A second pouring out takes place, and it is again replenished with water; and so on alternately pouring out and filling up as long as there are any guests to be served.

" You may then judge, Mr. Editor, what is the nature of the liquid when poured into the cups. Still on the same principle of economy, you are not allowed to sweeten your own tea, lest you should be too profuse of the sugar; nor to cream it, lest you should draw too largely upon the precious milk and water which is used as substitute. The presiding goddess of the teapot puts into your cup a bit of sugar, the size of a hazel nut, and five drops of milk. If you should not be satisfied with this quantity, and should have the impudence to send your cup for more, she puts in another bit of sugar of the size of a pepper

D

corn, and three more drops of milk, —but at the same time looks sour enough to turn the sugar to tartaric acid. But, although so sparing of the milk and sugar, it is but justice to say, she deals bountifully with you in the article of tea, and will give you as many cupsful as you desire ; for pump water is cheap, and the process of pouring in very easily supplies the exhaustion of pouring out. In short, the tea is furnished you, ' in one weak, washy, everlasting flood.' It now only remains for me to conduct you to your bed; and I will do it at once, since the strength of your tea will not be likely to keep you awake. There are half a dozen beds, perhaps, in your room, where you and your fellows may snore in concert; or, if more agreeable, keep one another awake. As for that whereon you lie, there is usually a plentiful scarcity of feathers; but to make up the deficiency you may have as much straw as you please, and so thrown up into ridges, lumps, and bumps, that you feel as if you were stretched across a pile of rails, or over a heap of cobble-stones. To add still further to your comforts, ever and anon your nose is assailed by the odour of one of those bloody-minded animals that come travelling over your pillow, and insist not upon a pound of flesh, but upon having Christian blood. Sheets changed once a month, and a towel that wipes your hands and face for three weeks, complete the furniture of your lodgings. Thus, Mr. Editor, having given you a picture of a New York boarding-house, I bid you good night, barely hazarding a single remark, that there is not perhaps in the world a place where, in the articles of meat, drink, and lodging, one is more thoroughly Jewed than at the New York boarding-houses, nor where there is need of a more speedy and complete reformation."

Mechanics pay twelve shillings per week ; and, from what fell under my own observation, as well as what I learnt from individuals of that class, they have value received; their tables not lacking beef-steaks, and other dishes equally substantial, three times a day. As Americans will not be servants, the domestics in all these establishments, and in private houses, are either blacks, or coloured persons—as all the intermediate shades between the former and white are designated—and Irish.

The blacks are styled servants, and appear a civil, good-tempered, happy race. They perform their duties better or worse, according to the treatment they experience from their em-

ployers, and the previous advantages they
have possessed. The men show great tact
in acquiring a genteel address. As to the fair
daughters of the Emerald Isle, they being
almost all of the poorest description of emigrants, it will not be expected that previous
education has done much for them in household matters. They do not allow themselves
to be called servants, but prefer the American
term, help; and knowing full well that they
are in the land of freedom, and that the obligations of mistress and servant are mutual,
they do as they please, and go where they
please. It is no uncommon thing for these
damsels to be *requested* to remain at home on
the Sunday afternoon, should their services be
particularly required. They fall into the
American habits of dress with great ease, and
soon doff their humble caps for Parisian hats
and flowers; which, by the bye, they can well
afford to purchase, as they receive from twelve
to sixteen pounds sterling a year wages.

In allusion to the impatience under control
which is so common to this class, an Irish
lady wittily remarked to me, that her country's impudence, mixed with American independence, made the worst compound in the
world for a servant. To my great astonish-

ment, I only met with two Englishwomen in this capacity in America. These were sufficiently conspicuous in their neat frilled caps, to say nothing of their clean persons and northern complexions. A sort of Paul Pry curiosity to gain information prompted me to have a chat with these individuals, both of whom I found were from the neighbourhood of Manchester. They had not lost their Lancashire dialect, nor any of their attachment to their native soil; for although they received nearly double the wages they could earn at home, and were perfectly satisfied with their cheering prospects, it might easily be discovered that foreign habits were not congenial, and that they thought—to use their own language—there was no place like *ould* England.

CHAP. III.

Among the public edifices of New York, the City Hall stands proudly pre-eminent.

This splendid building, which is situated in an extensive area, planted with trees, and laid out with walks, is of white marble, which, in this dry, clear atmosphere, unpolluted by coal smoke, preserves its original purity. The dimensions of the edifice are 216 feet in length by 105 feet in depth, and 65 in height. From the centre rises a lofty cupola, which, like all such structures we saw, is of wood painted; and its four sides exhibit handsome dials, which at night are illuminated. A statue of Justice crowns the whole. The expense of this erection was above 100,000*l.*

From the gallery of the cupola the spectator enjoys a magnificent panorama of New York and its surrounding scenery; the eye embracing the whole extent of the city, the noble rivers, the spacious bay enlivened by the numerous vessels constantly arriving and departing, the town and heights of Brooklyn on the one hand, with the romantic Hoboken and Weehawken on the other; together with the woody undulations of Staten, Long, and New York islands, and the gray frowning precipices of the Jerseys, which bound the range of vision.

The City Hall is appropriated to the various courts of law, as well as to the uses of the corporation. An elegant rotunda staircase of white marble leads to the principal apartments; but this, like the floors of the lobbies, and even of the courts, is kept in a most disgusting state, being constantly bespattered with the saliva of the tobacco chewers.

In the council chamber, which is furnished with small neat desks for the use of the members, are full-length portraits of Washington, and several other of the worthies of America.

The great object of attraction, however, in this room, is the identical chair in which the Liberator sat when inaugurated as the first President of this great republic.

Although this precious relic is merely an old-fashioned mahogany sofa chair covered with red morine, yet the associations connected with it are such as to give it an in-

describable degree of interest; and, in my
eyes, it was worth all the bespangled and
gewgawed thrones in Christendom, the venerable worm-eaten Gothic chair of our own
Westminster Abbey into the bargain. The
banner which waved over the head of the
illustrious president on the glorious occasion
alluded to, and which may be not improperly
styled the American Oriflamme, is suspended
on the wall, with an inscription over it in
letters of gold. The various court-rooms are
not distinguished by either advantageous arrangement, or elegance of decoration; and
the absence of wigs and gowns on the bench,
and among the counsel, as well as of liveries
and all appearance of state in the subordinate
officers of justice, had a singular effect upon
the English spectator; although, probably,
not more so, and most assuredly not so ridiculous a one, as our courts must have in the
eyes of an American. Justice is, nevertheless,
as promptly and impartially administered in
these undecorated walls as amidst the imposing pomp of British judicial proceedings;
and, what is of importance, at a cheaper rate
too; and I had, in the course of my oft repeated visits, abundant opportunities of proving that a knotty point might be ably argued

by a counsellor, and a case summed up with perspicuity by a judge, although both these personages might be attired in the unpretending costume of brown frock coats and black silk handkerchiefs. In short, I saw that it did not require the use of wigs and gowns " to steady our habits, and teach us to know distinctly what we are about."

The simplicity of dress in those who administer the laws is also accompanied by a corresponding simplification of their forms, which, being disencumbered of many technical and antiquated absurdities, are made intelligible to all.

In one of the courts, I noticed a marble cenotaph to the memory of the late distinguished Counsellor Emmett, who emigrated from Ireland during the civil troubles in which his talented brother fell a sacrifice to an imprudent but patriotic zeal. This amiable gentleman practised the profession of the law in his adopted country with great success, and died deeply and generally lamented.

Of the edifices dedicated to commercial purposes, the Merchants' Exchange, and the Bank of the United States, are the most considerable. The façades of both these structures are of white marble, and in a good style of architecture.

The former contains a noble room or hall, eighty-five feet in length, and proportionably lofty, open to the public, and in which the merchants and others assemble at a stated hour, as in the seats of business in England. The communications by the telegraph are also here displayed for general inspection, as soon as received.

Adjoining this resort, is the public sale room, where auctions of land and buildings, or what is termed real estate, are daily held. Here may be seen, at the same hour, and to the utter confusion of the stranger, one auctioneer, elevated on his rostrum, expatiating on the quality of land in an almost *terra incognita*, inviting his attentive audience, in the most friendly manner, not to lose so favourable an opportunity of enriching their families or friends; a second equally energetic in praise of some corner lot, so eligible for stores, that he wonders how any man can hesitate a single moment; whilst a third vows, that if there is no immediate advance upon the offer for the lease in question, he will take it himself.

To afford some idea of the different value of the property brought to the hammer in this bustling mart, I may inform my readers, that I have often witnessed hundreds of acres, woods, game, and all, knocked down at the paltry price of four to five shillings per acre ; and perhaps at the adjoining rostrum a lot of one hundred yards was even bought in at the enormous price of ten pounds per yard. The former was, of course, in a part of the interior, distant from navigable rivers or canals ; the latter in the very best situations of the wealthy city of New York.

Not less different, according to English classification, is the composition of the audience at these sales.

The banker, the merchant, the mechanic, and the carter in his white frock, are here beheld *en masse ;* and the highest bidder is as likely to be found among the last description of personages as the first.

Underneath the Exchange is the Post Office; contiguous to which is a large bar room, where, for the trifling sum of threepence, the thirsty "business man" is refreshed with a tumbler of claret and iced water ; or, should his habits be less abstemious, with the same quantity of more stimulating liquors.

In the immediate vicinity are concentrated almost all the principal banks, insurance offices,

newspaper offices, as well as those of the cal-
culating class, — the money changers ; the
fronts of which last are liberally placarded
with such notices as the following, all in the
largest and most attractive letter : —" Highest
price given for gold and silver. —Wanted immediately, sovereigns, for which the highest
value will be given.— Bills of broken banks
bought here. — Uncurrent bills taken." And
others more or less intelligible to the stranger.

As in London, a man is not under the necessity of travelling far from this focus of business in search of a beef-steak. Chop-houses of
every grade abound ; and a good dinner of one
dish, with vegetables, bread, and half a pint of
vin ordinaire de Bourdeaux, may be had for a
shilling, which covers all demands.

The oft-repeated assertion, that without a
religious establishment in connection with the
state, or laws to enforce the observance of the
Christian Sabbath, religion itself would be
extinct, is most completely disproved in the
United States of America. Whatever may be
said on the score of *practice*, — which is perhaps, upon the whole, much the same in all
countries, however different their modes of
faith, — the public *profession* of religion is no
where more conspicuous than in that country.

The city of New York alone contains above one hundred places of worship, or churches as they are called.

All sects, whether Trinitarian or Unitarian, Jew, or Philosophical Unbeliever, enjoy the same political privileges ; and each maintains its own ministers by voluntary subscriptions, none being taxed to support religion in any shape.

The Presbyterians are the most numerous body ; but the Church of England, or, as it is more correctly styled, the Protestant Episcopal Church, is the richest sect in proportion to the number of communicants.

This arises from the endowments of land made by the Crown previous to the revolution not having been molested, and the land itself having now risen greatly in value.

The bishop and clergy are elected by the popular voice; and although they are liberally, they are not extravagantly paid. The emoluments of the former, whose see is nearly as large as all England, his jurisdiction extending over the state of New York, are little more than 1000*l.* per annum. The crying sin of the Church of England — pluralism — is unknown ; as also the unjust and odious impost of tithe.

The clergy are strict in their outward demeanour, neither visiting theatres, balls, or any diversions, or indulging in a rubber at whist, as their brethren of the old country; and a fox-hunting or a sporting parson would be considered, as Falstaff says, " little better than one of the wicked."

Clerical magistrates are also unknown, the duties of the Christian pastor being very properly limited to spiritual matters. Although spacious and convenient, few of the churches have any pretensions to architectural beauty.

The spires and belfries are of wood, and are all provided with lightning conductors, which are insulated from the buildings. The summits, as in England, are generally crowned by vanes, in lieu of the more appropriate termination to Christian temples, the cross.

I observed a difference in the interior arrangements of the Episcopal churches from those of the mother-country; the pulpits being placed against the wall in the rear of the communion table; and that important personage, the clerk, is dispensed with.

The windows are provided with green Venetian blinds; and one or two of the churches are hung with glass chandeliers, which have, as may be imagined, a gay effect.

The cemeteries surrounding two of these sacred edifices, but which are now no longer used, contain fine elms and weeping willows, which, in this delightful climate, seem to flourish in town as well as country.

In the Golgotha of Trinity, or the mother-church, in which the dust of hundreds of the loyal subjects of King George is mingled with that of thousands of his enemies, is a monument to the memory of the brave Captain Lawrence, who was killed in the conflict with the British frigate Shannon, and finally here interred. The design is a fluted column, with its capital fallen; and on the pedestal is a suitable inscription. Unfortunately, this national tribute to the hero was not executed in a substantial manner; for the whole is fast hastening to decay, and in a few years will be no more.

In the vestry of Trinity Church, unknown to the crowds who hourly pass the window, I found two portraits of English divines, who, by the fashion of their wigs, show themselves to have been, in their day, preachers of passive obedience and non-resistance; doctrines little likely to be revived in the pulpits of republican America, and daily becoming less palatable even in monarchical England.

The cemetery of St. Paul's is interesting to the Englishman, as containing the remains of that great illustrator of Shakspeare, Cooke, who closed a life of inebriety in the city of New York.

Over the grave of this talented but foolish man is a white marble monumental pillar, surmounted by an urn. On one side is the following inscription, from the pen of one who unfortunately has inherited the follies as well as the mantle of the individual honoured : —

ERECTED

TO THE

MEMORY

OF

GEORGE FREDERICK COOKE,

BY

EDMUND KEAN,

OF THE

THEATRE ROYAL DRURY LANE,

1821.

THREE KINGDOMS CLAIM HIS BIRTH;
BOTH HEMISPHERES PRONOUNCE HIS WORTH.

This monument, not being protected by rails, is much defaced by idle scribblers. The propensity to scratching autographs is as common among the Americans as it is among the English, and it is one of the few customs of the mother-country which they have not rejected.

Under the portico of the church is a marble cenotaph to the memory of the gallant Montgomery, who fell in the unsuccessful attack on Quebec at the commencement of the revolutionary war. The body of the general, after having laid interred in that city for nearly half a century, was, in the year 1818, exhumed and removed to New York, where it is now deposited immediately in front of the monument in question. General Montgomery was an Irishman by birth, but took a decided part in favour of the colonies in their contest with Great Britain.

The cemetery of St. Paul, likewise, contains the remains of the late Counsellor Emmett, to whom I have made allusion in describing the City Hall. A monument, upon a considerable scale, is about to be erected over the grave of this eminent individual. The design is an obelisk, upon one side of which is the American eagle sheltering a harp unstrung, with a medallion of the deceased, and two hands united; the wrist of one being encircled by a wreath of stars, and the other by a wreath of shamrock. On two of the other sides are inscriptions in Latin and Irish.

E

The obelisk is to be thirty-two feet in height. The plinth, which is seven feet square, and composed of one piece of white marble, was placed in its situation in the year 1830.

As may be supposed, the Book of Common Prayer of the Church of England stood in need of considerable alterations at the period of the separation of the colonies; and so favourable an opportunity for a general revision of this work, as well in respect to phraseology as doctrine and arrangement, was not neglected.

The Liturgy of the Protestant Episcopal Church of America, so amended, and as at present used, was ratified by the bishops, clergy, and laity of the said Church, in convention assembled in the year 1789, the period also of the establishment of the constitution of the United States. The Preface, which may be interesting to the English reader, runs as follows : —

" It is a most invaluable part of that blessed liberty wherewith Christ hath made us free, that in his worship different forms and usages may without offence be allowed, provided the substance of the Faith be kept entire; and that in every church, what cannot be clearly determined to belong to doctrine must be referred to discipline; and therefore, by com-

mon consent and authority, may be altered,
abridged, enlarged, amended, or otherwise
disposed of as may seem most convenient for
the edification of the people ' according to the
various exigencies of times and occasions.'

" The Church of England, to which the
Protestant Episcopal Church in these States is
indebted, under God, for her first foundation,
and a long continuance of nursing care and
protection, hath, in the Preface of her Book of
Common Prayer, laid it down as a rule that
' The particular forms of Divine worship, and
the rites and ceremonies appointed to be used
therein, being things in their own nature indifferent and alterable, and so acknowledged,
it is but reasonable that, upon weighty and
important considerations, according to the
various exigencies of times and occasions,
such changes and alterations should be made
therein, as to those who are in places of
authority should from time to time seem
either necessary or expedient.' The same
Church hath, not only in her Preface, but
likewise in her Articles and Homilies, de-
clared the necessity and expediency of occasional alterations and amendments in her forms
of public worship; and we find accordingly,
that, seeking ' to keep the happy mean be-

E 2

tween too much stiffness in refusing and too
much easiness in admitting, variations in things
once advisedly established, she hath, in the
reign of several princes, since the first com-
piling of her Liturgy in the time of Edward
the Sixth, upon just and weighty considerations her thereunto moving, yielded to make
such alterations in some particulars, as in their
respective times were thought convenient, yet
so as that the main body and essential parts of
the same (as well in the chiefest materials as
in the frame and order thereof) have still been
continued firm and unshaken.'

" Her general aim in these different reviews
and alterations hath been, as she further declares in her said Preface, ' to do that which,
according to her best understanding, might
most tend to the preservation of peace and
unity in the Church; the procuring of reve-
rence, and the exciting of piety and devotion
in the worship of God; and finally, the cutting
off occasion from them that seek occasion of
cavil or quarrel against her Liturgy.'

" And although, according to her judgment,
there be not ' any thing in it contrary to the
word of God, or to sound doctrine, or which a
godly man may not, with a good conscience,
use and submit unto, or which is not fairly

defensible, if allowed such just and favourable construction, as in common equity ought to be allowed to all human writings ;' yet, upon the principles already laid down, it cannot but be supposed that further alteration would in time be found expedient. Accordingly a commission for a review was issued in the year 1689 ; but this great and good work miscarried at that time ; and the civil authority has not since thought proper to revive it by any new commission.

" But when, in the course of Divine Providence, these American States became independent with respect to civil government, their ecclesiastical independence was necessarily included ; and the different religious denominations of Christians in these States were left at full and equal liberty to model and organise their respective churches and forms of worship and discipline in such manner as they might judge most convenient for their future prosperity, consistently with the constitution and laws of their country.

" The attention of this Church was, in the first place, drawn to those alterations in the Liturgy which became necessary in the prayers for our civil rulers in consequence of the revolution. And the principal care herein was, to make

them conformable to what ought to be the
proper end of all such prayers, namely, that
' Rulers may have grace, wisdom, and understanding, to execute justice and to maintain
truth;' and that the people ' may lead quiet
and peaceable lives, in all godliness and ho-
nesty.'

" But while these alterations were in review
before the convention, they could not but with
gratitude to God embrace the happy occasion
which was offered to them (uninfluenced and
unrestrained by any worldly authority what-
soever) to take a further review of the public
service, and to establish such other alterations
and amendments therein as might be deemed
expedient.

" It seems unnecessary to enumerate all the
different alterations and amendments. They
will appear, and, it is to be hoped, the reasons
of them also, upon a comparison of this with
the Book of Common Prayer of the Church of
England; in which it will also appear that this
Church is far from intending to dissent from
the Church of England in any essential point
of doctrine, discipline, or worship; or further
than local circumstances require.

" And now the important work being
brought to a conclusion, it is hoped the whole

will be received and examined by every true member of our Church, and every sincere Christian, with a meek, candid, and charitable frame of mind ; without prejudice or prepossession, seriously considering what Christianity is, and what the truths of the Gosple are, and earnestly beseeching Almighty God to accompany with his blessing every endeavour for promulgating them to mankind in the clearest, plainest, most affecting and majestic manner, for the sake of Jesus Christ our blessed Lord and Saviour."

The most important alterations in respect to doctrine in the American Liturgy are the expulsion of the Catholic tenet of absolution of sins by the priest, in the office for the sick, and also that mystifying and damnatory creed erroneously attributed to St. Athanasius.

To enumerate all the various amendments in phraseology and arrangement would be tedious ; suffice it to say, therefore, that in the morning and evening services, the repetitions of the Lord's Prayer are avoided, thereby rendering its effect, when read, more impressive ; the Gloria in Excelsis is introduced, as well as an exhortation of the Saviour after the last commandment ; and the President of the United States and Congress are substituted

for " our most religious and gracious King,
and the Lords of the Council." In the articles
of religion, the authority of the civil power in
spiritual matters is properly rejected. In performing the service, more is left to the discretion of the officiating minister than in the
English Church; and in the office of the Communion he does not leave the reading desk,
nor is the head bowed at the name of Jesus in
either the Nicene or Apostle's Creeds, only one
of which is read in the same service.

The responses are made by the choir; some
being said, others sung; and in those prayers
where the people join, the minister is allowed
to finish each sentence before the repetition
is commenced; an example worthy of imitation in the Mother Church. The organs are
in general well played, and the singing and
chanting in a corresponding style of excellence.

CHAP. IV.

THE two Unitarian churches, one of which possesses a classical façade, exhibit much elegance and some novelty in their interior arrangement. The pews, in lieu of the high, unsightly, box appearance of those in all the modern places of worship in England, have an agreeable inclination at the backs, which, with the seats, are well stuffed. The doors are about two feet in height; the ends of the pews being finished with a scroll or arm, something in the style of a sofa, lines or ranges of which luxurious pieces of furniture they indeed represent. The pulpits are open at the sides, having no doors, and are ascended by double flights of stairs or steps. They bear no resemblance to the tea-caddy pieces of carpentry so common with us, being much larger, and altogether in better taste. A sofa stands in the rear for the accommodation of the ministers.

One, which appeared to me particularly chaste and classical, was not unlike an altar, with a semicircular projection in front, immediately behind which stood the preacher. It was handsomely panelled, and painted in imitation of light veined marble, and was elevated but a few feet above the floor of the church. On each side stood large bronzed candelabra, on marbled pedestals, between which and the pulpit or rostrum were the steps; and at the back was a spacious niche or recess, the walls being covered with fluted crimson drapery, through which were the entrances into the vestry. The cushion and edge of the pulpit were covered with purple velvet. A little in advance stood a beautiful Italian alabaster font or tazza, for the baptismal water.

The clergy of this denomination wear gowns, and some conform to the episcopal habits so far as to wear bands.

In these Unitarian churches I had the good fortune to hear one of the most celebrated preachers of America, the Rev. Dr. Channing, whose name stands deservedly high even on this side the Atlantic. This eminent divine resides and officiates at Boston, but visited the city of New York on an autumnal tour, and preached four times to crowded congregations.

In these discourses he displayed much in-

genious speculation on a future state; arguing in favour of the doctrine of the soul's im-
mortality, even from reason; " because," said
the reverend preacher, " nothing in nature is
annihilated. Every thing, upon decay, resolves
itself into new combinations; therefore, why
should mind be an exception?"

He rejected the doctrine of a local hell,
substituting the idea of the stings of conscience tormenting us. Upon the subject of
the atonement, the reverend orator attacked
the orthodox notion of the redemption of
mankind by the act of shedding the blood of
Christ. He considered, that Christ dying
for us, and saving us by his blood, was to be
understood in the light of a most virtuous
teacher setting a perfect example, and falling
a martyr for his principles, " just as we Americans," said he most eloquently, " are saved
by the blood of our patriot forefathers who
died for us."

Dr. Channing is in person slender, and of
a delicate constitution, although his voice is
sufficiently powerful. His manner in the
pulpit is exceedingly engaging and impressive,
riveting the attention of his hearers; his style
of thinking and mode of illustration display
much originality; and when he happened to

touch a chord, as, in alluding to those who fought for the liberties of his country, the effect was electrical.

Of the several Catholic places of worship, that dedicated to Ireland's tutelar protector, St. Patrick, stands at the head. It is a very spacious edifice of stone, and contains a fine organ, which, together with an excellent choir, renders it peculiarly attractive to those who have music in their souls. The Catholics of New York are chiefly Irish, or of that extraction, as are the clergy. The spacious cemetery surrounding the church in question, is crowded with tenants, and the inscriptions on the head-stones or boards, bespeak almost all of them to have been natives of Ireland.

One or two of the Presbyterian churches exhibit a peculiarity which seemed more adapted for the display of the Catholic service, than for the simple forms of the former faith ; the floors being sloped towards the pulpit in the manner of the pit of a theatre towards the stage.

I heard the most eminent ministers of this persuasion introduce the word prayerful in all their supplications ; and in giving or announcing the hymn, they, as well as the Unitarians and others, omitted the conjunc-

tion, " and," in numbers above one hundred
as modern custom has decided with respect to
those under. Thus they announced the singing of the one hundred second psalm, or one
hundred twenty-third, in lieu of one hundred
and second, or one hundred and twenty-third.
The effect upon the ear of a stranger was un-
musical.

In the religious edifices of the various shades
of Methodism, I saw nothing particularly worthy of observation : Stentorian lungs, however,
as at home, seemed to be necessary qualifica-
tions for the teachers of some of these sects.

Freedom of speech and of the press in
America are in no way more conspicuous
than in matters of religion, and, as might be
expected, every mode of faith and every
shadow of opinion number their professed
followers. Deism has, of course, its share of
public as well as its more numerous private
disciples. A society of the former held their
meetings every Sunday in a ci-devant church
which received the new appellation of the
Hall of Science. In this metamorphosed
temple, lectures on natural philosophy in its
various branches usurped the place of religious
services ; and even within hearing of the loud
hosannas of some neighbouring evangelical

congregations, the throng of shrewd mechanics, with their families, were intent upon
the wonders of the Leyden phial, or the Voltaic pile. One Sunday evening, early after
our arrival in New York, we attended the
Hall in question, to hear a Miss Frances
Wright, an Englishwoman, the proprietress
of the building, and a great promoter of the
scheme, deliver a lecture on the present state
and future prospects of society. The Hall
was lighted up, and, although in the month
of June, crowded to excess. The thermometer at the time stood above 80° in the
building, so that it required matter of no ordinary interest to reconcile the hearers to sit
thus cribbed and confined.

Miss Wright displayed the immense advantages of the diffusion of education and useful
knowledge among the labouring classes with
great force ; and although her projects of reform might appear somewhat Utopian, she
had evidently the welfare of her fellow-crea-
tures at heart.

Miss Wright's delivery is exceedingly clear,
and her manner dignified and imposing. The
most novel feature of the evening's arrangements, however, was the introduction of verses
set to lively, nay to Anacreontic airs ; and a

choir, accompanied by harp and lute, sung hymns in praise of science to the music of " Away with melancholy," — " Auld lang syne," and " Will you come to the bower I've shaded for you?"

To say nothing of the bad taste of introducing music, and bad music too, at a lecture, the effect was ludicrous in the extreme; and suppressed laughter was visible in the countenances of numbers, particularly among the strangers like ourselves.

As an accessory to this establishment, and situated in one of the great thoroughfares of the city, literally opposed to the principal Bible repository, is a book and print store or shop, where are vended the theological writings of Paine, as well as those of Carlile, Taylor, and others of the same class. It is worthy of remark, that although the press is under no censorship or restriction in America, such publications are not more diffused than in England, where more publicity and notoriety have been given to that class of writings by the repeated prosecutions which have taken place from time to time, and which have invariably tended to excite curiosity, and promote the circulation of the works they were intended to suppress.

In connection with the subject of religion, I may allude to those of marriages and funerals.

The rite of marriage, by the American laws, is a civil, not a religious contract; and is equally binding, whether performed by a clergyman or a magistrate.

Persons about to be united in the bonds, usually employ the minister of the denomination or congregation to which they belong, to tie the sacred knot, although many choose the mayor of the city in which they reside.

In either case, in genteel, or even middle life, the ceremony is performed at the residence of the lady, generally in the afternoon or evening, and is followed by a gay party, in which the happy couple are the principal personages.

The marriage service of the Episcopal Church exhibits judicious curtailment, and the husband is not enjoined to worship his better half, although the latter has to pronounce the awful word " obey." That little matrimonial badge, the ring, is only used by the Episcopalians, and with them it is generally of an ornamental description, the simple but significant English gold circle being unknown. No licence from surrogate, or even parent or guardian's permission, is required for the lovers to join fortunes ; and the union of young couples whose united ages scarcely exceed thirty, or at most thirty-five years, is an every day occurrence.

The system of living so generally in boarding-houses may be said to afford additional facilities to these early marriages, as no outlay or establishment of any kind is requisite in the first instance.

As a sequel to this matrimonial picture, I may add that divorces are easily obtained, if both parties desire it, just as dissolutions of partnership in mercantile matters take place in England.

By a late sanitary law, interments are now only permitted in the older and more crowded parts of the city of New York, upon payment of a fine of 50*l.* sterling ; consequently the new burial grounds, which are neither picturesque, nor in general neatly kept, are situated in the environs, or at least in those parts which at present may be so designated. One of these humiliating receptacles of humanity is wholly devoted to vaults for the wealthier classes, by whom the design was completed. These silent mansions are built in rows, a few feet below the surface of the ground, and are entered by strong stone doors, the approaches to which are covered with flags ; and upon these is the grass-green turf. The names of the families and numbers of the vaults appear on white marble slabs fixed in the surrounding wall ; which, however, together with the entrance, are quite unworthy of this well-planned patrician cemetery. Coffins are invariably made of mahogany, and are finished in the true French style of polish, but without any tinsel, angels, crowns of glory, or gewgaw ornaments. These useful articles are kept ready made of all dimensions ; and large assortments of them are constantly exposed for sale in coffin-shops, as commonly as any article of furniture at the cabinet-makers'.

The English superstitious custom of burying the body with the feet to the east, is not always observed.

The wearing of mourning is fast growing into disuse ; the Americans arguing, that, independent of the folly of such outward demonstrations of grief, it forces unnecessary expense upon many who are perhaps ill qualified to bear it ; " the trappings and the suits of woe" are therefore almost confined to the Episcopalians, who, in this and other particulars, show a reluctance to abandon the rules of the old country, England. Palls, scarfs,

and other funereal badges, are seldom, if ever,
seen ; escutcheons or hatchments, never ; all
these, from their aristocratic origin, find no
favour in the eyes of the people.

Interments for the most part take place the
day after the decease. The announcement to
the relatives and friends of the hour of the
funeral is given generally, not individually,
through the medium of the newspapers, and
in the same paragraph which states the death.
Black coaches are not used ; but hackney
coaches, which in New York are all elegant,
and drawn by beautiful horses, are provided
by the friends or family of the deceased, if
they are in a station of life to afford the expense. These remain at the various stands,
agreeably to the advertisement ; and as they
are filled by persons wishing to attend the
obsequies of their departed friend, they are
driven to the residence, where they remain in
line, sometimes to the number of thirty or
forty, and filled with individuals of both sexes,
in their ordinary habits, until the arrangements are complete, and the hearse moves
forward. This last vehicle is open, devoid of
ornament, shabby, and drawn by one horse,
which is not uncommonly a white one, and
the driver often attired in coloured jacket and

trowsers. The pace is usually a quick walk. After the body is deposited in the ground, — which ceremony is not always performed with that solemn decorum distinguishable in England, — the followers disperse to their respective houses or places of business.

Divested as these sad offices are of every thing like sombre state or adventitious solemnity, yet I could not witness the long trains of oftentimes really mourning friends, without admiring the rationality of the system, as opposed to that of my own country ; and reflecting, that one of these unbought attendants was worth all the processions ever marshalled by the heralds.

At the head of the establishments for education is Columbia College, founded by the British Government in the reign of George II. ; and, until the period of the loss of the colonies, called King's College. It is a large and handsome stone building, surrounded by noble trees. The number of students is considerable ; and they enjoy the advantages of a good library, as well as an extensive philosophical apparatus. The plan of study being considered by many too strictly classical, and the constitution of the college in some points being otherwise objectionable, a new university, upon an extensive scale, is about to be established.

This latter will be modelled more in accordance with the spirit of the age, and better adapted to the wants of the people, who are not favourable to the cultivation of classical studies to the exclusion of what is well understood by the term useful knowledge. The public schools supported by the state, and of which there are many, are numerously attended and well conducted. Infant or preparatory schools abound ; and no pains are spared " to teach the young idea how to shoot ; " indeed, education is considered a matter of such primary importance, that no parent neglects to furnish his offspring with at least the rudiments of learning, the means of obtaining which are within the reach of all. No youth of either sex are to be met with, who cannot read and write, except perhaps the children of newly arrived European emigrants. It may be worth remarking, that the Americans, in their aversion to the use of the terms master and mistress, have attacked those antient and honourable compound words school-master and school-mistress ; the former being superseded by preceptor, the latter by preceptress, or more commonly by the awkward appellation of school-madam.

It cannot be expected that in so young a country as America, moreover in one so far removed from the great monuments and galleries of Europe, that the study of the fine arts should have been extensively prosecuted ; nevertheless a growing taste is observable, and annual exhibitions of pictures by native artists are among the most attractive of the public places of resort. In that which was open on our arrival in New York, as well as in a subsequent one, I saw enough to convince me that there was no lack of talent ; nor did I see reason to doubt, that had the young American students in the fine arts European advantages, the fruits of such would soon be apparent in their productions. This opinion is confirmed by the labours of those now resident in Europe, — need I mention the names of Leslie, Cole, and Greenough ?—and is further strengthened by the efforts of a humbler class of aspirants to the title of artists, I mean the painters of signs, the admirable execution of which, in New York, must attract even the most ignorant. Whatever is intended to be represented in these pictorial advertisements, is not only well drawn, but the management of the chiaro scuro is generally excellent; and in some instances I observed a tone and keeping really surprising, when the disadvantages under which these painters work is taken into consideration. The very superior style of carving, exhibited in the decoration of the heads of American vessels, and which are in general the work of self-taught individuals, likewise corroborates the opinion I have advanced.

The Academy of the Fine Arts contains a selection of casts from the antique; but I am grieved to record that they were so mutilated and disfigured as to even render them improper to be exhibited in the presence of females. This remark also applies to some paintings from the frescoes found in Herculaneum, and presented to the Academy by Napoleon when First Consul. That wonderful personage made a further splendid donation to the Academy in a copy of Piranesi's works, accompanied with an autograph letter, which, to the credit of those concerned, has been framed, and is hung in the same room where the volumes are deposited. The hand-writing is rather difficult to decipher, yet more legible than some documents which I have examined, written by the same illustrious man at a later period of his too short life.

A full-length portrait of West, by Lawrence, and an excellent French bronze bust of Voltaire, likewise grace the apartments.

The Lyceum of Natural History, which numbers among its members a Mitchell, Hosack, and Dekay; and the studio of that venerable patriot and artist, Colonel Trumbull; are also under the same roof with the Academy of the Fine Arts.

Colonel Trumbull was a soldier of the revolution, and enjoyed the distinguished honour of being private secretary of Washington, with which immortal man and the present generation he is one of the few remaining links.

The principal Museum of New York is private property; but open to the public by payment at the doors.

In one of our visits to this interesting display of the wonders of nature, we were accompanied in the survey by those wonders themselves, the Siamese twins.

These youths had made their tour of England, as well as of the United States, and were about to return to their native country.

They had acquired considerable fluency in the English language, and appeared in good health and spirits.

The New York City Library was founded

under the British authorities, nearly a century ago ; but the books having been purloined and dispersed at the commencement of the civil troubles, it was replenished after the establishment of the new government, and now contains above 20,000 volumes of well-selected works.

I observed over the fire-place a copy of a charter from that bigoted tyrant James II., to whom the country was granted, and in honour of whom it received its present name.

Among the various other libraries which the city contains, none are perhaps more useful than those devoted to clerks and mechanics.

The low price of books also tends materially to facilitate the diffusion of knowledge. No impolitic duties on paper, or other obstructions, exist.

In addition to the literature of America itself, all works of utility or general interest published in England are reprinted in a cheaper manner ; in general, at about one fourth of the English prices.

In many instances, I found the difference to be still greater : for example, Scott's Life of Napoleon, a work which has not elevated that distinguished writer's fame, in 2 vols. 8vo, may be had, bound, for eight shillings ;

Moore's Life of Byron, in 2 vols. 8vo, fifteen shillings; Bibles, in quarto, printed so that those who run may read, five shillings, and not unfrequently for a less sum at the numerous book auctions which nightly invite the passenger.

At these crowded rendezvous of literary mechanics, I was pleased to notice that the purchasers of cheap books, as well as maps and stationery, were sometimes boys, who, as soon as they had made their little calculations, commenced selling and bartering with a judgment and keenness quite inconceivable to the natives of other countries, and strongly illustrative of the national character and state of society.

Immense quantities of Bibles are disposed of at these sales; for the printing of the sacred volume not being a monopoly, as in England, competition is excited, as in any other article; and the result is its greater diffusion, at a less cost.

The version is that of the reign of James I.; but the dedication to that prince is omitted.

CHAP. V.

THE institution called the Athenæum contains a library and a collection of medals, and is also supplied with foreign and domestic newspapers and periodicals.

The Exchange has also its news-room, which is furnished with papers from every part of the Union, together with those of the Canadas, and an irregular supply from Great Britain. The circumstance of those from the latter country not being received in regular files, is a serious disappointment to the English stranger.

The Journals are fastened to high sloping desks, to which the reader is obliged to stand. This system, which is general in America, is extremely convenient for the hasty perusal of particular papers, which may always be found in the same place; but is very fatiguing to the reader of debates, or politician, who would not lose a single phrase of his favourite speakers. In this, and many other particulars, the Americans do not seem to study what the Englishman terms comfort.

Nothing in America is perhaps more striking, than the rapid and general diffusion of information through the community by means of newspapers, the daily circulation of which is immense, and very far exceeding that of Great Britain.

A daily paper only costs about two guineas per annum. I saw them every where, from the counting rooms, as the merchants' offices are called, to the smallest stalls of the sons of Crispin; and often observed the carters reading their papers whilst waiting for a job, either in the streets, or in small news-rooms purposely opened for that class opposite their usual stands.

Advertising is proportionably cheap, as there is no duty on either materials, publication, or contents; and the facilities given to trade by this liberal policy are very great.

The newspapers of the great cities are issued twice a day; namely, at six o'clock in the morning, and three or four in the afternoon.

The delivery is accomplished with great rapidity, by numbers of active messengers.

At private houses, the papers are either thrust under the doors, or thrown into the areas, or even left upon the step, should the newsman's knock not be immediately attended to ; and during the absence of a servant, or of the family, they sometimes remain untouched for hours, even in a crowded street or thoroughfare. None are so poor as not to have their own newspaper.

The diurnal press is, generally speaking, respectably conducted, and the leading articles well written. European news is copiously reported, and is as eagerly read ; but no namby-pamby trash of fashionable movements, routes, and dinners, finds its way into the columns of American papers, such absurdities being justly held up to ridicule.

In treating of political subjects, allowances must unquestionably be made for writers under the influence of party or strong national feelings ; but no excuse can be offered for the illiberal abuse and wilful misrepresentations in which some of the editors, when speaking of the parent country, delight to indulge.

I remarked an instance of national egotism in one of these journals, so egregious that I cannot resist giving it a place in these pages, although its insertion may cause a smile at the expense of the author. In allusion to the English Tory press, foolishly asserting that the newspapers of America were devoid of interest, the sapient writer, in his desire of revenge, launched into an hyperbolical flourish, from which I have extracted the following *morçeau :* —

" We thank Heaven that our papers are barren of interest to the recorders of midnight assassinations, of accidents by flood and field, of the tale of strife and blood, and of titled profligacy. We reprint; they (the English) originate."

Mark how plain a tale shall put him down! Within a few months from the date of the publication in question, the same paper, among its domestic intelligence and the every-day reports of the courts of justice, had to announce the horrid midnight murder of a gentleman of fourscore years and upwards, by a set of young men of highly respectable connections; the blowing up, with considerable loss of life, of several steam vessels ; the robbery of a bank of an immense amount; the robbery of a mail, under such aggravated circumstances that one of the culprits suffered death ; the execution of several pirates, who not only plundered the vessel, but murdered the captain and mate ; and, lastly, the apprehension of a barrister, of highly respectable and genteel family, for purloining wearing apparel from the house in which he boarded.

How far these crimes coincide with the classification of the New York editor, the reader will judge.

The drama in the United States, like the press, is not subjected to any censorship, save that of public opinion ; and managers are at full liberty to produce, as Polonius says, " Tragedy, comedy, history, pastoral, pastoral comical, historical pastoral, scene individable, or poem unlimited," without let or hindrance, when they please.

The consequence of this free trade in theatricals is, that in no country is the drama more liberally patronised.

The two principal theatres of New York are of large dimensions, and are elegantly decorated and fitted up. They have each four tiers of boxes, the fronts of the bases of which were hung with silk drapery in festoons, which had a good effect.

The scenery, machinery, dresses, and, technically speaking, the properties, appear equal, in style and execution, to what are exhibited in the patent establishments of London. The curtain of one of these temples of Thespis was of the richest crimson silk damask, ornamented with gold fringe and tassels ; and, in lieu of being drawn up, it was gracefully gathered to the sides of the proscenium.

The members of the *corps dramatique*, with a few exceptions, are English; and are as effective as any provincial companies in Great Britain.

Coffee and refreshments are served in the saloons at moderate prices; and in the winter season, these apartments, as well as the lobbies, are all kept agreeably warm by large stoves. As a precaution in case of an accidental rush to the doors from an alarm of fire, they are all made to open outwards, so that a pressure from within would not produce serious consequences, as such must inevitably do in the English theatres or crowded places of public resort.

For a similar reason the orchestras are not surrounded with spikes. The audience in the lower circle do not all appear in dress, which detracts somewhat from the elegant appearance of the houses; and neither females, nor even men of genteel appearance, frequent the pit, as in Europe.

The performances are, generally speaking, the stock or new pieces of the London stage; which last are sometimes altered, the better to suit the political atmosphere of America.

Nothing complimentary to John Bull (and it is but too true that the English pieces abound in such egotisms) would be tolerated for an instant, but the flattery reversed is of course highly relished. The country people of the state of Massachussets, or Yankees, as all the natives of that district of the Union are called, are introduced on the New York stage as the rustic Yorkshireman is on the London boards, and with as much effect : his dialect and modes of expression are his own, and his keenness in all his dealings is proverbial. To outwit a Yankee is considered no easy matter ; and such a triumph in the dramatic plot is sure to be duly appreciated by the audience.

The price of admission to the boxes of the principal theatre is one dollar, or four shillings and sixpence sterling.

French plays are performed for a short period in the summer by the company from New Orleans, who make an extensive theatrical tour during the unhealthy months at that city.

One of the most spacious as well as ornamental edifices of New York is the Freemasons' Hall ; erected, as may be supposed, for the accommodation of that ancient fraternity, the Free and Accepted Masons, but occa-

G

sionally diverted from its legitimate object.
Among other uses, it is now annually opened
for the exhibition, or fair, as it is termed, of
the American Institute of New York. The
society under that title is formed for the express object, as the address of its committee
declares, " To promote improvements in the
mechanic arts; to encourage American industry in agriculture, manufactures, and commerce; and to sustain such a system of policy
as will protect the great national interests of
our country."

As a member of a great commercial community, I felt considerable interest on the
subject of the rising manufactures of America,
and was well pleased to have an opportunity
of visiting one of the fairs in question, which
was held during the autumn of 1829.

The spacious hall was fitted up in the style
of those modern attractive scenes, charitable
bazars; and specimens of goods of every description produced in the United States were
exhibited for inspection and sale. To contribute to the effect, looms were seen in active
operation, and the national flag patriotically
displayed, with allegorical designs; the whole
studiously got up in order to produce an impression, particularly on the opponents of the

American protective system, who are pretty numerous in this metropolis of the importers. To enumerate the multifarious articles of the catalogue is unnecessary, as they comprised, with the exception of china and earthenware, specimens of almost every thing useful as well as many ornamental.

The staple articles, and those which were most attractive on account of their importance, were the woollen broad and narrow cloths and flannels, calicoes, plain and printed, carpeting, hats, cut and beautifully moulded glass, saddlery, ironmongery, and the more common description of general hardware, furniture, piano-fortes, small cabinet work, pocket-books, and paper; among the coarse qualities of which I was shown some made from straw, also some from the stalks or tops of the potato. The whole of the goods in the various branches mentioned were highly creditable to the different establishments in which they were produced, being mostly equal in point of execution to the same descriptions, and as cheap as the same qualities of goods imported under the high duties from the manufactories of England. The most novel article was the pressed glass; which was far superior, both in design and execution, to any thing of the kind I had ever seen either in London or elsewhere. The merit of this invention is due to the Americans; and it is likely to prove one of great national importance.

I observed, in my inspection of the hardware, that the locks and keys, as well as hinges, were manufactured of brass, a material of which the Americans make great use; but in small cabinet work, where the locks were likewise small, the keys were of steel of English manufacture. This application of foreign to domestic or home manufacture was visible in a variety of instances, when the object introduced could be imported cheaper than it could be made in America.

The specimens of joiners' tools exhibited several variations from the forms of those used in England. The claw ends of hammers had a greater curve, so as to afford more lever power to the handle; the augers were wormed like cork-screws; and the saws were all of the kind sometimes used by cabinet-makers, the blade being narrow, and kept straight by upright ends of wood, braced at the upper ends by twisted cords.

Among the numerous specimens of fancy goods, I recognised some to be the production of English workmen; great numbers of whom are now employed in every branch of manufactures in the States. We did not see any specimens of jewellery, although the Americans excel in this article. The hall during the few days of exhibition was crowded to excess; and an address in favour of the American protective system, and lavish in abuse of the Huskissonian theories, was distributed gratis to the visitors. The feeling created by these patriotic exhibitions may be best understood by the communication of the fact, that I repeatedly overheard such expressions as, " We are already equal to the English in our manufactures ; " — " Our domestic goods are much better than any imported ; " — " In a little time we shall have no occasion to import any thing from England."

I heard one gentleman, who was evidently a stranger, attacked in no very measured terms, for presuming to doubt the genuineness of a sample of Carolina indigo ; and an ultra-tariff man roared out, with stentorian voice, as he quitted the room, " Now, thank God, we are physically as well as politically independent."

I must not forget to mention, that some careful housewife, imbued with the same feelings of amor patriæ and preference to domestic manufactures, had sent a patchwork quilt or spread, as the Americans call such useful articles, which was conspicuously displayed.

The public markets for the sale of provisions are conveniently situated, but are not distinguished either for extent or architectural beauty. They are named after the great men of the country, as Washington, Fulton, &c. Although the Englishman in his strolls through these busy places of resort does not find the prime fed beef of Smithfield, the mutton of Leicestershire, or even the hare, pheasant, or partridge, yet the abundance of good things, and their comparative cheapness, satisfy him that he is in the land of plenty.

I found the prices of eatables about half as much as those of the markets in the large towns of England. Some things, however, which with us would be accounted luxuries, are, from the nature of the climate and country, among the cheapest in the markets of America. Venison, at four-pence a pound, forms a striking contrast to the price of such meat in the shops of London ; as does a fat turkey, which will not always command the sum of four shillings. The descriptions of fish vary considerably from those of the British seas. The turbot, sole, and bret, are unknown; and although salmon is occasionally to be found, it is sold at a high price, being brought from Nova Scotia. Shad, mackerel, and several other kinds, peculiar to the American waters, abound in their respective seasons. The smaller fishes are brought to the market alive; and are kept in that state in tubs of sea water until wanted, as is the custom in some parts of Europe. The places of the muscle and cockle are supplied by several other shell-fish, of which great quantities are consumed. The crabs and shrimps are small, and not plentiful; but compensation is made by the abundance and excellence of the lobsters and oysters, both of which are often very large; the former, including the claws, sometimes measuring three feet in length, and the circumference of the shell of the latter as much as eighteen inches. Smaller lobsters are, however, preferred. The oysters are all well fed, and of the finest flavour. Both are extremely cheap; particularly the former, which are generally sold at two-pence to three-pence a pound.

Oyster cellars abound; and immense quantities of these luxuries are likewise vended from small waggons in the streets; at which locomotive shops, the pedestrian may be supplied with biscuits, pepper, and ginger beer; in short, for a few pence, the carter or mechanic has a whet which might satisfy even a gourmand.

The house where midshipman Prince William, now the reigning monarch, William IV., was wont to carouse, was standing in 1830, but has since been pulled down. It was for many years a celebrated oyster house, and much frequented by the British officers.

Among the great varieties of wild and cultivated fruits which the long summers of the surrounding country ripen, the peach and the apple are the most plentiful. They are produced in the greatest abundance, and are sold at prices which astonish the English emigrant. The peaches are grown on standard trees, and, although excellent, are neither superior in size or flavour to those on the tables of France or England, but the apples are, generally speaking, finer. Great quantities of both are dried for winter use. Grapes are small and scarce, but melons of many kinds abound, as do raspberries, strawberries, cranberries, whortleberries, and blackberries, all of which grow wild. The introduction of the latter fruit in desserts forcibly reminds the Englishman of his boyish days.

Pine apples are brought in bulk in small vessels from New Providence, and other parts of the Bahamas, and are sold at the low rate of sixpence to a shilling each. Two of the favourite vegetables for the table are the Carolina or sweet potato, and maize or Indian corn. The latter is used when green and boiled: it is exceedingly palatable, although most awkward to be eaten, unless the seeds are previously removed from what is termed the cob. It is thus mixed with kidney, or what the Americans call string beans; and so served, is called succutash, and is much esteemed. The word corn invariably means maize, unless with a qualification, as bread-corn, which signifies wheat. The common potato is called the Irish potato. The beet-root is much eaten, as is cabbage, in a variety of forms, introduced, no doubt, by the early Dutch settlers. The common English bean is unknown; but a large species, and of good flavour, lately imported from Peru, called the Lima bean, is already much in vogue. Cauliflowers are comparatively dear ; but asparagus, of the finest quality, is abundant and cheap. The markets of New York present few attractions for the florist: every article on sale therein being actually for use ; but establishments for the supply of the requisites for ornamental gardening exist.

The most interesting of such is the conservatory and seed store of a Mr. Thurburn, a native of Scotland, who emigrated to America many years ago, and who, I was told, had no reason to repent of his speculation.

On a space of ground of very trifling extent, and situated in a narrow street, Mr. Thurburn has concentrated a choice selection of the plants of various countries and latitudes; and so fine is the climate, and so free from smoke the city, that the parterre exhibits all the floral beauties in succession, in as healthy a state as they would appear in the most rural site in England. Behind the conservatory is an extensive seed store, not more distinguished for the great variety in the stock than for the admirable classification and arrangement. Rakes, hoes, and other gardeners' implements on sale, are tastefully displayed on the walls in the style of agricultural emblems; and in a gallery there is an aviary, containing hundreds of canary birds, whose little throats make the welkin ring with their volume of song.

Considering the wise precautions under the sanitory laws as respects interments, to which

I have already alluded, I was much surprised
to find that nothing had been done to remove
the nuisance of slaughter-houses, which are
scattered over many populous districts of the
city, impregnating the surrounding atmosphere during the long hot summers with
the most noxious effluvia. In addition to
the annoyance which the organs of smelling
receive, the feelings of the passenger occasionally suffer in beholding the necessary but disgusting work of blood, which is carried on in
buildings exposed to the public thoroughfares.
Having sometimes passed through these districts, I had opportunities of witnessing the
American mode of killing cattle ; which, as it
appeared so much quicker, and humane, than
the ancient method still preserved in England, revolting as the topic is, I may nevertheless be allowed to describe.

The animal intended to be slaughtered is
placed under a strong beam, from which de-
scends a rope, connected with a powerful
hoisting apparatus at a little distance. A noose
being fastened to one of the hinder legs, and
the hook of the rope attached, the animal is
suddenly raised or suspended, with the head
downwards. The arteries of the neck are immediately severed ; and the blood flowing

copiously, life is soon extinct. A civil and intelligent operative butcher, to whom I had addressed some questions, remarked, in regard to the English system of knocking down the oxen by repeated blows with hatchets, " that it was a cruel method; and in fact, a double murder of the harmless beast, and after all not convenient." To hear a man of his profession argue on the score of humanity to the brute creation was not less pleasing than novel.

The only public establishments which remain to be noticed are the General Hospital and the Arsenals. The former is a spacious edifice, situated near the centre of the city; but being upon high ground, and having a large area in front, it possesses the advantages of good air and quiet, two things not generally found in bustling cities. Several of the medical officers attached to this institution stand deservedly high in their respective branches of the healing art, as well as on subjects of general science and literature; and although the title of Doctor stares the passenger in the face on the door of every petty retailer of salts and rhubarb in New York, the legitimate members of the profession have all passed the ordeal of rigid examinations previous to their adoption of that honourable appendage to their names.

The Military Arsenal occupies part of a large space, which in the olden time was generally covered with water, and in winter afforded the youth of the city a glassy surface for the amusement of skating. It is recorded, among the events connected with this spot, that his present Majesty, King William, was one of the number who thus enjoyed themselves, when, as a *middie*, on the New York station, he had leave of absence from his ship.

It is worthy of remark, that this great depôt of cannon and arms is entirely unprotected by either fortifications or guards; a striking contrast to the state of such establishments in the cities of monarchical Europe.

The Naval Arsenal, or Navy Yard, as it is styled, is situated on the margin of the East river, adjoining the rising and cheerful town of Brooklyn, and opposite the upper part of the city of New York. In these piping times of peace it presents an almost deserted appearance, the government keeping the establishment on as low a scale as possible.

I saw in the wooden building houses two noble sixty-gun ships, or frigates of the first class, on the stocks, and finished, and at the moorings the ship Ohio of 120 guns, also the Washington and Franklin, each of 90 guns, which, from the want of protection from the weather, were hastening to decay.

The ships on the stocks had what are termed flush decks, the Americans having abandoned the old system of building, both in their vessels of war and those of the merchant service.

The frigate United States had been converted into a receiving ship, in lieu of the celebrated steam battery called the Fulton, which was accidentally blown up a few days previous to our arrival. The guns on board all bore the royal initials and crown, having been taken out of the British frigate Macedonian.

A sloop of war was the only vessel in commission for service at the period of my first visit.

The few sailors and marines whom I saw bore an appearance so British, that had it not been for the difference in the uniform of the latter, I could easily have supposed myself among the brave defenders of old England's wooden walls.

The ship-building yards for the merchant

service are situated on the city side of the river.

Great activity generally prevails in them, and the workmen receive very high wages. These last are counterbalanced to the ship owner or merchant by the cheapness of timber; and as iron, copper, and canvass, are likewise afforded at a lower rate in England than in America, the vessels trading thither are usually coppered on their first arrival out, and are also supplied with chain cables and the heavier sails.

Vessels of war are sometimes built in these yards for the Russian and other governments.

As the rise of the tide is slight, there are not any docks, so that vessels in want of repair are drawn up inclined planes by powerful machinery.

Before I conclude my sketch of New York, I must not omit to mention its fire police, the efficient organisation of which is the admiration of every foreigner.

This excellence, which is common to all parts of the Union, arises, no doubt, from the frequencies of fires, a calamity unavoidable in cities abounding in wooden tenements, and where timber, or what are denominated shingle roofs, are yet so common.

By the laws of the state, every citizen must either be enrolled in the militia, and serve if called upon, or he must act as a fireman for a certain number of years, which exempts him from the duties of either office for the remainder of his life.

Strange to say, the arduous and dangerous one of a fireman is held in the highest repute, and at all hours and seasons the utmost alacrity is shown in hastening to the scene of conflagration. The fire-engines are numerous, of the best construction, and finished in a very superior style of workmanship, being not only powerful, but handsomely painted with devices, and highly ornamented with brass, which is kept bright and clean. They have a certain quantity of hose wound round a cylinder or axle fixed for the purpose, and, together with the pipes, hatchets, and drag-ropes, are always kept in the engine houses ready for instant use.

To obviate any confusion or delay in the night, torches and strong lanterns fixed on poles, are also kept with them ready to be lighted.

The engines are numbered, and the firemen, who have appropriate dresses, form corresponding companies.

Very broad ladders, of various lengths, placed on light wheels, are also in readiness for use at the different stations. The alarm of fire is given by calling the word " fire" aloud, which is instantly repeated by hundreds in the streets ; and by ringing the bell of the nearest church, the key of the belfry being either kept adjoining, or in the immediate neighbourhood.

If the flame is visible at a distance, the signal of alarm is likewise given by a watchman, who, agreeably to the old Dutch custom, is stationed in the cupola of the City Hall, and who holds out a lantern in the direction of the danger.

The summer and autumn of the year 1829 were distinguished by numerous fires of great magnitude ; some of them, upon good grounds, supposed to be the work of incendiaries.

The repetition of the calamity afforded me repeated opportunities of witnessing the promptitude alluded to. None but those who have witnessed a fire in America can form an idea of the rapidity with which all the extinguishing apparatus, as well as safety ladders, are brought to the spot, and how quickly the firemen assemble. No sooner is the alarm

H

sounded, than the engine-house doors are
thrown open, and the engines dragged by the
populace at full speed — workmen, tradesmen, boys, of which there is never any lack,
all exerting their utmost efforts to bring up
the particular number; the spirit of emulation
among the various companies being carried
to an exceedingly high pitch. Water is obtained either from the pumps, which are
placed at regular intervals in the streets, or
from the rivers, if the conflagration is in their
vicinity. A chain of engines is often formed
to carry the water to a greater distance. The
orders are all given by the officers of the
companies, through the medium of speaking
trumpets ; and engines, called by their respective numbers, are moved in front or rear
with the swiftness of flying artillery ; ladders
are placed, and, should the danger be immi-
nent, houses are unroofed, or the parts com-
municating with the burning mass are pulled
down, with astonishing alacrity, and with such
a total disregard to their own personal safety,
by those employed in the operation, as to be
quite appalling.

As a proof of the enthusiasm with which
the firemen act, the direction of the water-
pipe or tube is claimed by the man who

arrives first, to gain which post of honour no exertion is too great; and as regards the discipline of the establishment, I never witnessed any neglect or disobedience of commands, or, indeed, any confusion but such as arose from the nature of the catastrophe.

Order on these occasions is maintained by the civil power, which is very effective.

The watchmen, who are a fine body of men, wear firemen's hats when on duty, and carry thick cudgels. They do not annoy the citizens with calling the hour or the particular state of the weather, — a custom which, in the old country, would be more honoured in the breach than in the observance.

CHAP. VI.

A T the latter end of the autumn or fall or
1829, I gladly devoted a few weeks of leisure
to a visit to the sublime wonders of Niagara,
which, since the introduction of steam vessels
and the cutting of canals, are no longer the
exclusive property of the wealthy traveller.
Previously to entering upon the particulars of
this most interesting tour, I must say something in regard to those floating mansions
which navigate the great rivers of America,
and which, viewed either as respects their
scale or elegance, have no parallel in Europe.

The steamers, — for the term boat seems
improperly applied to vessels of so large a description, — are from 150 to nearly 200 feet in
length, of proportionate width, and have often
three decks. They are generally propelled
by two engines, which, with the boilers and
the stock of wood for fuel, are placed on each
side of the middle deck, and enclosed in panelled chambers, so as to be almost wholly
screened from view. The machinery is all
of the most approved construction, and ex-

tremely powerful. The wheel, or apparatus
for steering, is fixed in an elevated chamber
or round house, with windows, on the upper
deck, and as near the bow of the vessel as
convenient. From this elevation the pilot or
helmsman has a full view of every object
ahead of or before the vessel. The communication between the wheel and rudder is made
by concealed ropes running under the decks;
and the captain's or pilot's orders respecting
the movements are communicated by means
of a bell, fixed in the engine-room, the number of strokes designating the nature of the
command. In lieu of a bowsprit, a long pole
projects from the stem, upon the end of which
is a cone something like a school-boy's dunce's
cap, but which is dignified with the title of
the Cap of Liberty. Although the interior
arrangements vary in different vessels, the
main cabin often occupies the whole of the
lowest deck, and is lined with a double tier of
sleeping berths, to the number of a hundred,
or more, sometimes enclosed by latticed doors,
but oftener hung with rich damask furniture,
the rods supporting which can be drawn out,
so as to form so many screens.

Two long sets of mahogany sliding tables,
with cane-seated benches and chairs, a Brus-

sels carpet, with a score of japanned spitting boxes, and a neatly furnished bar at the bow-end of the vessel, with handsome mirrors, and Argand lamps, complete the arrangements of this dormitory and refectory. The viands for the different meals are lowered by a mechanical contrivance from the kitchen, which is situated in the proximity of the great furnaces and boilers.

The cabin appropriated to the ladies communicates with the other by means of a private staircase, and occupies what in a ship would be termed the quarter-deck. This apartment is even more elegantly furnished than that of the gentlemen, besides having a supply of handsome rocking chairs, of which the American females are passionately fond.

Upon the same level are a number of small chambers devoted to various purposes, as the captain's office, pilot's room, steward's room, washing room, provided with every requisite; and lastly, a barber's shop, where Mungo is ready to officiate on all comers at all hours.

In lieu of masts there are light, neat poles and flag-staffs, from which the stars and stripes of young America float gracefully on the breeze.

The number of passengers depends much

upon the season; but it is no uncommon occurrence for these leviathans to convey as
many as six or seven hundred each trip. The
average speed is about twelve miles an hour,
although fifteen is often accomplished. Very
little detention is experienced at the various
towns on the route; passengers being landed
or received on board by a boat attached to the
steamer by a strong rope, which being run out
until the operations at the wharf are completed,
is drawn in by the engine, the steamer all the
while having moved forward with the motion
it had acquired previous to stopping the ma-
chinry

A bell is rung on approaching a landing
place, and if there are any passengers desirous
of proceeding by the steamer, a flag is hoisted
on shore.

In one of these splendid locomotive palaces
we embarked on a fine autumnal morning for
Albany on the river Hudson, a distance of one
hundred and forty-five miles.

The bustle incident to departure, the arrival
of hackney coaches and porters with all the
kindred of trunks and portmanteaus, was succeeded by the embraces, the shaking of hands,
and those poetic sensibilities of parting, which
may be imagined in a crowd of passengers,

many of whom were about to travel, or perhaps locate, as far in the great regions of the west as is the distance from London to Constantinople.

The signal bell loudly rang its final warning, the hissing of the steam ceased, and the vessel, on being released from its fastenings, majestically ploughed its way.

Soon after leaving the wharf, a man with a bell, after the manner of an English town crier, summoned all the gentlemen to pay their passage money at the captain's office ; which being done, we received the numbers of our respective beds.

Rapidly leaving the environs of New York, and the fine wooded parts of the island, as well as the interesting promontories of New Jersey, we soon reached the bold shore of the Hudson, called the Palisadoes. This natural wall, or range of rocky precipices, which vary from three to four hundred feet in height, extends for many miles, and is covered with woods. The sloping base in some places affords room for a few fishermen's cabins, which seem momentarily in danger of being overwhelmed by the masses of rock separated by the frost.

At this stage of our voyage we were invited to a breakfast, which seemed to combine all the substantials of a dinner, with the liquids and lighter matters of the former meal. In fact, the long tables exhibited a succession of dishes of well cooked victuals, from the English beef-steak to the fricassée of Monsieur, as well as several favourite items peculiar to the American bill of fare, among which may be enumerated buckwheat cakes and baptized toast. The former of these luxuries are eaten hot from the bakestone, a slice of butter being first put between each cake, forming a species of Voltaic pile. The baptized toast, which I at first mistook for spoiled toast, is the ordinary old-fashioned English buttered toast saturated with milk.

A regiment of waiters found that full demand upon their services, which might be expected from persons who had been inhaling the fresh air of the morning, and whose appetites were the better whetted for the encounter.

About twenty-five miles from New York we passed the scenes of Major André's arrest and execution; which events, it will be recollected, took place during the revolutionary struggle. — The melancholy fate of this accomplished but unfortunate gentleman, with the circumstances which led to it, as well as the subsequent promotion of the traitor Arnold, are related with conciseness and fidelity by the author of the "History of the American Revolution," in one of the publications of the Society for the Diffusion of Useful Knowledge; a society which owes its existence principally to the colossal and truly philosophic mind of a BROUGHAM, and which is contributing most powerfully to dispel the mists of ignorance.

The interest of this subject, even in the present day, will be a sufficient apology for its insertion. Under the head of " Treason of Arnold, and Death of André," the writer in question thus proceeds : —

" Washington, on the retreat of General Clinton, withdrew to West Point, — an almost impregnable position, situated about fifty miles to the northward of New York, on the Hudson river, by means of which he kept up a communication between the eastern and southern states ; and having occasion, towards the end of the month of September, to go to Rhode Island, to hold a conference with the French admiral and Count Rochambeau, he left the command of this important post to General Arnold, unconscious that in so doing he intrusted the fortunes of the infant republic to a traitor.

" Arnold was brave and hardy, but dissipated

and profligate. Extravagant in his expenses, he had involved himself in debts ; and having had on frequent occasions the administration of considerable sums of the public money, his accounts were so unsatisfactory, that he was liable to an impeachment on charges of peculation. Much had been forgiven, indeed, and more would probably have been forgiven, to his valour and military skill. But, alarmed by the terrors of a guilty conscience, he determined to get rid of pecuniary responsibility by betraying his country ; and accordingly entered into a negotiation with Sir Henry Clinton, in which he engaged, when a proper opportunity should present itself, to make such a disposition of his troops as would enable the British to make themselves masters of West Point. The details of this negotiation were conducted by Major André, the adjutant-general of the British army, with whom Arnold carried on a clandestine correspondence, — addressing him under the name of Anderson, whilst he himself assumed that of Gustavus. To facilitate their communications, the Vulture sloop of war was moved near to West Point ; and the absence of Washington seeming to present a fit opportunity for the final arrangement of their plans, on the night

of the 21st of September, Arnold sent a boat
to the Vulture to bring André on shore.
That officer landed in his uniform, between
the posts of the two armies, and was met by
Arnold, with whom he held a conference
which lasted till daybreak, when it was too
late for him to return to the vessel. In this
extremity, unfortunately for himself, he allowed Arnold to conduct him within one of
the American posts, where he lay concealed
till the next night.

" In the mean time, the Vulture, having
been incommoded by an American battery, had
moved lower down the river, and the boatmen
now refused to convey the stranger on board
her. Being cut off from this way of escape,
André was advised to make for New York by
land; and for this purpose he was furnished
with a disguise, and a passport signed by
Arnold, designating him as John Anderson.
He had advanced in safety near the British
lines, when he was stopped by three New
York militiamen. Instead of showing his
pass to these scouts, he asked them ' Where
they belonged to ?' And on their answering,
' To below,' meaning to New York, with singular want of judgment he stated that he
was a British officer, and begged them to let

him proceed without delay. The men, now
throwing off the mask, seized him ; and, notwithstanding his offers of a considerable bribe,
if they would release him, they proceeded to
search him, and found upon his person, papers
which gave fatal evidence of his own culpa-
bility and of Arnold's treachery.

" These papers were in Arnold's hand-
writing, and contained exact and detailed returns of the state of the forces, ordnance, and
defences of West Point and its dependencies,
with the artillery orders, critical remarks on
the works, an estimate of the number of men
that were ordinarily on duty to man them,
and the copy of a state of matters that had,
on the 6th of the month, been laid before a
council of war by the commander-in-chief.
When André was conducted by his captors to
the quarters of the commander of the scouting
parties, still assuming the name of Anderson,
he requested permission to write to Arnold,
to inform him of his detention. This request
was inconsiderately granted ; and the traitor,
being thus apprised of his peril, instantly
made his escape.

" At this moment Washington, arriving at
West Point, was made acquainted with the
whole affair. Having taken the necessary

precautions for the security of his post, he referred the case of the prisoner to a court-martial consisting of fourteen general officers. Before this tribunal André appeared, with steady composure of mind. He voluntarily confessed all the facts of his case. Being interrogated by the Board with respect to his conception of his coming on shore under the sanction of a flag, he ingenuously replied, that 'if he had landed under that protection, he might have returned under it.' The court, having taken all the circumstances of his case into consideration, unanimously concurred in opinion, ' that he ought to be considered as a spy; and that, agreeably to the laws and usages of nations, he ought to suffer death.'

" Sir Henry Clinton, first by amicable negotiation, and afterwards by threats, endeavoured to induce the American commander to spare the life of his friend; but Washington did not think this act of mercy compatible with his duty to his country, and André was ordered for execution. He had petitioned to be allowed to die a soldier's death; but this request could not be granted. Of this circumstance, however, he was kept in ignorance till he saw the preparations for his final catastrophe; when, finding that the bitterness of his destiny was not to be alleviated as he wished, he exclaimed, ' It is but a momentary pang!' and calmly submitted to his fate.

" Soon after this sad occurrence, Washington, in writing to a friend, expressed himself in the following terms : — ' André has met his fate, and with that fortitude which was to be expected from an accomplished gentleman and a gallant officer; but I am mistaken if Arnold is not undergoing at this time the torments of a mental hell.' Whatever might be the feelings of the traitor, his treason had its reward. He was immediately appointed brigadier-general in the service of the King of Great Britain; and, on his promotion, he had the folly and presumption to publish an address, in which he avowed that, being dissatisfied with the alliance between the United States and France, ' he had retained his arms and command for an opportunity to surrender them to Great Britain.' This address was exceeded in meanness and insolence by another, in which he invited his late companions in arms to follow his example. The American soldiers read these manifestoes with scorn; and so odious did the character of a traitor, as exemplified in the conduct of

Arnold, become in their estimation, that
' desertion totally ceased amongst them at
this remarkable period of the war.' "

The following extract from a letter written
at the time by Colonel Hamilton, of the
American army, portrays the unfortunate
André in so feeling a manner, and does so
much credit to the head and heart of the
author, that I cannot resist its insertion : —

" There was something," says Colonel H.,
" singularly interesting in the character and
fortunes of André. To an excellent understanding, well improved by education and
travel, he united a peculiar elegance of mind
and manners, and the advantage of a pleasing
person. It is said he possessed a pretty taste
for the fine arts, and had himself attained
some proficiency in poetry, music, and paint-
ing. His knowledge appeared without osten-
tation, and embellished by a diffidence that
rarely accompanies so many talents and accomplishments, which left you to suppose more
than appeared. His sentiments were elevated,
and inspired esteem : they had a softness that
conciliated affection. His elocution was
handsome ; his address easy, polite, and
insinuating.

" By his merit he had acquired the unlimited confidence of his general, and was making rapid progress in military rank and reputation. But in the height of his career, flushed with new hopes from the execution of a project the most beneficial to his party that could be devised, he is at once precipitated from the summit of prosperity, sees all the expectations of his ambition blasted, and himself ruined."

The remains of Major André were interred on the spot where he suffered. But a few years ago they were exhumed by order of the British Government, brought to England, and recommitted to the dust in the sacred precincts of Westminster Abbey. A ridiculous story has been circulated in America, that the remains were deposited in the royal vault at Windsor, and that a large cypress-tree, which had twined its roots round the skull, was transplanted to the gardens of the Castle. How this tree, which was, perhaps, of fifty years' growth, was conveyed alive across the Atlantic, I could not learn.

Before I close this digression on the subject of André, I may mention, as a further instance of the feelings of the Americans towards him, that the daughter of one of the captors, with whom we had the pleasure to become

I

acquainted, assured me that her father never mentioned the name without painful sensations.

A little farther, on the left bank of the river, is the great state prison of Mount Pleasant, or Sing Sing, as it is termed from the neighbouring village. This immense structure, which is of a quadrangular form, is built of a coarse-grained white marble, procured on the spot by the convicts themselves.

It contains 800 cells, besides a chapel, and all the necessary apartments and work-shops of the establishment. The principle kept in view, in respect to its unhappy inmates, is their reformation, and restoration to society; to effect which, a system of moral instruction is combined with the pursuit of various handicraft trades; and, as a terror to evildoers, the whole is carried on under the efficacious but terrible discipline of solitary confinement.

The periods of imprisonment, of course, vary according to the crime. They are generally from two to ten years; sometimes even longer; but their duration may be lessened, according to the deportment or apparent promise of amendment of life in the culprit.

The punishment of death is only applicable in America to murder in the first degree, or what in England is termed wilful murder; to arson, and robbing the mails under aggravated circumstances; but I was happy to find a growing opinion amongst the most enlightened persons of that country, that it ought, even in these cases, to be abolished. The sentiments of the wisest and best men of the age are opposed to its continuance. The excellent Lafayette, in a speech delivered by him in the Chamber of Deputies, on the subject of the motion of M. de Tracy for the abolishment of the punishment of death, thus emphatically expresses himself: — "Je persisterai à la demander tant qu'on ne m'aura pas prouvé l'infaillibilité des jugemens humains:" — "I shall persist in demanding it (this abolition) until human judgments are proved infallible."

The sensible Count De St. Leu also, a member of the talented family of Bonaparte, in his clever little work, entitled, "A Reply to Sir Walter Scott's History of Napoleon," which he justly styles "a vast libel upon the glories of France and Napoleon," has the following condensed and sublime sentiment: — "War and the pain of death, which society draws down upon itself, are but organised barbarisms; an inheritance of the savage state, disguised or ornamented by ingenious institutions and false eloquence."

Though last, not least in value, is the opinion of the late venerable historian of the Medici, Roscoe, who, in a conversation I had the honour to enjoy with that illustrious philanthropist a few days previous to my departure for America, in which I mentioned the proposal then recently made in that country, that executions should take place in the prisons, in lieu of making them public spectacles, thus expressed himself, " There should not be executions at all."

So admirable is the management of the prison of Sing Sing, and the other great prisons of the United States, that, in lieu of convicts being a grievous tax upon the community, as in England, the labour of the prisoners serves not only to cover the expenses of the establishments, but in some instances yields a surplus.

The river, which had varied from one to four miles in width, and exhibited on its banks fertile and populous districts, suddenly became narrower, as we entered the passage through the highlands.

The scenery, for some miles, became bold and grand ; the hills rising from their rocky bases in the water to a thousand, and even fifteen hundred feet in height.

We stopped for a short time at West Point, the scene of numerous revolutionary recollections, and now the seat of the United States Military Academy,—

" The nursery of men for future years."

The patriot Kosciusko resided for some time at this spot; and a small garden is shown, once cultivated by the hero's own hands, and in which he was wont to ruminate upon the oppressions of his unfortunate country.

From the termination of the highlands, the river again widens; and we passed a succession of thriving villages, as well as handsome country seats; among the former of which was Hudson, the site of some very extensive calico printing works. Although this place is situated 120 miles from the sea, it is accessible to vessels of large burden; and several ships sail from thence to the whale fisheries of the Pacific Ocean. The bold outlines of the Kaatskill Mountains on our left were picturesque objects during the remainder of the day, at the close of which we landed at Albany,

I 3

the capital of the state of New York. The fare for the whole distance of 145 miles, including the breakfast alluded to, as well as dinner and tea in a corresponding style, was only four shillings and sixpence sterling each person; but this, it must be stated, was considerably below the usual price, on account of the opposition among the steam navigation proprietors at the time.

We soon found ourselves comfortably lodged at an excellent hotel, and retired to rest full of reflections upon the revolutions produced by the power and application of steam. The distance we had so easily and agreeably accomplished in one day was formerly the labour of a week, or even a fortnight.

Albany is one of the oldest settlements in the country, having been founded by the Dutch above two centuries; and we noticed several houses yet standing, built of bricks brought from Holland, and bearing the dates of their erection in rude ornamental iron-work on their lofty pediments. From a comparatively insignificant place, it has become a populous city, its trade having rapidly increased since the introduction of steam navigation, and the opening of the great western and northern canals, for both which it is the entrepôt. The capitol, or state house, is a handsome building, and is finely situated, being on an eminence, and at the extremity of a long and wide street. The interior is conveniently arranged for the meetings of the legislature, as well as for the superior courts of justice. It likewise contains the state library. The public seminary is a spacious edifice, and accommodates 200 students.

CHAP. VII.

It was our intention to have proceeded from Albany by the canal; but in consequence of its circuitous course to Schenectady, the second town on the line, and the number of locks which intervene, the packets start from that place, the passengers being conveyed thither in stage coaches. The distance is sixteen miles through an uninteresting country, and over a partially and badly macadamized road; nevertheless, we performed the journey in about two hours.

There was no " Please to remember the chambermaid! please to remember the waiter!" when we left the hall of the hotel, nor even, in the voice of humility itself, any " Please to remember the porter!" when we were seated in the coach, and the luggage properly fastened behind. Each and all of these personages, who had performed their respective duties, were well paid by their employers; and although they might, with the Quaker in the play, think there was no harm in a guinea, nor would they, perhaps, have rejected a douceur, they would not degrade themselves by begging as mendicants.

The stage which called for the passengers at the hotel was a roomy vehicle, holding eight or nine persons comfortably. The upper part of the sides was of painted canvass, which is either rolled up or let down, according to the weather. The luggage, or baggage as it is more commonly called, was stowed behind; and the whole rested upon strong leather straps placed laterally in the manner of the old French diligences. There were no outside seats, except one next to the coachman.

This last-mentioned personage, who was exceedingly friendly as well as attentive, bore no resemblance to the fraternity in England, either as to rotundity or the envelopes of his person; in short, his profession could not have been recognized by external appearances; and at the end of the stage he did not ask for or receive a fee, but politely wished the passengers good morning.

The horses were strong and fleet, and their harness as simple in its construction as it was devoid of ornament.

On our arrival in Schenectady, I was not a little surprised to hear myself loudly called by name; but the mystery was soon explained by a polite message from Judge H——, with a request that we would join himself and lady in the packet in which they were about to proceed. These worthy individuals had sailed up the Hudson in the same steamer as ourselves; and in the course of the promiscuous conversation which arises when numbers are so associated, had learnt our surname, and the object of our excursion. Having passed us as we were entering the stage at Albany, and having arrived first at Schenectady, they had stationed the messenger in question to await our arrival, and tender the invitation.

Our worthy friend's civilities did not even stop here; for after two more days of agreeable travelling in their company, we were entreated to pay them a visit at their residence; and it was with feelings of regret that circumstances prevented our acceptance of their hospitality, which was the more valuable, because it was perfectly disinterested. I mention this as the first of a series of similar instances of politeness and kind feeling which we experienced in travelling in the United States, the recollection of which will never be weakened by time or distance. Schenectady is situated upon the great river Mohawk, on the site of an old Dutch settlement; but it is only within these few years that it has become a place of much importance. It now possesses a college with two hundred students, who are well boarded, and instructed in classical and useful knowledge, for thirty pounds sterling per annum each.

The hotels are commodious, and very well kept. That at which we stopped to dine could readily accommodate about a hundred guests.

The packet-boats on the canal are eighty feet in length and fourteen feet in breadth. Handsomely furnished cabins occupy the whole length, except a space at the bow for the heavy baggage, and a kitchen and berths for the crew at the stern. They are drawn by three horses; and being provided with lamps, travel day and night at the speed of four miles an hour. The charge is twopence per mile for each passenger, excellent board included, and you eat, drink, read, or chat, play whist or draughts; in short, do as you like.

In one of these agreeable conveyances we pursued our route, which was rendered intensely interesting from the novelties which presented themselves in succession. There were about thirty passengers on board, and at

seven o'clock we were summoned to tea, or
supper, as it was called. There, as in the
steamer, on the Hudson, the females were
ranged on one side at the upper end of the
table before the signal was given to the gentlemen, the seats opposite them being reserved
for their husbands, or travelling protectors,
each for each.

There was a formality in this arrangement
not very inviting; and yet, upon the whole,
it was perhaps the best that could be devised
for the comfort of those for whom it was intended. The ladies chiefly sat in their own
apartment, which was in the day time open to
that of the gentlemen. At nine the order
was given to prepare the beds, when a trans-
formation took place not unlike those exhibited
in pantomimes. A screen or painted drop-
curtain fell between the two cabins, and the
ladies were left with their female attendants.

The benches along the great cabin were
opened and formed into beds; another range
of cots were suspended like so many shelves
above; and by an arrangement of light frame-
work there were three long tiers of berths in
the centre. All these were supplied with
clean bedding; and the whole in a few minutes
had a most unique appearance. The choice

of beds was determined by the priority of
the names in the captain's book, the early
entry in which I found in a crowded boat was
of importance ; and here our friend the Judge
rendered us essential service.

The strangeness of the scene kept me
awake for some time after, as the sailors say,
" turning in ;" but, had I been an American,
I might have attributed the anti-drowsy feeling to the circumstance of the blankets
bearing the ominous mark of a crown, with
the initials G. R.   How these royal comforts
found their way thither I could not decide :
be this as it may, they were of the very
best quality, and the democratic republicans
snored between them most melodiously.

Anxious to view the scenery of the pass
of the Mohawk, called Little Falls, I arose
even before dawn of day. The canal, for
upwards of 100 miles, follows the course of
that noble river, of which beautiful views are
obtained. At the point in question, where
the latter flows through a branch of the Al-
leghany chain, the canal is carried by means
of locks and embankments, or through exca-
vations in the rocky precipices, on the margin
of the torrent, which pursues its rapid and
broken course in wild grandeur.

The scene strongly reminded me of some of the approaches to the Alps.

Beyond this romantic pass the country gradually opened and displayed high cultivation; but dear hawthorn hedges for the division of the land were ill supplied by the rough uncouth snake fences of the American farms, to say nothing of the black burnt stumps of trees which remain thickly studded over the country like so many monuments of the native forests.

Whilst musing on the varying scene, the welcome sound of breakfast saluted my ears, and I hastened to the again transformed chamber, which, of its late occupation, left not " a wreck behind." We reached Utica, the first of the hundred classically named mushroom villages on this route.

By the term " village" must not, however, be understood any thing like the sequestered nooks of England, where the venerable ivy-grown Gothic church and spire, the trim parsonage with its parterre and its honeysuckles, the snug ale-house and its swinging sign, displaying the many-quartered shield of the lord of the soil, the winding but well macadamised road, bordered by humble white-washed cottages, with their blacked oak frame-work, combine

to form a picture as captivating as it is soothing and poetical. No such scenes await the
traveller in America, where every thing is of
yesterday, and planned by active spirits with
utility and profit for their motto.

Utica, although denominated a village, is
a considerable town, containing not less than
10,000 inhabitants. Its streets are straight
and wide, and the edifices mostly of brick.
We saw several large hotels, six or eight
churches, and many spacious stores. There
are a number of cotton and other manufactories in the neighbourhood, which is populous;
and I was informed by an English settler,
whom I met at the hotel, and who had resided
in Utica several years, that the whole district
was extremely fertile, and agriculture and
trade generally in a most flourishing condition.

This individual closed his remarks in the
following emphatic words: — " Sir, you little
know in England the power of this country."

At Utica, we changed packet boats, and
proceeded on the line to Rochester.

We passed among a succession of places
of minor importance, — Rome, Syracuse,
Canton, Jordan, Byron, Montezuma, Lyons,
and Palmyra; all flourishing villages, but
bearing no more resemblance to the ori-

ginal cities from which several derive their titles, than the meanest hovel to Windsor Castle.

They are chiefly built of wood, and the edifices painted white, or often yellow; and the churches have cupolas or spires of the same material, with green Venetian blinds, or weather-boards, in the steeple windows; all looking very neat, certainly, but at the same time most unpicturesque.

Rome stands near the site of a colonial fort, the scene of some fighting in the war of the revolution; and further celebrated from a successful stratagem of the American General Arnold, by which the British commander was so duped and panic-struck as to give up his undertaking, and make a retreat.

The latter was commenced with such rapidity, that the viands under preparation for the officers' mess on the same day were abandoned to the enemy; a veteran of which, now living, assured me that he never relished a dinner more; for, independent of their excellence, he, with his comrades, had been for some time on what are called short commons.

The country displayed patches of cleared and cultivated land, here and there sprinkled with the primitive log cabins of the wood clearers, or the frame-houses of the settlers; the former being admirably in keeping with the surrounding scenery.

A great portion, however, was almost impenetrable forest; and the banks of the canal all along exhibited the novel spectacle of huge trees felled, half-burnt, or broken, lying, as it were, in ruins, and in majestic confusion; while eagles and other birds of prey, hovering about, gave additional wildness to the scene.

Among the most striking parts of the line were the marshes of Montezuma, through which the canal passes, the towing-path being carried near three miles on a timber bridge; and the great embankment of the Irondequoit, which is carried two miles, at the height of seventy feet above the surrounding country.

Rochester, which we reached at noon on the third day, is in some respects the most wonderful place on the face of the globe. It was only founded twenty years ago, previous to which the country was a perfect wilderness.

In 1815, the population but consisted of about three hundred persons; whilst in the year 1829, at the period of our visit, it had risen to thirteen thousand, and was rapidly progressing.

K

The local advantages of Rochester are very conspicuous. Seated upon the fine river Genesee, which flows through a fertile country, and is navigable for barges nearly one hundred miles above, and for sloops from Lake Ontario, seven miles below, to within two of the town, intersected by the great western canal; possessing in abundance what the Americans denominate " hydraulic privileges," but what in plain English would be termed inexhaustible water power : it is destined to become a place of great importance.

The flour, or, as they are called, flouring, mills, are numerous, and several of them are erected upon a most extensive scale; one of these immense structures containing more than four acres of flooring. They were all in full operation, and are a source of much wealth to the place.

I was informed that more than twelve thousand bushels of wheat were daily ground in these mills. The produce is chiefly sent to New York; but should the Montreal or Quebec markets offer inducements, the facilities of transport to those places are now very great, the water communication being perfected by the completion of the Rideau canal in Canada.

The streets and public buildings are upon a handsome scale; and besides a number of large churches, banks, hotels, and other erections of an ornamental nature, Rochester has its athenæum, museum, and other scientific institutions.

The most singular feature of this bustling infant town is the condition of the environs, which are still very much in a state of nature.

The transition from a crowded street to the ruins of the forest, or to the forest itself, is so sudden, that a stranger, by turning a wrong corner in the dark, might either be in danger of breaking his neck over the enormous stumps of trees, which, as yet, there has been no time to clear away; or, escaping that calamity, might soon be entangled in the labyrinth of wood which environs this unparalleled place.

Amidst all this grinding of corn, shipping of flour, unpacking and retailing of manufactures, felling of trees, and building of houses, we found the refinements of life were not neglected. Music was taught to all the young misses, as young females in the sphere of society above the labouring classes are styled; and, in a ball-room over the apartment in which we dined at the hotel, Monsieur was giving lessons to a number of pupils in the art of " tripping on the light fantastic toe." The sensations produced by hearing sounds associated with the most polished life, in view of the labours of the pioneer of the forest, would not be easy to describe; suffice it to say, I more than once found myself in a prospective reverie, excited by the strangeness of the scene.

At Rochester we removed to a third boat, and, crossing the river Genesee by a handsome stone aqueduct of eleven arches of fifty feet span, we pursued our route. From hence to Lockport, near sixty miles, settlements seemed more rare; and we sailed for many miles through dense forests, —all, however, destined at an early period to the unsparing axe or the devouring flame. At Lockport the canal is carried up what is called the mountain ridge, to the height of sixty feet, by a double set of five locks. One set is used for boats ascending, and the other for those descending. The whole of this stupendous work is finished in the most durable and scientific manner; and the scene, from the number of boats passing through the locks, is extremely animated.

This rise of the canal is succeeded by a deep cutting of three miles, through limestone rock, at the depth of twenty to thirty feet, and soon after the canal enters a creek which flows into the Niagara river, near a place called Tonnewanta, twelve miles farther, and opposite Grand Island.

Here we arrived soon after breakfast, and bade adieu to our friends in the packet, which proceeded to Buffalo on Lake Erie, a distance of eleven miles. The whole length of the Erie canal is three hundred and sixty-three miles. It has eighty-three locks, and eighteen aqueducts of various dimensions, and also several branches, some of which are twenty to forty miles in length. The longest level is about seventy miles, and the height of the waters of Lake Erie above those of the Hudson river is five hundred and sixty-eight feet. This grand work, which was projected by the late De Witt Clinton, the Bridgewater of America, was commenced in 1817, and finished in the year 1825, at a cost of about seven millions of dollars. The traffic upon this canal is yearly and rapidly increasing: indeed, we met or passed trading boats along the whole line, in great numbers ; and although all the boats are by law obliged to carry lamps, yet, from carelessness or obstinacy, the concussions at meeting in the night were sometimes very disagreeable. The same observation applies

to passing through the locks ; but perhaps the
nuisance in this latter case is unavoidable.
The expense of travelling by the second class
of boats, by which the foreign emigrants are
conveyed, is only one penny per mile, for
which they are bountifully fed.

The sociable style of American travelling
easily admits of the formation of intimacies,
and these in many instances soon ripen into
friendships. We had an agreeable proof of
this in the tour in question ; for soon after
leaving Schenectady we were joined by a medical gentleman from Philadelphia, whose ardent love of knowledge can only be appreciated
by those who have witnessed his devotedness
to its pursuit ; — need I name to the American
reader that distinguished naturalist, Doctor
Harlan ? Finding, from casual conversation at
an early period after our meeting, that the objects of our journey were, to a certain extent,
the same, we soon decided upon visiting the
great natural wonder of the western world in
company.

Tonnewanta is the nearest point of the canal
to Niagara, being only distant from thence
eleven miles. Here we engaged a small light
wagon, with young and sprightly horses and
driver ; and, trotting merrily through woods

and wilds, with ever and anon a jolt over a
decaying stump, and a drag through a slough,
we descried the thick white mist, which, like
the pillar of smoke of old, pointed out the way;
and soon afterwards reached Manchester, —
most unappropriate and unpoetical name! —
the small village situated at the American side
of the falls. We alighted at the principal hotel
or tavern, within hearing of the awful roar
of the cataract.

CHAP. VIII.

THE intensity of feeling on the stranger's approach to Niagara is such, that in my own case I could only have described it by comparison with that on my first approach to those architectural glories, St. Peter's at Rome and the Coliseum, or to the exhumed wonders of Pompeii, had not the pages of that popular writer, Captain Basil Hall, furnished me with an illustration still more forcible.

Captain Hall had visited the magnificent Napoleon, the Cæsar of the age, in his exile; and, in the work of the former on America, the author compares the sensations he experienced just before beholding the falls of Niagara, to those on first arriving in the presence of that wonderful personage. By a most singular coincidence, I had also visited Napoleon in exile; and the mingled sensations of tremulous expectation and awe I experienced on that occasion, making due allowance for the difference in the nature of the objects, were repeated in my breathless approach to the falls of Niagara.

A short walk from the inn brought us in full view of the grand panorama of nature. Our ideas of Niagara, of the pyramids, ·of St. Peter's, and other wonders of the world, are so magnified from infancy, that it is by no means surprising if a certain degree of disappointment is the immediate result of the first gaze; but, as in the familiar instance of the great cathedral alluded to, as soon as the spectator has had time to dwell upon the scene before him, it seems to expand, and he stands mute in astonishment.

I had watched the fiery evomitions of Stromboli and Vesuvius at midnight, had witnessed the most glorious spectacle of sunrise from Mount Etna, had tracked the solitary footsteps of the wolf midst Alpine snows, and read the starry heavens on the boiling surges of the Atlantic; but none of these lessons to the soul surpassed, if equalled, in solemn grandeur the falls of Niagara.

In viewing them I felt abstracted—humbled, —and the mind, overwhelmed with the immensity of the scene, was absorbed in the contemplation of eternity.

Reflections apart, and to pursue descriptions in detail, we visited Bath and Goat Islands, which separate what is called the American from the Canadian or British fall, the platform which overlooks the abyss, as well as descended the staircases which conduct to the base of the cataract.

Goat Island is covered with wood, and is altogether a most romantic situation.

Until a few years ago, it was inaccessible, except at very great personal risk; but it is now reached by a bridge across the rapids, in the construction of which considerable ingenuity was shown by the spirited projector, General Porter, of the American army.

On Bath Island we were agreeably surprised to find a pretty museum of natural history. Several mills have been erected on this advantageous site, and were in busy operation, possessing " hydraulic privileges" with a vengeance!

Reluctant to leave such scenery whilst a ray of light remained, it was not until late in the evening that we found our way back to the hotel, the accommodations of which were extremely good.

As the night was cold we ordered a fire in the parlour we occupied; and a man in coarse attire, the same who had received us on our arrival, and who had assisted to carry the portmanteaus and cloaks, Caliban like,

brought in the logs and made the fire.   Whilst
he was engaged in this operation, conceiving
him to be one of the porters of the house, I
asked some questions relative to an individual
who had recently exhibited feats of jumping
into the river from extraordinary heights.
Leaning upon the chimney or mantel piece,
as it is commonly called in America, evidently
quite at home, he answered my interrogatories,
and began to enter upon the subject of the
laws of falling bodies, and the force of gra-
vitation, with much acuteness, and talked as
familiarly of squares as if he had been a graduate of Cambridge.

We soon ascertained that our friend was
not only " mine host of the garter," the proprietor of the hotel, but also a general of
militia; and our compagnon de voyage,
Dr. H., good-humouredly told us, that in
our next encounter with brother Jonathan,
we might meet the general, at the head of his
division, applying his mathematics to serious
purposes.   That English Bonifaces would
" not carry coals" is certain; and it may be
doubted whether they pay as much attention to the laws of falling bodies as they do
to falling prices.   The anecdote is strikingly
illustrative of the state of society in the newly

settled parts of that wonderful country, the United States.

Taking leave of our scientific and military host, we followed the course of the river Niagara down to Lewistown, a distance of seven miles. The river pursues its rapid way between lofty and precipitous banks, exhibiting in several places what the French would style, "belles horreurs." One of these frightful chasms, called after his Satanic majesty, is close to the road, and nearly two hundred feet deep. In the French Canadian war, a number of unfortunate British soldiers, who with their wives and children were retreating in the night, and ignorant of the country, were driven into the abyss by their pursuers, and all miserably perished except a solitary drummer, who was discovered at daylight suspended by his belt which had caught some of the projecting branches from the rocks. On the road near this terrific gulf we were suddenly surprised by the appearance of a wild and haggard young female, almost in a state of nudity. Her ravings proclaimed her a maniac of the most hopeless class. Our young driver, nothing desirous of a closer intimacy with this unfortunate creature, urged his horses to their utmost speed, nor could we prevail upon him to stop a few minutes to satisfy our curiosity.

Strange to relate, on the opposite bank of the river, another unfortunate being of this description was pointed out to us. The individual, who was of the other sex, was apparently busily employed sawing wood; but in lieu of a saw he had only a stick or stave, contenting himself, poor soul, in passing his days rubbing one piece of wood against another, leaving the rest to the imagination.

The character of these incidents added no little to the wild effect of the surrounding scenery.

At the cheerful village of Lewistown, we embarked in a small ferry-boat, and crossed the river to Queenstown, in Upper Canada, not without some fears of the numerous whirlpools and the drifting timber with which the surface of the river is here covered.

Queenstown is advantageously situated at the head of the navigation of the Niagara, below the falls, and vessels of considerable burden can approach the place.

Near the village are the heights where General Brock and his aide-de-camp, Colonel

M'Donald, were killed in an action with the enemy, at an early period of the late war.

The Americans crossed the river before daylight, and stormed the British posts; but were finally driven back, upon the latter receiving reinforcements. We were told by an eye-witness to the action, that the result would have perhaps terminated differently, had the American commander been properly supported by the militia, many of whom absolutely refused to cross the river, on the grounds that they were acting defensively, not offensively. The real motive was, probably, a panic which spread through their ranks at the sight of their wounded and dying comrades, whom their general had humanely sent to Lewistown for their better accommodation and comfort.

On the heights alluded to, which are nearly three hundred feet above the level of the river, a column has been erected to the memory of the gallant Brock, whose remains, with those of his aide-de-camp, moulder under its base. The column, which is of stone, is one hundred and twenty-six feet in height, and a spiral staircase leads to the summit, from which there is a most extensive prospect. We distinctly saw York, the capital of the province, at the opposite side of Lake Ontario, which last

seemed " vexed with storms " and regretted
that the steamer's having ceased to ply for the
summer season prevented our visiting that
young but flourishing settlement. Over the
entrance to the monument is the following
inscription : —

" The Legislature of Upper Canada has dedicated this monument to the many civil and
military services of the late SIR ISAAC BROCK,
Knight Commander of the most honourable
Order of the Bath, Provincial Lieutenant-
governor and Major-general commanding his
Majesty's forces therein. He fell in action,
on the 13th of October, 1812 ; honoured and
beloved by those whom he governed, and de-
plored by his Sovereign, to whose service his
life had been devoted. His remains are deposited in this vault, as also those of his aide-
de-camp, Lieutenant-colonel JOHN M'DONALD,
who died of his wounds, the 14th of October,
1812, received the day before in action."

Around the column are a number of double
hillocks, marking the silent mansions of many
brave fellows sleeping the sleep of death.

Taking a last look at these melancholy me-
morials, we again hired a wagon, and, after an
agreeable ride of seven miles, were set down
at the house of Mr. Forsyth the younger, one

of the two large hotels kept by the family of
that name, and situated opposite to Manchester, where we had spent the previous
day.

The approach to the falls by this road is
decidedly the best, as the whole bursts upon
the sight in all its grandeur. The celebrated
Table Rock is situated on the Canada side,
between which and Goat Island the river falls
one hundred and sixty feet in one great concave of six hundred yards in width. This,
from its form, is denominated the Horseshoe
Fall. It has receded in the memory of man ;
although the present range is about the same
as it was in the year 1822, as appears by a stone
placed for the purpose of observation. The
waters, after dashing and roaring among rocks
for nearly two miles, all breakers and foam,
here make a graceful bend over the edge of the
precipice, and present in their descent a curved
and unbroken surface of green water, for
the depth of twenty or thirty feet. The abyss
is a boiling chaos, the white mist from which
rises several hundred feet, and often presents
to the spectator the most beautiful iris.

The American fall, which is here seen to
great advantage, is convex, and three hundred
yards wide. Some idea may be formed of the

effect of the whole, when I state, that a detached branch, between Bath and Goat Island, is equal in volume to the justly famed cascade of Terni, which, in the opinion of Byron, and must be in that of every European traveller, was worth all the cascades and torrents of Switzerland put together.

The great projection of the upper stratum of rock, with the curve of the fall, enable persons to proceed for a considerable distance behind the sheet of water ; and although there is little danger in the attempt, it is an affair requiring considerable strength of nerve. Determined to explore the hidden wonders, and encouraged by the statements of our guide, we attired ourselves in oilcloth dresses provided for the purpose, and descended the staircase which conducts to the base of Table Rock. After passing amongst the huge fragments which are scattered in every direction, we followed a track which has been made at the foot of the overhanging precipice, and soon came within reach of the spray, which met us, both as to quantity and force, precisely as if we had been stationed on the forecastle of a ship in a storm.

By dint of exertion, and in spite of a ducking, we made our way for a considerable dis-

L

tance in the rear of the mighty torrent.   The gloom, the thundering sound, the tremendous blasts of air, the dashing of the waters, and the difficulty of respiration, soon oblige the curious visitor to quit this Neptunian scene ; and we gladly hastened to the light of day, and comparative stillness of the banks of the river.

Unlike an old Scotch settler, who coolly informed us, that he had passed the falls half-a-dozen times every year for as many years, and never turned to look at them, we felt an increased interest with every hour's contemplation of the sublime spectacle, and, after a lingering last look, we started for Buffalo on lake Erie.

The road lies parallel with the margin of the river, and we had a charming view of the rapids, but accidentally missed an examination of the burning spring which rises on the brink.   The water at this spot is warm, and surcharged with sulphurated hydrogen gas, which being collected in a vessel having a tube, and lighted, burns with a brilliant flame.

In this ride we passed over the battle grounds Lundy Lane and Chippewa, and halted to refresh the horses at a small tavern near the latter. The battle of Chippewa was fought on the

5th of July, 1814, and terminated by the retreat of the British, whose loss in killed and wounded amounted to 514, while that of the Americans is stated to have been 328. The still more severe conflict of Bridgewater or Lundy Lane took place twenty days after the former, and was so desperately contested that neither party could claim the victory, or were able to renew the engagement.

The respective losses were about equal; that of the British being estimated at 878, and that of the enemy at 860. Our wagon-driver, as well as the host of the tavern, were in these engagements, and described the last in particular, which was fought at night by the light of the moon, and the cannonade as a most sanguinary affair.

The following extract from a letter written by a medical officer attached to the American army, is terribly descriptive of the work of blood.

" In the afternoon," says this writer, " the enemy advanced towards Chippewa, with a powerful force. At six o'clock General Scott was ordered to advance with his brigade, and attack them. He was soon reinforced by General Ripley's brigade ; they met the enemy above the falls. They had selected their ground for the night, intending to attack our camp before day-light. The action began just before seven, and an uninterrupted stream of musketry continued till half-past eight, when there was some cessation, the British falling back. It soon began again, with some artillery, which, with slight interruptions, continued till half-past ten, when there was a charge; and a tremendous stream of fire closed the conflict. Both armies fought with a desperation bordering upon madness; neither would yield the palm; but each retired a short distance, wearied out with fatigue. Such a constant and destructive fire was never before sustained by American troops, without falling back. The enemy had collected their whole force in the Peninsula, and were reinforced by troops from Lord Wellington's army, just landed from Kingston. For two hours, the hostile lines were within twenty yards of each other, and so frequently intermingled that sometimes an officer would order an enemy's platoon. The moon shone bright; but part of our men being dressed like the Glengarian regiment, caused the deception. They frequently charged, and were as often driven back.

" Our regiment, under Colonel Miller, was

ordered to storm the British battery. We charged, and took every piece of the enemy's cannon. We kept possession of the ground and cannon until twelve at night, when we all fell back more than two miles. This was done to secure our camp, which might otherwise have been attacked in the rear. Our horses being most of them killed, and there being no ropes to the pieces, we got off but two or three. The men were so excessively fatigued they could not drag them. We lost one howitzer; the horses being on full gallop towards the enemy to attack them, the riders were shot off, and the horses ran through the enemy's line. We lost one piece of cannon, which was too much advanced, every man being shot that had charge of it but two. Several of our caissons were blown up by their rockets, which did some injury, and deprived our cannon of ammunition. The lines were so near, that cannon could not be used with advantage."

The greater part of the slain were collected and burnt, and the grass now waves luxuriantly on the sites of their funeral piles. A few skulls thrown up by the plough, or found among the underwood, were shown to us by the veteran innkeeper. Unlike young Siward, who had his hurts on the front, one of these scalped

trophies had a bullet hole at the back ; another
had been gnawed by racoons, or other wild
animals, the marks made by the teeth of the
ravenous tenants of the forest being perfectly
visible.   The sight instantly brought to mind
the horribly fine lines of the ever-to-be-lamented
Byron, in the poem entitled " The Siege of
Corinth."

" And he saw the lean dogs beneath the wall
Hold o'er the dead their carnival,
Gorging and growling o'er carcass and limb ;
They were too busy to bark at him !
From a Tartar's skull they had stripp'd the flesh,
As ye peel the fig when its fruit is fresh ;
And their white tusks crunch'd o'er the whiter skull,
As it slipp'd through their jaws when their edge grew dull ;
As they lazily mumbled the bones of the dead,
When they scarce could rise from the spot where they fed ;
So well had they broken a lingering fast
With those who had fallen for that night's repast."

The population at Chippewa, and along this
route, with whom we happened to come in
contact, were chiefly Irish, and seemed very
well satisfied with their situation and prospects.
One or two miserably daubed representations
of the royal arms of England met our view in
the shape of signs.   Royal emblems did not
appear to have been within the scope of the
artist's talents ; and perhaps the cap of liberty

would have been better suited to his pencil, if not to his feelings.

At Waterloo,—for this name has travelled wheresoever John Bull has a footing, — we were obliged to wait some time for the ferry-boat; and during the period of our delay had the misfortune to witness a very affecting scene. Near the fire in the room into which we were shown stood a fine looking young man, his eyes fixed upon the ground, and apparently abstracted from all around him. A female, nursing an infant, sat in the same apartment; and her dejected look bespoke a sympathy with her partner, as the man proved to be, which strongly excited our curiosity, and prompted us to enquire the cause of their grief. " My brother, with my wife and myself, and our little ones," replied the young man, " were on our way to locate farther west, and had got so far yesterday, all well. We had, for convenience, stowed our furniture and baggage in a small boat which was to be towed down the Niagara river and up the Chippewa, whilst my wife and the babes were to follow in the wagon. My brother and another man were in the boat, and had reached the mouth of the Chippewa, a short distance above the commencement of the rapids, when the tow-rope broke, and away drifted the boat towards the falls. My poor dear brother, terrified at the moment, jumped over-board, but could not gain the shore, and was soon hurried into the breakers: and," added he, with faltering voice, " miserably perished over those tremendous falls. Alas! there's no mistake — there's no mistake," he reiterated, at the same instant wiping the big tears from his manly cheek : " had you seen the dear orphans," said he, " cling to my knees, crying, yet doubting the truth, saying, ' No, no, uncle ; daddy is not gone, he will come again ; you are playing with us,' it would have melted the firmest heart.

" Nothing served to comfort them after they were made to believe the fact, until I promised them to be their father ; and," added he, with great emphasis, " I have promised it, and I will perform. God bless them and all of us."

As soon as the distressed man became a little composed, he informed us, that the boat with his brother's companion was almost miraculously drifted upon Goat Island, when within one hundred yards of the precipice.

This simple tale of woe brought tears from all around ; and deeply sympathising with the afflicted group, and wishing them health and prosperity in their anticipated settlement, we bade them adieu, and entered the ferry-boat which was to convey us back to the United States.

The river is here a mile in width ; and such is the rapidity of the current, that although we were in a boat propelled by machinery, worked by two horses, yet I could scarcely divest myself of the idea of some accident happening, and of our being drifted to the falls below.

We landed at Black Rock, unquestioned by the authorities of the Custom House, and in half an hour alighted at the Eagle Hotel in Buffalo.

CHAP. IX.

PREVIOUSLY to entering upon a description of this place, I may remark, that we did not, like a celebrated traveller to whom I have alluded, find the air, the sky, the land, and the whole scenery of the Canadian side of the river differ from the same things on the American side. The land is, indeed, a little more cleared. We were attended at the hotel by an English female servant, in her frilled cap, and our bill was twice as much as it was for the same meals at the Generals, at Manchester village. As for the rest, it was, to use the words of Pope, " all but leather or prunello." Buffalo, like Manchester and Lewiston, fell a prey to the flames during the last war ; having been set on fire by the British, in retaliation for a similar outrage committed by the Americans at Newark, on the Canadian frontier. It has since been rebuilt, and is rapidly extending. Its situation, as the point of junction between the great western canal and Lake Erie, gives it immense advantages ; and the

day is not far distant, when Buffalo will become one of the most important places in the
state. A commodious harbour has lately been
constructed ; and besides a number of schoon-
ers and trading sloops, steamers of large burden sail regularly during the season between
this place and the various ports on the coasts
of Lake Erie ; among others to that of Cleave-
land, the entrance of the Ohio canal lately
finished, which, after passing for the distance
of three hundred miles through the fertile
and now populous state of that name, communicates with the great river Ohio, one of the
grand tributaries to the Mississippi. These
vessels also visit Detroit, a populous district,
and occasionally make trips to the new settlements, as far as Lake Michigan, a distance of
nearly one thousand miles. The neighbourhood of Detroit, which was founded by the
French, nearly two centuries ago, was represented to me as being a most desirable location.

The squares and streets of Buffalo are
planned upon an extensive scale, and the
buildings are pretty good.

The Eagle Hotel, that at which we took
up our quarters, is not only very large, but is
equal in most respects to the best in Great
Britain.

Nearly one hundred persons of both sexes sat down to meals, most of whom were store-keepers and their assistants.

The females were first shown to their usual station, the upper end of the long table, and then came the eager rush of hungry " business men," summoned from all parts of the village by the great alarm bell fixed on the summit of the building. We invariably noticed, that the American females had delicate appetites, and ate very little, although they permitted their plates to be loaded unmercifully, seldom re-fusing any thing, however opposite in taste. We often saw half a dozen different meats and vegetables upon the same plate, the chief of which was sent away untouched ; and children appeared to be excessively indulged in regard to food, nothing being denied them. The charge for wine at the hotels is extravagant, when it is recollected that the duty is so trifling. The consequence is, very little, if any, is called for. We were charged at Buffalo nine shil-lings for a bottle of Madeira, although half that sum would have afforded the proprietor of the hotel an ample retail profit.

The charge for board and lodging, in fact, for every thing of the best and in great abun-dance, except wine, was about five shillings per day each person for transient visitors ; and, as I have already remarked, no servants' fees of any description, notwithstanding which, all were exceedingly attentive and polite. We found this to be the usual charge in the best establishments out of New York, in which city the terms are rather higher.

This infant settlement contains a pretty museum, in which we saw some fine and lively rattle-snakes. These being secured in wire cages, we were enabled to study their movements and mode of attack, as well as to hear the warning rattles from which they derive their name.

On introducing a cane through the wires, the snakes made a low rustling sound with the rattles, not unlike that produced by a person walking amongst dry leaves, and darted their fangs at the object of their annoyance in a manner sufficiently indicative of what would have been the consequence, if a limb in lieu of a cane had been in contact with these venomous reptiles. The Indians have an antidote which renders the bite perfectly innoxious, and they sometimes, for the purpose of exhibition, allow themselves to be bitten severely in the extremities until the limb is swollen by inflammation ; and, on applying the

remedy, feel no subsequent bad effects. Above
the museum is a lecture room, where lectures
on the various branches of natural philosophy
or on ány other useful subjects are occasionally
delivered.   All this, touching the confines,
indeed still in the midst of forests and wilds,
presented a cheering spectacle, and a striking
lesson to the people of older countries, upon
whose heels, if not as respects some matters,
upon whose toes the Americans are treading.

We saw at Buffalo, numbers of Indians, of
the Seneca, Tuscarora, and other tribes, the
remnants of that division of the aborigines,
called the Six Nations.   They were all of a
copper hue, and had long coarse black hair.
The women wore loose cloth pantaloons, ornamented with embroidery at the ankles, and
large blue bordered blankets covered their
heads and enveloped their persons.   The ears
and necks of these bronzed damsels were
bedizened with silver ornaments, whilst their
feet, cold and wet, had no other protection
than soft shoes or moccassins manufactured by
themselves from the skins of the wild deer;
but not having soles, the water penetrates as
in a sponge, rendering them extremely un-
comfortable.   Some of the squaws, as the
wives of the red man are called, had infants

or papooses in swaddling clothes braced to
boards, and carried on the back under the
blankets.

We asked permission or rather, as the squaw
did not understand us, we made signs that we
wished to see her infant, and proceeded to
unfold the blanket. The little copper-faced
brat being suddenly awoke, gave us each a
look of surprise which I shall not soon forget,
and then set up a scream which pierced the
ears of all around. The men were attired in
long frock coats and trowsers, and wore hats.
Most of them wore large red worsted sashes
round the body, as is the custom in some parts
of the south of Europe. During our stay at
Buffalo, we made excursions to the village of
the Seneca tribe of Indians, which is situated
about three miles from that place. The road
was so bad that it was scarcely passable either
for wagons or for persons on foot. On our way
thither, we met an Indian in a small vehicle
driven by an American boy. On asking the latter the distance we were then from the village,
and happening to state that we were strangers
and English, the Indian jumped out of the
wagon, and, to our great surprise, shook hands
with us very cordially, stating, in no very bad
English, that he had been in our country and

was delighted to see us. On explaining to him the object of our pilgrimage, he insisted upon being our guide, and, allowing the boy to proceed to Buffalo, walked with us to his village. Upon further conversation we found we were indeed highly honoured in the person of our Cicerone, who proved to be the nephew of the celebrated chief Old Red Jacket, then in the eightieth year of his age, and since dead, to whom he promised we should be *presented*. Thus escorted, and full of wigwam anticipations, we visited some of the cottages, in which we were not a little disappointed, as tourists, to find every thing in a comparatively advanced stage of civilization.

In one of these humble habitations, the squaw, who could not speak a word of English, was highly decorated with silver chains and other pendent ornaments; and, in this gala attire, was busy making cakes of Indian meal, while the papouse or infant lay sleeping.

The different articles of furniture were such as are found in the cabins of the white settlers; but what more particularly attracted our attention among the moveables, was the display of Birmingham tea-trays, and blue and white Staffordshire crockery, which with us were associated with such an opposite picture of rural life.

Many of the Indians are converted, or rather have been persuaded to profess particular systems of Christianity; for how is it possible that the dogmas taught by the missionaries, and which have been fertile subjects of dispute among the most learned, from the first to the present century of the Christian era, should be comprehended by the unlettered child of the forest. Was the pure morality of the Gospel alone inculcated, by practice as well as precept, leaving speculative opinions to man's own bosom, the result would probably be much more favourable to virtue, and consequently to happiness.

We were told that the old chief of the tribe resolutely maintained his own religious opinions, and his nephew wisely declined any discussion on the subject.

This otherwise communicative individual informed me, that the tract of land they occupied was ceded to them by the state, together with a pecuniary compensation; and he seemed to feel a degree of pride on declaring, that nobody dared to cut down one of the trees on their little territory without their permission.

M

It would, perhaps, be much better for the possessors, however, if more were cut down; but semi-civilized Indians make indifferent husbandmen; and the vice of intemperance, for which they are indebted to the white man, is very prevalent.

On our return to Buffalo, our guide entertained us with an account of his English travels. He informed us, that he had been one of a party who visited England some years ago, to exhibit the Indian war dances, and had made the tour of the country. He expressed himself as having been delighted with all he saw; and that his reception had been flattering, was evident from the satisfaction with which he alluded to it.

Among several public characters who had witnessed his performances, and whose titles he had not forgotten, was his late Majesty, George the Fourth, whom he enquired after with all the familiarity of an old acquaintance. He also mentioned, with glee, the late Duke of York, who, it seemed, had ordered the knights of the tomahawk and scalping knife to be regaled with their darling liquor, gin.

" The Duke of York very much please with dance," said he; and added with a burst

of laughter, in which we heartily joined,
" He give us plenty — plenty of gin!"

When we arrived at Buffalo, we found that
his majesty, Old Red Jacket, had left the
village on his return to his residence, and
were consequently disappointed in regard to
the expected presentation. Having shook
hands with his obliging nephew, thanked him
for his kindness, and treated him to as much,
or perhaps more, of his favourite beverage
than was good for him, we parted.

However averse to labour the red man
may be, the squaws were represented to us
as being very industrious; and, besides the
performance of their domestic duties, they
manufacture many ornamental articles of dress,
among which are the moccasins before alluded
to. These curious species of shoes are tastefully embroidered with the quills of the American porcupine, which they dye with various
brilliant colours of their own preparation.

The knowledge of this interesting race is
not confined to their own productions; for
we learned from one of the principal store-
keepers of Buffalo, that the Indians were all
excellent judges of foreign goods, particularly
of broad cloths, which, if their means allowed,

they would always purchase of the finest quality.

At Buffalo, our agreeable and scientific travelling companion, Dr. H., left us, to pursue his journey to the great metropolis of the western states, Cincinnati; whilst we, not able to extend ours at that period, and warned by the sudden approach of winter, were reluctantly obliged to commence retracing our steps to New York. Taking a last look at Lake Erie, and its shores, as far as the eye could embrace from the elevated belvidere of the hotel, we embarked in the packet for Rochester, which happened to be the identical boat in which we had been conveyed from that place to Tonewanta, on our route to the falls.

On entering the cabin, I was not a little surprised to hear myself welcomed by the title of Colonel, to which I certainly had no more claim than I had to that of Mi Lord, a term liberally applied to English travellers on the continent of Europe some seventeen or eighteen years ago, and to which one actually became accustomed. To explain the mystery, it is necessary to inform the reader, that in travelling in America, we found persons, whose appearance did not bespeak them to be hewers

of wood or drawers of water, often styled Captain, and by such title I had been addressed
on the voyage from Albany. Whether I had
ingratiated myself with our commander, by
conversation, jest, or tale, I know not; but it
seemed he thought proper to dub me by
brevet, and the superior title of Colonel was
soon echoed by his assistant and others, to my
great annoyance at the moment, although the
sound conveyed little of its English signification in a country where we had so lately found
the landlord of an inn to be a general. At
the commencement of our route, we passed a
man in rough attire, returning from gunning,
as the phrase is, and attended by a black servant. They had just killed a fine buck, which
the negro bore over his shoulder, whilst his
master was so hung round with wild ducks, and
other birds, that it required no great stretch
of imagination to identify the group with poor
Robinson Crusoe, and his faithful Friday.

As we approached Rochester we found all
the population assembling to witness a surprising feat, at the performance of which it
was also our melancholy fortune to be present.
This grand attraction was no less than the
fatal jump of the individual named Patch,

which furnished a subject for the newspapers of the time.

A little below the village of Rochester, the river Genessee pours over a precipice one hundred feet in height, and close to the cascade, a scaffold of twenty-five feet in height had been erected, so as to make the eminence exactly one hundred and twenty-five feet above the surface of the river below.

From this great elevation the foolish man jumped, and striking the water with tremendous force, disappeared. The time occupied in falling was not quite three seconds.

The precipitous banks of the Genessee were crowded with almost the whole population of the village and neighbourhood, and the sight was one of uncommon interest. Patch was dressed in a white suit, with a black belt or sash round his loins. He sprung fearlessly from the platform, and kept himself perfectly upright, with his feet close together, until nearly reaching the water. As he had before jumped from the height of one hundred feet at the same place, as well as a little below the falls of Niagara, and had experienced no bad effects, it was believed, had he been sober at the time in question, which, unfortunately for himself, was not the case, he would not have met with his untimely end.

The termination of the scene was more affecting to us, from the circumstance of our having seen him in the packet-boat a few days previously, with his favourite companion, a fine young bear, when we had the curiosity to question him upon his manner of jumping, the management of his limbs, and state of his feelings, at the time of his performances. The poor fellow, who it seemed was too idle to work, pursued the occupation for a miserable pittance, and the better to attract the populace, had advertised this as being positively his last jump, the coincidence of which with the catastrophe caused an impression that he contemplated suicide. The spectacle of the descent, in front of a black precipice, and the breathless anxiety manifested by the assembled multitude for some minutes, were awfully grand.

The body of the unfortunate man was discovered in a perfect state, at some distance from the place of his death, upon the breaking up of the ice in the following spring.

It was our intention to have proceeded from Rochester by the stage to Utica, visiting Geneva on the Seneca Lake, Auburn, celebrated

for its state prison, and other places of interest
on the route ; but the bad state of the roads,
which made travelling by land exceedingly
fatiguing, obliged us to resume the aquatic
mode of conveyance. A jolting ride of sixteen miles through a tolerably cleared country,
brought us to a station on the canal just as
the night set in, and before the packet, whose
course from Rochester to this spot was circuitous and interrupted by locks, had arrived.
The evening was cold, but as the inn where
we alighted was in the neighbourhood of
forests, and the fuel being in abundance for
the labour of " hewing and splitting," we
experienced the cheering influence of a fire
which would have done credit to the wide
hearths of the baronial castles of the olden
time. The blazing mass before which we
supped was no less than eight feet wide by
three feet in height, and presented a truly hospitable appearance.

Reluctantly quitting this attraction, and the
assembled guests, just when reserve was giving
place to anecdotes and good-humoured disputation, we again embarked, and had not proceeded many miles before an accident to the
rudder obliged us to halt in our career.

The boat was secured by ropes to stumps

of trees on the bank of the canal, whilst messengers were despatched with the broken apparatus to the nearest smithery, as it was
termed, a distance of three miles. Before
retiring to my cot for the night, I happened
to take a peep at our location, which contrasted strongly with the snug comforts of
the packet, causing one to enjoy them so
much the more. That part of the canal in
which we were detained was cut through
dense forest, the trees of which were at least
eighty, and some even one hundred feet in
height; the ground was covered with snow,
and the scene viewed by the lamps of the
boat, midst the most profound stillness, save
an occasional cry from some tenant of the
woods, was one of utter loneliness. The
effect produced by a bugle horn in these wilds
was particularly striking; and Weber's fine
hunting chorus, played by one of the boatmen
at my request, was a musical treat of no ordinary character. The necessary repairs being
completed in the course of the night, we
pursued our " winding way," and in the
morning found ourselves again in the neighbourhood of comparative civilisation.

Unlike the custom of the great seaports of
America, where, as in England, separate esta-

blishments exist for the sale of distinct branches
of manufactures or other commodities, most
of the stores in the smaller towns and villages
contain a general assortment of goods of the
most heterogeneous description ; and the customers may be supplied at the same counter
with a pound of young hyson, a pair of scis-
sors, or a copy of Scott's Life of Napoleon.

A still inferior class of stores is to be found
located along the lines of the canals, wherever
the junction of a branch, the proximity of
locks, or the establishment of some factory
has attracted settlers.   Rude as the signs of
these humble tenements in general were, and
varied as regarded the stocks in trade, I
certainly was not prepared for the following
jumble of articles of prime necessity, the catalogue of which I copied verbatim from the
front of a store as we were passing one of the
locks.

Pork.	Snuff.
Lamp Oil.	Dried Beef.
Crockery.	Nutmegs.
Tobacco.	Whiskey.
Shot.	Cinnamon.
Salted Shad.	Gunpowder.

Many of the hucksters to whom these little
stores belong were poor Irish emigrants, who

happening to arrive at the period when the
canal was commenced, laboured in its execution; and having saved a little money, bought
their acres, built their frame-houses, and are
now enjoying the fruits of their industry free
from the assaults of gamekeepers, or the periodical visits of either tithe-proctors or excise-
men.

On transferring ourselves at Utica from the
packet which had brought us from Rochester
to that which was to convey us to Schenectady,
we experienced an instance of good feeling on
the part of the captain, which was the more
appreciated by us as it was perfectly disinterested. Having expressed our satisfaction at
the comforts of the boat, and the attention
paid to the wants and wishes of the passengers,
the individual alluded to, on shaking hands
with me, not only assured us of his desire to
see us again on that route, but in the most gentlemanly manner begged, that if it was agreeable to us to make another trip, he should
consider us as his guests both going and returning.

The accident of mislaying a bunch of keys
at Utica, obliged me to perform my toilet for
the day at the nearest hairdresser's or barber's
store I could find. On entering a respectable-

looking shop of this description, I was immediately requested by the sable, woolly-headed
Figaro who received me, to be seated; so
pulling off my coat and stock, I accordingly
sat down, when, in an instant, I felt the back
of the chair, as I thought, giving way. In
this I was deceived; poor Mungo had discovered that the best position for his customers, whilst under the operation of shaving,
was precisely that so favourable for the dentist,
and his chairs were accordingly constructed,
so that the backs could be elevated or depressed
at pleasure. It would be an act of injustice
were I to omit to state, that no Parisian valet
could have performed his task better, even to
the concluding part of handing me my hat,
cane, and gloves, as well as making his obei-
sance on my wishing him good morning. This
trifling act of civility on my part was, probably, the more acceptable, because it is one
which an American is not in the habit of bestowing upon his darker brethren.

Proceeding onward, we passed the romantic
scenery of the Little Falls by moonlight, thus
enjoying its wild beauties under varied aspects;
and after a most delightful day's sail, in view
of the enchanting Mohawk, we landed at
Schenectady, and taking the stage, in a few

hours were again comfortably seated at the American Hotel in Albany.

The morning following we once more embarked, in one of the splendid steamers, for New York, and rapidly pursued our voyage down the broad and noble Hudson. The company was numerous, and the fineness of the weather, although it was now the middle of November, permitted us to enjoy the ever-varying landscape from the upper deck, the seats on which were all in requisition.

Among the passengers was a young female of exceedingly interesting appearance, but who sat abstracted in the midst of the throng, apparently insensible to the remarks of the lover of the picturesque, the reasonings of politicians, or the sallies of wit. Curious to learn the cause of this evident indifference, I took an opportunity of making some observation to the gentleman who was seated beside her, and under whose protection she appeared to travel. This led to further conversation, in which he informed us that the young lady in question was his sister, who had the melancholy misfortune to be a mute, and that she was returning to the school for the deaf and dumb, near New York, after a few weeks' recreation among her friends. At our request we were instantly

introduced to the afflicted young creature, as
strangers travelling to see America.   Her
countenance beamed with pleasure at being
thus noticed ; for the brother had, by signs,
signified that we deeply sympathised with her
in her affliction.   Pencils and pocket-books
were immediately brought forth, and we, for
a time, forgot the moving panorama in the
novelty of our mode of converse, and the interest it excited.   Her first questions were, as
to our names, place of abode, and its distance
from New York.   The answer to the latter
seemed to strike her forcibly, for it was immediately followed by the question, " Have
you friends so far behind you ?"   On reading
the affirmative she shook her head slowly, and
wrote, " How far you are from them !"   After
asking the favour of her name, I wrote down,
" Will you tell me a secret, that is, your age ?"
She smiled, and wrote, " I am fifteen years."
Desirous to know whether she had any knowledge of those celebrated men, the Abbé
de l'Epée or the Abbé Sicard, I put the
question ; but, incautiously and in haste, wrote
down, " Have you *heard* of them ?"   She
wrote in reply, " I don't hear."   I then used
the phrase, " Have you read or been told of
those good men ?" She answered, " Yes, sir."

Some interruption occurring, I wrote, "We will chat again after dinner." This word caused her to knit her brows, and show evident signs of having met with a difficulty. After thinking for an instant she wrote, "What is chat?" I answered, "Chat is to converse in an easy familiar manner." The girl's eyes sparkled, and, with significant nods, she wrote, "Yes, yes." During our resumed colloquies, a lady enquired "Whether she could work with the needle?" She wrote, with hasty satisfaction, "Yes, madam; and I can make bead bags." In reply to the question of, "How long have you been at the school?" She wrote, "I have been four years, and shall stay one year seven months." We complimented her on her proficiency; at which she appeared to be much gratified, and expressed a great desire to see us again before we returned to England. The shades of evening having gradually thinned the crowded decks, we enjoyed the pleasure of a twilight promenade, until the steward with his bell announced that supper was on the table.

A dense fog coming on soon after, we were unable to proceed, and the vessel was accordingly anchored. It so happened that this was about the spot where the British sloop of war, the Vulture, lay when she was to have received Major André on board, upon his return from his visit to Arnold.

When all was still, and as I lay in my berth, rather in a musing than a sleeping mood, I indulged in a thousand associations connected with past and present times; with America, as she was, at the period to which I allude, empoverished and struggling in the noblest of causes, The Rights of Man; and America, as she now is, the beacon and the watch-word of Liberty; and, in energy and successful enterprise, the rival of the powerful nation from which she sprung. My musings were soon interrupted by the hissing of the steam, and the noise occasioned by weighing the anchor; and in a few hours after, I found we were at New York. In this extended excursion of nearly eleven hundred miles, we had met with most intelligent and agreeable society, had received invitations and various civilities from persons to whom we were wholly unknown, and who, in all probability, we may never meet again; and, although we had travelled in public conveyances alike open to all, had not witnessed any drunkenness or riotous be-

haviour, nor heard an oath, or any indecent
or objectionable word. Such as were of congenial tastes, or whose conversation suited,
naturally associated together ; in short, those
talked together, who *could* talk together ; all
was good-humour and perfect civility ; and if
the Americans do not do the thing exactly in
the French style, we observed they were invariably polite to the softer sex, let their age
or attire be as they might. I could not help
thinking that this general good deportment
must be attributed not only to the diffusion of
education, but in some measure to the constant amalgamation of the different classes in
hotels, boarding houses, and particularly in
travelling, in which there are no aristocratic
modes. Every individual knows that he is
expected to conduct himself with propriety ;
and whatever he may be at home, he conforms
to the rules of decorum abroad. I often
wished, however, that the very prevalent
habits of chewing, smoking, and, worse than
either, their effect, spitting, had been dispensed with : but it is proper to remark, that
these are not the habits of the best educated
persons ; and except it might be for the convenience of some particular individual, who,

N

like the late worthy and learned Dr. Parr, could not exist without his whiff of the Indian weed, I do not remember to have seen that disgusting article, a spitting-box, in any private drawing-room in America.

CHAP. X.

Anxious to reach Washington, the seat of government, before the freezing of the rivers, we left New York, for Philadelphia, on the morning of December 24th, 1829.

The air was as mild as the month of May in England; and our sail across the charming bay, and up the little river Rariton, was delightful. A most bountiful breakfast was served in the steamer; after which, on paying our fares, we were presented with tickets, bearing numbers, which entitled the passengers to seats in the coaches bearing corresponding numbers. The distribution of these tickets, in which considerable tact is displayed, is the business of the captain of the vessel.

Those gentlemen who had ladies or children under their protection, were requested to name their party, and were assigned to the same coaches, so that no separations took place; and this rule was extended to others, by making a request to that effect.

A further and more delicate classification took place in putting those together whose

N 2

sphere of life or manners appeared to assimilate; yet this was so adroitly managed as not to excite general notice, still less to cause any unpleasant feeling among the passengers. On approaching New Brunswick, a signal was made, notifying the number of stage coaches required, which in this instance was nine; and at the same time passengers were requested to select their baggage, each article of which was immediately marked with chalk, agreeably to the number on the ticket. All the vehicles were ranged on the wharf in numerical order; and the instant we landed, we hastened to ours; and the packages being brought on shore, and secured behind, off we drove, each coach, under all circumstances of watering or changing horses, keeping its relative station.

The last vehicle was appropriated to blacks or persons of colour, who, in spite of their degraded position, wore the happiest faces in the whole procession. The distance from New Brunswick to Trenton, on the Delaware, is about twenty-six miles, and the road tolerably good.

The country appeared well cultivated; and every farm had its peach-orchard. This tract was the scene of several conflicts in the war of independence; and I found the name of

Tarleton, one of the few officers of the British army who served in that quarter now alive, still remembered.

Princeton, sixteen miles from New Brunswick, has, in addition to the State College, founded by the royal government, a large establishment for the education of youths intended for the Presbyterian ministry.

Trenton, which is ten miles further, is beautifully situated near the first rapids of the Delaware, which here, at the distance of one hundred and twenty miles from the sea, ceases to be navigable for vessels of burthen.

The road crosses the river on a covered wooden bridge, above four hundred yards in length.

Trenton was the theatre of two of the most brilliant exploits in the military career of the great Washington; the particulars of which are extremely interesting, and are related with spirit in the same publication to which I have before alluded, as emanating from the society of which the present Lord Chancellor is the corner stone.

" On the approach of the British to the Delaware," says the writer, " Congress adjourned its sittings from Philadelphia to Baltimore ; and it was expected that General Howe would speedily make his triumphal entry into the Pennsylvanian capital; but a bold man-œuvre of Washington suddenly turned the tide of success.

" On his arrival at the Delaware, his troops were dwindled down to the number of 3000; but having received some reinforcements of Pennsylvanian militia, he determined to en-deavour to retrieve his fortunes by a decisive stroke.

" The British troops were cantoned in Bur-lington, Bordenton, and Trenton, waiting for the formation of the ice to cross into Penn-sylvania.

" Understanding that in the confidence produced by a series of successes they were by no means vigilant, he conceived the possi-bility of taking them by surprise. He, ac-cordingly, on the evening of Christmas Day, conveyed the main body of his army over the Delaware, and falling upon the troops quar-tered in Trenton, killed and captured about 900 of them, and recrossed into Pennsylvania with his prisoners. On the 28th of Decem-ber, he again took possession of Trenton, where he was soon encountered by a superior force of British, who drove in his advanced parties, and entered the town in the evening, with the intention of giving him battle the next morning. The two armies were separated only by a narrow creek which runs through the town.

" In such a position, it should seem to be impossible that any movement on the one side or the other could pass unobserved. But in the darkness of the night, Washington, leaving his fires lighted, and a few guards to attract the attention of the enemy, quitted his encampment, and crossing a bridge over the creek, which had been left unguarded, directed his march to Princeton; where, after a short but brisk engagement, he killed sixty of the British, and took 300 prisoners. The rest of the royal forces were dispersed, and fled in different directions.

" Great was the surprise of Lord Cornwallis, who commanded the British army at Trenton, when the report of the artillery at Princeton, which he at first mistook for thunder, and the arrival of breathless messengers, apprised him that the enemy was in his rear. Alarmed by the danger of his position, he commenced a retreat; and being harassed by the militia, and the countrymen who had suffered from the outrages perpetrated by his troops on their advance, he did not deem himself in safety

N 4

till he arrived at New Brunswick, from whence, by means of the Rariton he had a communication with New York." *

On our reaching the point of embarkation on the Delaware, we were transferred on board the steamer with as much celerity as we had been handed into the coach at New Brunswick, and immediately sat down to a bountiful dinner. The charge for meals on board these packets was two shillings each person. Nothing was required by the waiters, or even by the porters who removed the baggage. Near Bordenton, we passed the residence of Count Survilliers (Joseph Bonaparte); but the only object visible from the river was an elevated chapel, the mansion being concealed by woods.

The banks of the Delaware are low, but highly cultivated; and the houses, many of which are of brick, are shaded by lofty poplars or weeping willows; which last trees grow to a size quite unknown in England.

---

* Since the completion of this work, the author has been agreeably surprised to find, that the excellent History of the American Revolution, from which the foregoing, as well as a former extract, were taken, is from the pen of the Rev. William Shepherd, the learned author of the Life of Poggio Bracciolini, and the consistent advocate of " The Eternal Rights of Man."

About half way between Trenton and Philadelphia, we passed Bristol and Burlington, two cheerful and populous villages situated on opposite sides of the river.

Near the latter we were informed that a certain London banker of notoriety had located himself.

Descending this beautiful river, spires at length became visible; the buildings on the right bank gradually increased in number, until at last they presented a continuous appearance; and passing the suburb of Kensington, with its ship-yards, its glass-houses, and other manufactories, we soon after landed in the city of the Penns.

The first sounds which saluted our ears on approaching Philadelphia, were those of church bells, which were ringing a peal on the occasion of Christmas Eve. It was the first time we had heard that national and soothing music since leaving England, and it instantly recalled to our remembrance, home, country, friends, so powerfully, that even the welcome with which we were received was not sufficient to banish these natural associations.

The circumstance forcibly reminded me of the sublime allusion of Napoleon to the effect of the sound of the bell of the church of

Rueil, and which is thus recorded by his biographer, Scott.

" Immediately after his, Napoleon's, elevation
to the dignity of First Consul, he meditated
the restoration of religion ; and thus, in a
mixture of feeling and policy, expressed himself upon the subject to Thiebaudeau, then a
counsellor of state.

" Having combated for a long time the systems of modern philosophers upon different
kinds of worship, upon Deism, natural religion,
and so forth, he proceeded : — ' Last Sunday
evening, in the general silence of nature, I
was walking in these grounds, of Malmaison.
The sound of the church bell of Rueil fell
upon my ear, and renewed all the impressions
of my youth. I was profoundly affected, —
such is the power of early habit and associations ; and I considered, if such was the case
with me, what must not be the effect of such
recollections upon the more simple and credu-
lous vulgar ? Let your philosophers answer
that. — The people must have a religion.'"

The city of Philadelphia, or Brotherly Love,
is situated between the noble Delaware and
the Schuylkill, a few miles above their junction.

The former river is rather more than a mile

in width, opposite to the city ; and the latter, something less than that of the Thames at London Bridge.

The streets, excepting the two centre ones in each direction, are rather narrow, but perfectly straight, and cross each other at right angles at equal distances. Those from river to river are about two miles in length, and are named after different descriptions of trees, as Chestnut, Walnut, Spruce, Pine; while those in the contrary direction, the length of which is gradually prolonged with the increase of buildings, are numbered. The houses are of brick, and regular in their architecture.

The steps, and the parts about the doors and windows, which, in England, are usually of stone, are of white marble ; which, with the white painted doors, silvered plates and knobs, have a very chaste effect. The side walks are paved with brick, and are kept remarkably clean ; and the shops are superior, as regards their external appearance, to those of New York ; more of them also are devoted to the sale of engravings, and other branches of the fine arts, than in that city. Among the number of public edifices which adorn Philadelphia, the most interesting, although not the most beautiful, is the State House; for in one of its halls was signed the document which separated thirteen of the American colonies from Great Britain.

The apartment in question, which I was grieved to find in a dirty and neglected state, contains a statue of the immortal Washington, carved in wood, and painted. Upon the pedestal is the oft-quoted but just inscription, as applied to this great man : — " First in war, first in peace, and first in the hearts of his countrymen."

On the steps of the principal entrance of the building, the Declaration of Independence was first published to the world ; and, as some atonement for the neglect of the consecrated hall, these worn relics have been religiously respected. From the cupola of the edifice, in which there is an illuminated clock, the stranger has a most interesting bird's-eye view of the city, — its handsome squares, its streets in long straight lines, and its populous environs. It was the bell in this cupola that proclaimed American freedom on the memorable 4th of July, 1776 ; and, by a singular coincidence, it bears an inscription in praise of Liberty, although cast in London some years prior to that event.

If the State House possesses the most interest, politically considered, the United States Bank certainly claims pre-eminence over all the other public edifices of the city on the score of architectural beauty. This grand building, which stands on a raised terrace between two of the principal streets, is of the Grecian Doric order, and is composed of white marble, partially tinged with a bluish shade, like the quality in general use in Philadelphia. It measures 161 feet in length, and 87 feet in breadth. Each of the two fronts contains eight fluted columns, 4 feet 6 inches in diameter, elevated upon six rows of steps. This beautiful temple was designed by the late ingenious M. La Trobe ; and, when viewed by the " pale moonlight," the effect is sublime.

The other public buildings of the same material as this *chef d'œuvre* are, — the Old United States Bank, the façade of which exhibits a portico of the Corinthian order, the columns of which are fluted ; the Bank of Pennsylvania, which is a beautiful Ionic temple ; the Freemasons' Hall, a pseudo-Gothic structure ; and the New Mint. This last edifice was not completed at the period of our visit ; but, judging from the design, as well as the execution of what we saw, it will be creditable to the Government and the architect, as well as an ornament to the city in which it is situated.

The Asylum for the Deaf and Dumb, the Naval Hospital, and the Pennsylvania Hospital, are all spacious and handsome erections, worthy of a large and philanthropic community. In the area before the last-mentioned building, which is surrounded by lofty trees, stands a statue of the illustrious founder of the city. This work of art is of lead bronzed, and was presented to the Institution by one of the noble descendants of the family of Penn in England. Although the figure is attired in the primitive Quaker dress, even to the broad-rim hat " of the order," yet the execution of the work is so good, and the effect so prepossessing, that I felt my faith in the propriety of classical costume in sculpture attacked, every visit which I made to this memento of the father of the country.

In our perambulations we visited the spot, on the banks of the Delaware, where Penn concluded his celebrated treaty with the aborigines, — the only treaty, it has been observed, ever made without an oath, and the only one which has not been broken. A neat marble obelisk, commemorative of the event, has recently been erected on this hallowed site by the Society of Friends, — the first instance, I believe, of that body patronising the fine arts.

The venerable elm, under the shade of which the treaty was ratified, was standing a few years ago, but is now no more; and the extension of the suburbs of the city has completely destroyed every vestige of the olden time.

We were much pleased to hear that the memory of Penn was still held in veneration by the Indians, whose fathers did not fail to transmit to their children the " golden opinions" which they entertained of that upright individual.

I cannot quit the subject of the great founder of Pennsylvania, without inserting the following very interesting account of the origin of the name, as given in a letter from Penn himself, dated January 5th, 1681 : —
" This day," says the writer, " after many waitings, watchings, solicitings, and disputes in council, my country was confirmed to me under the great seal of England, with large powers and privileges, by the name of Pennsylvania, — a name the King would give it in

honour of my father. I chose New Wales, being a hilly country ; and when the secretary, a Welchman, refused to call it New Wales, I proposed Sylvania ; and they added Penn to it, though I much opposed it, and went to the King to have it struck out. He said 'twas past, and he would take it upon him ; nor would twenty guineas move the under-secretary to vary the name ; for I feared it should be looked on as a vanity in me, and not as a respect in the King to my father, as it really was. Thou mayest communicate my grant to friends, and expect shortly my proposals. 'Tis a dear and just thing ; and my God, that has given it me through many difficulties, will, I believe, bless and make it the seed of a nation. I shall have a tender care to the government, that it be well laid at first."

The Philadelphia Museum, which is kept in a commodious and ornamental edifice called the Arcade, is particularly rich in Indian costumes and implements ; but it also contains many fine specimens in the department of natural history. Among the latter is, perhaps, the greatest treasure of the kind in the world, — a complete fossil skeleton of the mammoth. The size of this huge creature, which differs little in structure from the elephant, may be better conceived, when I state that a skeleton of an ordinary specimen of the latter animal stands under the head of the former. This unique relic of a former world was found imbedded in marl in Ulster county, in the State of New York.

The other most prominent specimens in the animal kingdom were, — an elephant; a turtle, of the fluted back sort, which measured above five feet in length; an alligator, fifteen feet; a ray, six feet in diameter; a lobster, above three feet in length; and several enormous rattlesnakes, and other species of the serpent family, which the southern and western territories furnish in great variety. In our survey of the articles of a mixed description, and which are kept in an appropriate division of the Museum, I found a MS. poem, composed by Major André, in whose handwriting it was stated to be. The subject was pastoral, and the versification corroborated what I had read and heard of that gentleman's poetic taste; but, after all, its chief interest arose from the fact, that it was the production of a leisure hour a short time previous to his fatal catastrophe.

On the walls of a gallery were displayed

o

a great variety of portraits of celebrated characters, painted by the ingenious individual
who founded the Museum, and whose talented
family are indefatigable in their exertions in
the cause of science and the fine arts.
Amongst the crowd of worthies I recognised
my countryman, and, I am proud to add,
friend of my family, the illustrious Priestley.
This great philosopher, and martyr to the
sacred cause of Liberty, closed his eventful life
at a place called Northumberland, situated at
the confluence of the branches of the Susquehanna, about 130 miles from Philadelphia, and
where some of his descendants remain.   I
could not help reflecting, whilst viewing the
portrait in question, on the great changes
which had taken place in the tone of thinking
among the English people, since the period
of the banishment of this early friend of Reform ; and it is gratifying to know, that the
very community with whom the penetrating
mind, the profound acquirements, and the mild
virtues of a Priestley could not insure his protection, is now among the foremost to uphold
those principles of political justice, for tem-
perately advocating which his threshold was
violated — the results of a life of laborious
study and experiment were given to the flames;

and, as if the powers of hell should triumph during this demoniacal Saturnalia, the house of God where he ministered was rased to the ground.

The Philadelphia Museum of Natural History, which is, however, in no way connected with the Museum to which I have alluded, contains a very extensive collection of minerals, fossils, shells, and also some fine specimens in the department of ornithology. Among these is the wild turkey, now well known in Europe through the splendid labours of that indefatigable naturalist, Audubon; to whom, as well as to other individuals of acquirements, I had the good fortune to be introduced by our travelling companion to Niagara; and I may here add, that the scientific information communicated to us by the latter gentleman during our sojourn in his native city was only exceeded by the kind and unpretending civilities which he, in common with his countrymen, show to the stranger, whatever may be his rank or clime.

The turkey is a native of the western hemisphere; but by one of those accidental circumstances, like that which gave the name of America to the country, it has received its appellation from a territory of which it is not indigenous.

The most conspicuous objects in this well-arranged Museum are the skeletons of a very large horse and man. The latter, having a dart in his hand, is astride the former, which is in the act of galloping. The group is terribly fine.

The Franklin Library, honoured with the name from the circumstance of that great philosopher and statesman having been among its early promoters, contains a large and useful collection of books; and in the front of the building is a well-executed statue of this wonderful man. The house in which he resided has, in the spirit of improvement, been pulled down; but the spot in the Episcopal cemetery, where " his body lies buried in peace," is designated by a memorial as unostentatious as were the habits of the philosopher himself. A plain, solid, white marble slab covers his dust, together with that of his faithful companion; and the stranger reads thereon, —

$$\left.\begin{array}{c} \text{Benjamin} \\ \& \\ \text{Deborah} \end{array}\right\} \quad \begin{array}{c} \text{Franklin,} \\ \text{1790.} \end{array}$$

There is a quaint accordance in the old-fashioned name of Deborah with Benjamin Franklin particularly striking; and although

one looked for some more elaborate memorial
of so great a man, yet I doubt whether any
thing could be devised more effective, and
certainly not more congenial to the expressed
wishes of the deceased, than the simple tomb-
stone I have described. I had spent hours at
the resting places of popes, of emperors, of
kings, and of doges, in admiration, and as-
tonished at the splendid efforts of art which
have been raised over their remains ; but in
many instances without bestowing a thought
on the individuals whose memories they were
intended to honour. Alas ! how different are
the feelings at the grave of Franklin ! His
whole life passes as it were before one, from
the periods of his juvenile and humble occupation of cutting and preparing the wicks of
candles at Boston ; his forlorn situation, when,
strolling up the streets of Philadelphia with
the rolls under his arm, he was observed by
his future wife ; to that when, " self-taught
and self-directed," as has been not less classically than truly said, —

Eripuit cœlo fulmen, sceptrumque tyrannis.

He snatched the lightning from heaven, and the sceptre
from tyrants.

The mansion where the stern republican

o 3

patriot, Jefferson, composed the charter of American freedom, has been more fortunate than that of his fellow labourer. The edifice stands unaltered, and the chamber in which he wrote was pointed out to us.

Besides the great debt of gratitude which America owes to her Jefferson, for that nervous and uncompromising state paper, the Declaration of Independence, and his share in its enforcement, she is under infinite obligations to his philosophical mind, which displayed itself in all the varied offices which he was successively called upon to fill. Will it be credited, that in return for such invaluable services, because he entertained some abstract opinions in matters which rested between himself and his Maker (and which, of course, ought to have been held sacred), not in unison with those of persons in authority, in the year 1830, his Life and Correspondence, then just published, were refused a place in the public Library of Philadelphia? — " Tell it not in Gath, publish it not in the streets of Ascalon." Such conduct is an insult to the manes of the immortal founders of the country.

Philadelphia possesses her Academy of the Fine Arts, as well as those of the Sciences ; and the increasing collection of antiques, casts, and paintings, together with their neat arrangement, proves the anxiety of the citizens to combine the refinements with the more useful arts of life, and realise the motto, " Utile dulci."

The gallery is indebted to the worthy Count Survilliers for several of the choicest pieces in the collection ; among which are, pictures of his brother Napoleon crossing the Alps, by David ; and a full length of himself as King of Spain, painted, I believe, for the palace at Madrid. What opposite destinies for the subject of the picture, as well as for the picture itself!

In the court before the building is a mutilated antique statue, presented by some American officer who had served on the Mediterranean station.

None but those who have whiled " the sultry hours away," in the voluptuous regions washed by that sea, and pondered amidst the wrecks of antiquity, can fully appreciate the feelings excited by even a passing glance of this isolated relic ; which, as often as I saw it, appeared like a connecting link between the old and the new world, and elicited a thousand delightful reminiscences of youthful days of travel.

CHAP. XI.

Of the various places of worship which we
visited during our stay in Philadelphia, that of
the principal Episcopal Church was the most
interesting, from its associations. Here the
pious Washington offered up his prayers to
the Great First Cause, to that Incomprehen-
sible Being in whose hands are the fate of
empires, and before whom the mightiest are
as dust.

The pew which he occupied was pointed out
to us by a member of the congregation, whose
politeness had been shown on our entrance, by
providing us with seats, -- an attention much
neglected by the same denomination of Christians in England, who in this particular seem
to forget that one of the first duties inculcated by the persecuted founder of the Christian religion was kindness to the stranger.

We were disappointed in our visits to this
church, in not having the pleasure of hearing
the venerable Bishop White, who, although
upwards of eighty years of age, occasionally

ministered to his flock. This patriarchal individual officiated as chaplain to the first Congress; every member of which, except one,
he had survived.

The spire of the building is surmounted by
a gilt Cap of Liberty, — an ornament very common even to the ecclesiastical edifices in American cities; and in the tower are the bells
which had saluted our ears on our arrival in
Philadelphia.

The Unitarian Church, which is a modern
and ornamental edifice, contains a pulpit or
rostrum of extreme classical simplicity, and
well worthy of being the model for those places
of worship where altars are not required.

The general plan is the same as that of the
one in the Unitarian Church in New York,
which I have attempted to describe; but the
effect, from the introduction of two Doric
columns supporting an entablature in front of
the recess, is heightened. This sect of Christians, whose numbers in Philadelphia, at the
period of Dr. Priestley's occasional ministry,
did not exceed fifty persons, is fast increasing.

The principles, although subject to fierce
attacks from the pulpits of what are denominated orthodox Christians, have taken deep
hold of the community; many of the most

literary characters of the Union being professed Unitarians; and numbers of individuals are gradually abandoning the system in which they were educated, and attaching themselves to this, in which reason holds a more prominent station.

At the evening services in this place, which were extremely well attended, we saw a considerable sprinkling of members of the Society of Friends, whose heresy was not concealed by any alteration of costume.

Whilst upon the subject of the Unitarian Church, I may relate a little mistake in regard to identity, which caused no small amusement at the time.

A report having been circulated one Sunday morning, that the talented author of the Sketch Book had just arrived in Philadelphia, it so happened that I had the honour to be taken for that charming writer; and whilst sitting in church, as well as on leaving, the supposed fact was whispered about.

The evening service was attended by increased numbers, prompted by a laudable curiosity to behold so bright an ornament of their literature; when, lo! even the supposed Washington Irving was not present, and the disappointed throng separated, informed of the innocent imposture of which I had been made the subject.

We were much surprised to find in this Quaker City, as Philadelphia is often styled, no less than three large and elegant theatres, as well as a newly erected concert room.

Only one of the former places of amusement, or schools of instruction, — for the latter is, perhaps, an equally proper designation, — happened to be open during our visit; and that was not, as I found, the one patronised by the fashionable world, although the best adapted for dramatic effect.

The better to study national manners and peculiarities, I generally made it a rule, in my visits to places of public resort, to arrive at the opening of the doors; and on the evening of that to the Walnut Street Theatre, I found myself seated solus on the third bench of the large pit, some time after the corps of money-receivers, cheque-takers, and box-keepers, were all at their respective posts.

By and by a few, not lean, but certainly unwashed, artificers seated themselves around me; one of whom, evidently not of the abstemious school, seemed disposed to be upon the very best terms with his neighbours; and addressing himself to me in the most familiar manner, began what was likely to be a very long story about a forged bill which he had taken in payment, and his good wife's anger at his conduct.

Not being anxious to cultivate the friendship of my new acquaintance, nor my English feelings exactly according with the spitting habits of the grade among which I had located myself, I cut the matter of the bill short by quitting the pit, and proceeding to what we denominate the dress circle.

The house, as the hour of performance approached, filled rapidly; but in vain did I cast my eyes to the doors of the boxes, as they opened, for damsels in all the pride of ornament, handed to their seats by spruce gallants; for no such sight met the eye. In lieu thereof, substantial tradesmen and mechanics, fresh from their counters or their workshops, poured in with their merry wives and daughters; and the curtain rose to as full, and certainly as free and easy, an assemblage as I ever witnessed. The principal performance of the evening was the musical drama of Rob Roy, which was well played by an English company. The scenery, dresses, music, all were good; and the illusion was complete. In the pantomime spectacle which followed,

some humorous satire was played off against
a resident empiric, an American Doctor Solo-
mon, who warranted his panacea to be the
true and veritable elixir of life : in short, to
cure all manner of diseases, and almost to re-
store the dead.

An individual, represented as a vender of
this Balm of Gilead, was introduced on the
stage ; and we certainly had ocular demon-
stration of its wonderful powers.

After taking a single bottle, blacks became
white, wrinkled old maids became blooming
nymphs of sweet eighteen, the halt and
maimed frisked about, and, lastly, the Siamese
twins were plucked asunder, and joined the
quack in a merry jig. The delighted audience
testified their approbation by many a round of
applause ; and when the curtain dropped, all
dispersed, evidently satisfied that, in the account of pleasure, they had had value received.

The greatest quiet reigned in the streets
contiguous to the theatre, strongly contrasted
with the like neighbourhoods in England, or
even in New York ; and scarcely half a dozen
coaches were in waiting at the conclusion of
the performance.

One of the largest edifices in Philadelphia,

or indeed in America, is the New State Prison, or Penitentiary, which is situated in a quarter of the city not yet built upon.

This great receptacle of crime consists of eight ranges of buildings containing solitary cells and workshops, which diverge from a centre; and the whole are enclosed by a lofty stone wall, forming a square, each side of which measures 650 feet.

The grand entrance is castellated, as are also the angles; and the design is highly creditable to the architect. I was informed that the system pursued in regard to the prisoners was, in most respects, the same as in the Penitentiaries of the State of New York.

Enlightened as the Americans are on this branch of civil polity, they are by no means inattentive to the opinions of the philanthropists of Europe; and at several conversations upon the subject of criminal codes and prison discipline, at which I happened to be present, it gave me pleasure to hear the authorities of a Romilly and a Roscoe alluded to with all that respect to which such minds are justly entitled; and it was a further gratification, on these occasions, to be enabled to claim the latter distinguished writer and advocate of liberal principles, not only as a countryman, but as a townsman and friend.

In the neighbourhood of the Penitentiary are the celebrated works which supply the city with that important article, water.

The reservoirs, which are situated on the summit of a hill, 100 feet above the Schuylkill, contain upwards of twelve millions of gallons, and are supplied by pumps worked by large water wheels, the river being dammed for the purpose.

The buildings containing the machinery, as well as the terraces adjoining, are kept in remarkably neat order. On the brow of a rocky and romantic precipice, which almost overhangs the works, a pretty little open temple has been erected, from which there is a charming view of the river, and the beautiful villa and domain called Lemon Hill, the summer residence of one of the most wealthy merchants of Philadelphia.

The grounds of this half Italian retreat, which we often visited, were laid out with much taste, and ornamented with grottoes, fish-ponds, and jets d'eau ; and the conservatory, which is very extensive, was well stocked with rare and curious plants from all parts of the globe. There was, however, an air of neglect

about the whole, which did not correspond
with the extreme neatness and order observable in the city.

A little below the water-works the Schuylkill is crossed by a timber bridge of one arch,
probably the largest in the world, the chord
measuring no less than 320 feet; and, somewhat further down, directly opposite the main
street of Philadelphia, in that direction, there
is another bridge of three large arches, the
piers of which are stone.   Both these structures are covered, and have windows or open-
ings at each side, at regular intervals.   The
road-ways are divided in the centre; and
notices are posted up, forbidding the drivers of
vehicles to pass over the bridges at a quick
pace.

In this quarter is an infant establishment
for the manufacture of china, the ingenious
proprietor of which is an American, who owes
his successful commencement to an unassisted
but ardent pursuit of the knowledge requisite
to his undertaking.   The quality of the specimens of china I examined was exceedingly
good, and the decorative part was tasteful and
well executed.

Although the projector of this interesting
little manufactory had met with very liberal

encouragement from his fellow-citizens, we were informed that he found a powerful opposition in the great import of French china, the extreme beauty of which, combined with its cheapness, notwithstanding a duty of twenty per cent., insures it a ready sale.

The great market of Philadelphia, which is above half a mile in length, has no pretensions to architectural beauty; it being, in fact, merely a succession of long commodious sheds in the centre of the principal street, separated or intersected by those streets which cross it in an opposite direction.

In this neat and well-supplied mart of provisions, where the best beef-steaks are sold at four-pence per pound; fatted turkeys, as large as eagles, for three to four shillings each; and all the good things the country produces in the same proportion; we saw the opossum, and also the tortoise, as articles of food,—the flesh of the latter being esteemed a great delicacy. It was impossible to view the former animal, with his long tail, without being reminded of the negro Hamlet's vocal episode, "Opossum up a gum-tree," so humorously introduced by that inimitable artist Matthews, in his "Trip to America."

The last public establishment of Philadelphia

P

which remains to be noticed is the Navy Yard, a place naturally interesting to a native of the isle whose hardy sons have so long ruled the waves. In one of the huge wooden building-houses I saw the leviathan of naval architecture, of which the Americans may justly feel proud, and of which description of floating castles their enemies, unless prepared with equal weapons, may perchance some day feel afraid. The ship in question is 228 feet long by 57 feet in breadth, has four decks, and is intended to carry about 140 guns of the largest calibre. This immense vessel is constructed of what is termed live oak,—a species of timber admirably adapted for ship-building ; and whether as regards size, model, strength, or excellence of workmanship, it may be accounted the *ne plus ultra* of the art.

The adjoining building-house was occupied by a sixty-gun frigate,—a class called into existence by the energies of the American Naval Board, previous to the commencement of the last war, and which, as it is too well known, caused the loss of two or three British frigates, whose " lion-mettled " commanders had the temerity to attack them.

The frames of several ships were stowed in large sheds, each piece of timber being marked, so that they could be put together at a short notice. The yard displayed long rows of cannon, whose stopped muzzles and touch-holes were quite in unison with the peaceful scene presented by the Delaware, whose placid tide was studded with white sails, from the little coasting sloop to the richly freighted merchantman from industrious England, from the lands of corn, wine, and oil, bounding the blue Mediterranean, or from the remote and fertile regions of Bengal or China.

As in the Navy Yard of New York, I spied a few cannon bearing the initials G. R., surmounted by a crown,—trophies of American prowess over the cocks of the sea, as the captain of a Genoese xebeck, in which I once made a short voyage, styled the English.

All this is fair ; and I never looked upon such mementos of my country's defeat with any feelings, save those of regret, that, in spite of early lessons, she should have pursued the same course of insult and injustice, which a second time ended in her disgrace, and elevated the power which it was her great object to humble.

A new era has, however, commenced : England at length possesses a Sovereign whose sentiments are more in accordance with the enlightened spirit of the age, and in whose advisers are concentrated unsullied integrity, splendid talents, the love of political justice, and the most extensive philanthropy. Guided by such, we may reasonably anticipate a long period of happy and beneficial intercourse between the two nations, whose only rivalry should be in the arts of peace.

During our sojourn in this charming city, I had the pleasure to be introduced to the literary conversaziones, called Wistar parties, from the name of an eminent physician of Philadelphia, with whom the idea of these agreeable meetings originated. The Wistar parties are held weekly, and alternately at the houses of the members, and afford great facilities for the bringing together residents, as well as strangers of the same pursuits in science or literature.

As I could not claim the privilege of *entrée* under any particular branch, I was kindly admitted as an amateur of all, although the title of stranger is sufficient in this friendly city to ensure a welcome. Among other literary characters, I had the good fortune to meet the learned Doctor Du Ponçeau, the countryman and early companion of that noble and consistent patriot Lafayette. Immediately after our introduction, the Doctor questioned me as to my first impressions on landing in America; and when I told him that the high character of the working classes, and the total absence of mob or rabble, seemed to me the distinguishing characteristic, he seemed much pleased, adding in his own way, "Sir, you have said a great deal; but why does not your countryman Captain Hall say so?" I replied, that I could not answer for the feelings of that gentleman. Perhaps the fact escaped his notice.

Having lingered in Philadelphia beyond the period when the rivers are usually closed by ice, we were suddenly warned, by a frosty night, to hasten our departure for Washington; and we accordingly embarked in the first steamer for Baltimore, which great city lies in the route. Acting upon the maxim, "Better an hour too soon than a minute too late!" I had directed the black servant to call us at six o'clock precisely, the packet leaving at seven. Sambo, mistaking the light of the moon, which happened to be at the full, for that of day, sounded the note of preparation somewhat earlier; and, to my surprise and vexation, came thundering at the door just as the deep-toned bell of the State House tolled two. Like Mercutio's soldier, roused by Queen

Mab, I swore a prayer or two, and slept again.
At six, we were once more awoke by salvos of
artillery in honour of the anniversary of the
battle of New Orleans, which is observed
with great enthusiasm ; and proceeding to the
packet, at seven were ploughing the Delaware.

The morning was bright and clear to a
degree scarcely conceivable to Englishmen
who have not witnessed American, or other
skies than those of their own weeping climate. The beautiful ships at anchor in the
noble river sat like swans, so gracefully and
so proudly, whilst the busy steamers plying
between the city and the shores of New Jersey gave animation to the interesting picture.

We had not been long on board before " a
goodly, portly gentleman," conceiving us to
be Americans, addressed himself to my wife,
next to whom he happened to be seated, as
follows : — " So, madam, you are not stopping
to keep the glorious anniversary."

Aware of his mistake as regarded our country, she replied jokingly, " It is to avoid the
festivities, sir, that we are leaving the city."

" What !" said he, evidently much surprised,
" not rejoice at such a triumph as the victory
of New Orleans, where twelve thousand of

Wellington's veteran troops were beaten by
a few of our young farmers?"

Thinking he had gone far enough under a
false impression, and not knowing what harsh
speech might come next, I at once explained
that we were English. Astounded at the
discovery, our friend coughed — hemmed —
and, not a little confused, apologized for the
mistake, but he thought — he ——"

Here I relieved him from his embarrassment
by requesting he would not make any apology,
as none was required; and, at the same time,
I remarked, that if his countrymen should
visit our shores in the same hostile manner,
we should, of course, give them a similar
warm reception.

The *éclaircissement* caused a laugh on our
parts, in which our new acquaintance, as well
as others, joined; and after some remarks
upon the disastrous issue of the expedition
alluded to, which I considered attributable to
the delays and blunders of the commander-in-
chief, he opened a discussion upon the state
of England and America, which was resumed
in the course of the day.

Like most of the Americans with whom I
conversed, to be independent of England
seemed the ultimatum of his ambition; for-

getting that the welfare of every country is most essentially promoted by intercourse and reciprocity of advantages. In his dream of this anticipated state of independence, he exultingly exclaimed, that in fifty years America would not import a single package from Great Britain. I somewhat damped this feeling by remarking, that, perhaps, in that time, England would not require a single bag of American cotton, or American flour; but I added, that I hoped the day was not far distant when the good sense of all nations would induce them to abandon the fallacious theory of what is styled the protecting system; and, throwing open their ports, buy where they can find the cheapest market, and sell at the dearest.

The recent removal of the oldest American Consul in Great Britain, and who had received his appointment from the hands of Washington himself, gave rise to a tough argument upon the policy of what the democratic republican party term rotation in office, — a system much more in favour with the *outs* than the *ins*. I expressed my doubts whether the uncertain tenure of office did not rather tend to repel men of steady, fixed habits, who would do credit to the stations to which they might be appointed, and to invite as candidates those of an opposite character. My friend's opinions, however, were not to be shaken, at least by any arguments I could wield.

Of the celebrated Cobbett, he spoke as one having a greater respect for his talents than his consistency.

The banks of the Delaware below Philadelphia are much less picturesque than those of the Hudson, but they are agreeably diversified by villages and farm-houses, which, being chiefly of brick, have something English in their general appearance.

We passed Newcastle, one of the oldest settlements in the country, having been founded by the Swedes in 1627, and for some time after called Stockholm. On an island, a few miles lower down the river, a very formidable fort has been erected, which commands the channels on both sides; and nearly opposite is the embryo city of Delaware, consisting of half a dozen houses. At this place, which is forty miles from Philadelphia, we left the steamer, and proceeded by the new canal which unites the waters of the Delaware and the Chesapeake. This communication has been made at a great expense; for although the distance is only fourteen miles, the marshy nature of the country presented many obstacles to the engineers. The usefulness of the undertaking is, however, very apparent; and the traffic on it will, no doubt, repay the outlay.

The packet-boat on this canal was drawn by six horses, and we performed the passage in two hours.

Near the western end is a deep cutting of seventy feet, over which a timber bridge has been thrown of 280 feet span.

The canal communicates, in the first instance, with a creek, the banks of which are thickly covered with wood. Here we again embarked in a steamer, and soon after entered the Elk river, which brought us into the great arm of the sea, called the Chesapeake, just at the point where it receives the noble meandering Susquehanna.

After a few hours' rather rough sailing, we found ourselves entering the Patapsco; and in an hour or two more we reached Baltimore, having travelled by rivers and canal above one hundred miles in the course of the day.

The accommodations and the fare, both in the steamers and on the canal, were excellent; and the charges, as usual, very moderate. At Baltimore we were lodged at the famed hotel kept by a spirited individual named Barnum.

This establishment is the largest of the kind in the New World: one of the fronts measuring 117 feet, and the other nearly 200 feet. It contains two hundred rooms, some of which are very spacious; also a news-room, well furnished with papers. On the basement story are the Post Office, and the offices for the mail-coaches and other conveyances.

The whole of the extensive arrangements reflect credit on the proprietor, who, we were sorry to hear, was not remunerated for his exertions.

One of the first objects which met our eyes, on strolling out the next morning, was a funeral. It was evidently of a person in genteel circumstances, from the number of private carriages in attendance; and some trouble had been taken to produce a solemn effect, but to little purpose. The carriages were very old-fashioned, and had seen their best days; and the coachmen and footmen, who were all blacks, were attired in rusty old crape hat-bands, which trappings harmonised most disadvantageously with the shining jet faces of the wearers.

Although the extensiveness of the black and coloured population had particularly excited our notice on arriving in New York, yet as we proceeded in the direction of the slave-holding States, their numbers evidently increased. At Philadelphia, we found the porters who attend the landing-places, and who carry the baggage of passengers, all of that class. The waiters in the packets on the Delaware and Chesapeake were coloured men; and at Baltimore not only the porters, but a gréat proportion of the hackney coachmen, carters, and others, were of the African race.

Deferring our inspection of this flourishing city until our return from the seat of government, we took the first conveyance to that skeleton of a metropolis, Washington.

The distance from Baltimore is thirty-eight miles. The country is uninteresting, but the road, for America, was good.

About five miles from Washington, we passed through the little village of Bladensburgh, rendered memorable from the brilliant affair of arms preceding the taking of the capital, and which was almost the only conflict of any importance during the last war, in which the Americans were not triumphant.

The British army lost above five hundred men in killed and wounded, in passing the little bridge, which here crosses the creek called the east branch of the Potomac. This severe loss was principally owing to the skill and bravery of Commodore Barney, of the American navy, who, with a party of sailors, and two heavy guns, planted on the opposite height commanding the village, swept the bridge with grape. The American militia stand accused of not doing their duty on this eventful day, and thereby abandoning the capital to its fate; be this as it may, however, it is agreed on all hands that the British commander caused a needless waste of life in forcing a passage of the river at Bladensburgh, when an unprotected ford was not far distant. The gallant Barney was wounded and taken prisoner, but afterwards exchanged for an English officer of rank who had met with a similar fate. In consequence of the subsequent precipitate retreat of the British, their unfortunate wounded could not be removed; but it gave us pleasure to hear, from the best authority, that they all experienced the most humane and generous treatment from the enemy, who, in this and other instances, proved, that they warred more with the government of England, than with the people. Like all battle fields of recent date, that of

Bladensburgh exhibits its melancholy tokens of the strife, in grass-grown hillocks covering the bones of the fallen combatants; and as night was just setting in, and some snow falling as we left, the scene looked chill and melancholy.

In less than an hour we were informed we were in Washington, although we had not noticed a single house; and looking through the window of the coach, beheld the Capitol in lonely magnificence. Passing close to this noble edifice, we drove down the principal avenue, and alighted at one of the hotels, where, before a blazing log fire, and surrounded by no less than half a dozen shining black faces of both sexes, we sat down to tea. These sable attendants, who were new in their vocation, caused us no small degree of amusement. If a bell sounded, or a call was heard for Antony, Cæsar, Laura, or Lily, away they all scampered together; and when we, in our turn, desired our wants supplied, the whole band, as if by magic, and grinning with delight appeared, again.

Our arrival proved to be opportune, and was matter of self-congratulation; for, the day after, there fell torrents of rain; and a north

wester springing up,—which wind in America,
produces the greatest degree of cold,—pene-
trated each chink and cranny ; and the morning following, the great Potomac, which is
here above a mile in width, was a firm
sheet of ice.

CHAP. XII.

THE city of Washington, the metropolis of the United States of America, was founded, at the close of the last century, upon a section of land ten miles square, which was ceded by the States of Maryland and Virginia for the purpose, and which is now under the special government of Congress, and termed the District of Columbia. The plan of the embryo capital is at once grand and unique. Very long and broad avenues diverge from centres, and are intersected by streets at right angles. Only one of the former, however, and not many of the latter, contain any buildings ; and these are, for the most part, as paltry as they are scattered, although the city contains a population of twenty thousand persons.

The chief architectural ornament of Washington, and, indeed, of the Union, is the edifice called the Capitol, in which are the Chambers of Congress, the Supreme Courts, and the National Library. This noble building, which stands on a most commanding site, is 350 feet in length, and is surmounted by a lofty but heavy dome. The style of architecture is Palladian, and the material freestone ; but, in consequence of the discolouration produced by the burning of the interior by the British, the whole of the outside has been painted white, — a very questionable proceeding as regards effect, to say nothing of the periodical expense which will be thereby incurred.

The principal entrance, which is under a magnificent portico, opens into a circular hall or rotunda, one hundred feet in diameter, and exactly the same in height. The walls of this classical apartment are ornamented with large paintings by the venerable Colonel Trumbull, to whom I have before made allusion.

The subjects of these pictures are illustrative of the principal scenes of the Revolution, and they are particularly valuable as containing undoubted portraits of almost all the leading characters of that eventful period, painted by the familiar companion of many of the individuals. The costume of the time is also strictly preserved, giving additional interest to the figures, whether civil or military. The signers of the Declaration of Independence, with the exception of the uncompromising Jefferson, who figures in a blue coat and scarlet waistcoat,

Q

have rather a courtly air. The virtuous and revered Franklin is represented in a suit of black, which I was delighted to imagine the identical one of Manchester velvet, worn before the Privy Council, when, with " a conscience void of blame," this great philosopher calmly received the insults of a Wedderburne; and which suit he again wore in Paris at the signing of the treaty which deprived Great Britain of her thirteen colonies, having then, indeed, received glorious " satisfaction."

In the pictures representing the surrenders of General Burgoyne and Lord Cornwallis the artist has not been unmindful to contrast the elated looks of the Americans and French, with the chap-fallen countenances of the beaten English, which certainly denote big Mars to have become bankrupt.

The smaller panels contain alto relievos allusive to the early settlement of America. One of these represents Captain Smith saved by the tender Pocahontas from the fury of her father, King Powhatan, a subject full of romantic interest. The subjects of the others are, — The landing of the persecuted band of English worthies at Plymouth in 1610 — The conference of Penn with the Indian chiefs on the banks of the Delaware, — and a conflict between the intrepid Boon, one of the explorers of the great western country, and an Indian chief.

The Hall, or Chamber of Representatives, the largest and most elegant apartment of the kind in the world, is semi-circular, and is ornamented with noble variegated marble columns, procured in the neighbourhood of the Potomac. The superb Corinthian capitals and bases are of statuary, and were wrought at Carrara. The ceiling is a semi-dome, and handsomely painted. The members, or representatives, sit in handsome arm chairs, at mahogany desks, which are provided with materials for writing, glasses of water, and, in spite of the protecting system, with penknives of real Sheffield manufacture. Every member has also a spitting box, which articles are indispensable to the chewers and smokers.

On the left of the speaker hangs a fine full length portrait of La Fayette, painted by a French artist. A gallery, free to the public of both sexes, without the imposition of fees, extends along the semicircle, from which the effect of the hall during the sitting of congress is exceedingly imposing.

The chamber appropriated to the senate, or that branch of the legislature not immediately popular, is upon the same general plan as that of the representatives, although upon a smaller scale. It is elegantly furnished, and, from the circumstance of being also much frequented by the fashionable visiters at Washington, presents a gay appearance. It is not the architectural magnificence of these halls, however, which constitutes their great interest in the mind of the reflecting spectator. It is the moral effect in beholding the freely chosen representatives of the freest nation on the face of the globe, that delights the heart and elevates the mind; and as a humble worshipper at the shrine of Liberty, I envy not the feelings of the man who can contemplate the sublime spectacle unmoved.

During a stay of five weeks in Washington, we had repeated opportunities of attending some of the most important debates, and consequently of hearing some of the best speakers of both the political parties of Congress. The fault of all seemed to be the disposition to extend the field of discussion beyond what was necessary to the subject-matter before the house, and the extreme proneness to digression; in short, the desire to be distinguished for much speaking, in contradistinction to the rules observed by those master spirits, Washington and Franklin, who, as Jefferson informs us, seldom spoke more than ten or fifteen minutes at a time; " seizing," says that distinguished patriot, " the strong points, and leaving the weak ones to fall of themselves." If I did not hear any specimens of what we term the highest style of oratory, — as the splendid harangues of a Chatham, a Fox, a Sheridan, or a Brougham, — I do not recollect to have heard much below mediocrity, or any thing at all approaching to the egregious nonsense occasionally uttered, or the disgusting cant which has so lately disgraced another assembly.

The order and decorum observed in the chambers of America are well worthy of adoption in those of Great Britain; where the present system of cheering, by way of expressing approbation, and coughing down, as it is termed, to denote the reverse, are at once disgraceful, and beneath the dignity of deliberative and enlightened senators. I must confess, however, that the absence of an occasional "Hear, hear!" to which significant expression of opinion one has been so accustomed, detracted somewhat from the effect of a bold period, or a happy and pointed allusion. The American legislators, more rational than those

of the mother-country, do not devote the
night to the business of the day. The hour
of meeting is twelve at noon; and the ad-
journment, except on particular occasions,
takes place at three. The punctuality with
which the motion for the latter is made, often
to the interruption of a speaker, surprised me.
The instant the clock told the appointed time
some member started up, and moved, that the
house should adjourn; which being promptly
seconded, all the members hastened to their
boarding-houses: the flags which floated during the hours of business over the roofs of the
chambers were lowered, and the doors closed.

When a spirited debate was anticipated, the
hall of the senate became the rendezvous of
beauty from all parts of the Union, as the
delegates of the people are often accompanied
to Washington by their wives or daughters.
The delicate paleness of the damsels from the
south was strikingly opposed to the blooming
complexions of the daughters of New England.

No placeman or holder of any office whatever
under the government can sit in Congress.
The members of both houses receive eight
dollars per day during the session, besides a
compensation for travelling. Those of the
senate are styled Honourable. This title,

together with that of Excellency, applied to the President, were bestowed at the period of the formation of the constitution, and whilst some of the " old leaven" of aristocracy yet remained; but how the enlightened republicans of the present day can consistently retain these high sounding terms I am at a loss to conceive. Their use is not, however, more absurd than that of esquire, which we found to linger in the older cities. Prostituted as this latter title may have become in England, where it is tacked to the names of all but the mere " hewers of wood and drawers of water," it has there some palliation in the circumstance of the government being monarchical, and so many relics of feudal times existing; but in free America, where liberty and equality is the motto, it is as tinkling brass, an empty sound, and unworthy of a reflecting people, whom its use subjects to merited ridicule. Jefferson protested against these follies years ago, and, in his true republican simplicity, even recommended the abolition of Mr. as prefixed to surnames. Whether this recommendation was attended to by the " business men" at the time, I know not, but I observed, that packages of goods at warehouses, or at wharfs for shipment, were invariably directed by the simple Christian and surname of the parties; no Mr., Messrs., or esquire, even appearing, such being reserved for correspondence.

The Library of Congress, which is a large and classical apartment open to the public, contains above 20,000 volumes; all supplied since the wanton destruction of the former collection by the British troops.

Many of the books now on the shelves were presented to the nation by Jefferson; and some of them contain marginal notes in the hand-writing of that acute critic. The Congress Library is the only one in the United States possessing a copy of that magnificent work, Audubon's American Ornithology. Great as the labours of this persevering individual have been, and much as he has done to illustrate the natural history of America, as well as to raise her scientific character, he has scarcely met with the slightest patronage amongst his countrymen; and has been forced to look to England and France for that remuneration which at home he sought in vain. It may be proper to mention, as some little extenuation for this apparent apathy in the cause of science and the fine arts, that the researches and the beautiful works of a Wilson and a Bonaparte had partly supplied the desideratum in the branch of ornithology.

In the supreme Court of Appeal, which is situated in the same building as the apartments described, we saw the venerable Chief Justice Marshall, author of the Life of Washington. The judges in this court wore black gowns, the only instance we observed in America of any official costume in the courts of law.

The view from the gallery on the summit of the dome of the Capitol is very extensive, and the broad Potomac is seen to great advantage ; but the city itself presents a straggling, unconnected appearance, and the eye traces a series of avenues and streets merely chalked out, as it were, on the wide waste.

Our cicerone pointed out a little brook, which has been dignified by the name of Tiber, but which, in the olden time, was known under the less classical appellation of Goose Creek ; and he further called our attention to a railed enclosure, which he denominated the Botanic Garden, although it did not then contain a single tree or shrub, save what nature herself had planted. Whilst musing on the panorama presented from this elevation, I could not avoid contrasting it with that exhibited from the Capitol of the ancient mistress of the world, which I had beheld not many

months before. How different were the sensations produced by the two scenes! In
contemplating the relics of the "Imperial
hearths," and the solemn wrecks of grandeur
which arrest the eye in the eternal city, the
mind is carried back through a series of ages,
until it is lost in remote antiquity. An empire
has risen, flourished, and decayed. There
every thing *has been*,—here, on the contrary,
every thing *is to be:* the reflections are all
prospective; and when we think upon the
gigantic scale of the American republic, her
free institutions, her wonderful progress in
arts and arms, and the unfettered energies of
her rapidly increasing population, it is not indulging in wild speculation to assert, that,
long ere the century of its foundation arrives,
Washington may be the metropolis of the most
powerful nation in the world.

The official residence of the President, or
the White House, as I occasionally heard it
termed, is situated on elevated ground about
a mile and a half from the Capitol. It is a
large and handsome edifice of stone; and
contains a suit of apartments furnished in a
genteel, but not extravagant, style. Having
suffered a similar fate with the Capitol in
1814, the exterior has, like that building, been
painted. The area in front, with the drives,

exhibited an appearance very different from
the grounds of English mansions, where neatness is carried to such excess, that even a
decayed leaf is not allowed to obtrude itself
upon the notice.

The railing to the road appeared as if it had
not received a coat of paint since it was fixed,
to use a verb in great favour with the Americans, and which is applied to any thing and
every thing under the sun : the walks were
unweeded and rough, the grass plot was strewn
with fragments of bones and other rubbish ;
and, to complete the coup d'œil, we sometimes
saw sheets, table-cloths, and sundry body
linen, displayed in true washerwoman's array
in the grounds immediately before the drawing-
room windows; all which things might be
conformable to republican simplicity, but assuredly did not meet our ideas of good taste,
when associated with Corinthian porticoes and
noble saloons.

During the sitting of Congress, the President holds levees or drawing-rooms ; the peculiar characteristics of which, as opposed to
those of European courts, are being open to
the public, and wholly divested of state.   On
the appointed evenings the doors are thrown
open at eight o'clock ; and the company, as

they arrive, pass into the drawing-room, where,
if it is their wish, they are presented to the
President, with whom it is usual to shake
hands. Some slight refreshments are occasionally handed by waiters in plain clothes;
and the whole, after promenading the apartments for an hour or two, retire. On the
evening of our visit, about 1000 persons of
both sexes were present, all of whom were
well dressed. Some of the foreign ministers
and strangers of rank wore their stars and
other decorations. The President, General
Jackson, whose bow would pass the ordeal of
the Tuileries or St. James's, is a tall thin man,
apparently about sixty-five. His visage is long
and pale, his hair grey, very bushy, and
combed upwards; and when we had the honour
of being presented, he was in mourning, having
recently lost his wife.

Although, as I have observed, the doors
are thrown open to all indiscriminately, we
only noticed two or three persons who had
the appearance of operative farmers or mechanics, and these ventured no further than
the entrance to the first drawing-room, where,
after gazing upon the brilliant throng for a
few minutes, and not anticipating amusement,
took their departure. We were informed that

the working classes prefer having their own evenings, particularly that of New Year's day, when they muster in full force to shake hands with the nation's chief magistrate.

The presence of guards of honour, of bands of gentlemen pensioners, and of livery servants, are, happily for the people, unknown in America; but the objection to music at the levees, as too closely approximating to royal state, seems less weighty, and the absence of sweet sounds certainly deprives them of much enlivening interest.

How a proposition for the introduction of a military, or, indeed, any band into the mansion of the President would be received, may be judged, when I state that the directions for the drivers of coaches, as to setting down and taking up the company, and which appeared in the Washington papers, were the subject of ridicule, although such regulations were absolutely necessary to prevent accidents.

To our surprise none of the Indians made their appearance at the levees, although several of rank were on a visit to the capital at the time. These interesting remnants of their race, whose fallen state was apparent in their " dejected 'haviour of the visage," were generally to be seen in the bar-room, or under the

portico of their hotel.   They were attired in
fashionable costume ; in which, however, they
did not appear at ease, and all wore Scotch
plaid cloaks.

Some laughable anecdotes were circulated
respecting the deportment of these strangers
at table, who, it seemed, were perfectly " at
home," and thought nothing of throwing the
bones from their plates upon a Brussels or
Turkey carpet, and committing other little
breaches of politeness, not exactly in keeping
with the rules of polished society.

Contiguous to the residence of the President
are the public offices of the government, in
one of which, that of the department of state,
is a collection of authentic portraits of Indian
chiefs in the territories of the United States.
The collection is particularly interesting, as an
exhibition of the pictures of individuals whose
characters are well known, and the physiogno-
mist may find much to attract his notice in
these lineaments of the sons of the forest.

In the same apartment are a great variety
of Indian dresses, ornaments, and weapons,
and we saw some silver medals of George III.,
which had been presented to chiefs by the
British government, and afterwards given by
these worthies to the Americans.   In the bu-

reau of foreign affairs are deposited the treaties
between the United States and other powers.
All these documents are on parchment, neatly
written, and are bound in velvet, richly ornamented with gold trappings, bearing the immense wax seals appended in silver boxes.

I was sorry to observe, for the credit of the
fine arts in my own country, that the seal of
Great Britain was by far the worst executed
of any ; while, strange to say, that of America was the best, both in design and execution.

It is not the gewgaw finery, however, but
the occasion and subject of these treaties, and
the autographs of the signers, which renders
them worthy of notice. One of the first in the
catalogue is that between Great Britain and
the United States immediately after the revolutionary war ; and in which, despite of bold
ciphers, I imagined I saw the subdued obstinacy of George III.

A treaty with France under the consulate
was highly interesting, from its bearing the
signatures of Bonaparte and Talleyrand. The
latter is curious, from its not commencing with
a capital letter. Those of the new republics
of South America inspired cheering anticipations, notwithstanding the occasional effer-
vescences of party spirit, and the intrigues of

ambitious men, to which they may be for a long period subject. Together with the treaties, we were permitted to examine a number of jewelled snuff-boxes, swords, and various articles presented by foreign powers to American ministers at their courts; who, by a wise law of the constitution, are forbidden to retain such, and they are in consequence given up to the department of state.

The great object of attraction in this division of the public offices, and which, to the lover of civil and religious liberty is alone worth a pilgrimage to behold, is the original Declaration of Independence. This sacred and precious roll, the most valuable civil document in existence, is of parchment, and for its better preservation has lately been framed and glazed. The writing is very distinct, but the signatures have suffered a good deal from the fingers of well-meaning but thoughtless individuals. The secretary, to whose care the document is intrusted, informed us that he had only just time to convey it to a place of safety, before the British troops commenced the destruction of the public buildings; and that, but for his exertions, this invaluable relic must have fallen a prey to the flames. We also learnt from another officer of government the important fact, that, upon the occasion of Captain Hall's visit, that gentleman held his infant child to the suspended parchment, which he, to the astonishment of the Americans present, obliged it to kiss.

The other public edifices of Washington, devoted to civil purposes, are, the City Hall, and the General Post Office, the first of which, when completed, will present a handsome appearance. The latter is a large brick building, defaced, as is too common in America, by a covering of bright yellow paint. In one wing of the structure is the Patent Office, where are deposited and arranged models of all the machinery for which patents have been enrolled in the United States.

The preservation of this valuable collection of mechanical ingenuity from the melancholy fate of the stores of literature in the Capitol, was owing to the timely interference of a British officer, who, with a mind superior to that of his commander, arrested the hand of the soldier about to apply a torch to the building.

The churches are upon a small scale, and presented nothing particularly worthy of notice. In one of them, the Unitarian, we saw that accomplished scholar and statesman, the

R

ex-President Adams, who is a member of the
sect. The present chief of the republic is
attached to the Presbyterian denomination.
For the convenience of the members of Congress, the noble Hall of the Representatives is
opened on Sundays as a place of worship, but
we found the attendance very small.

The Navy Yard of Washington is situated
near the mouth of what is called the eastern
branch of the Potomac, which is navigable for
a short distance for vessels of the largest class.

A sixty gun frigate, bearing the name of
the river, had been recently launched, and
another vessel of the same description was on
the stocks.

At the entrance of the yard are two immense brass guns, highly polished, and bearing
the arms of Spain, by which power they were
presented to the American government.

In the area of this arsenal is likewise a
rostrated column of white marble, surrounded
by emblematical figures, erected, as the inscription states, to the memories of the officers
who fell in an attack upon Tripoli. A more
recent inscription states that this monument
was mutilated by Britons in the year 1814.

Without dwelling upon the folly of a nation
thus recording its own disgrace, in allowing an

enemy to pollute its sanctuaries, I must be permitted to remark, that the damage alluded to is not, after all, of a very serious nature; being nothing more than what might have been done by any tipsy soldier with the end of his bayonet.

Had the demolition of this monument been meditated, it could easily have been effected by half a dozen men in as many minutes; but that such was not the case, is evident from the circumstance of it alone having been left standing, while all the magazines and warlike stores in this government establishment were either burnt or destroyed.

Happy would it have been, had the invaders, who, in the capture of Washington, respected private property, limited their powers of destruction to the legitimate objects of warfare; then would not England have to bear the deep and lasting disgrace of an act of Vandalism unparalleled in modern times, — the deliberate burning of a splendid library.

Notwithstanding the anxiety of the Americans to be independent of other countries in respect to what are styled the useful arts, they by no means exhibit the same zeal in matters of taste, or even in those of science, not directly bearing upon the advancement of wealth; and the United States stand alone among civilised nations in not possessing a national Observatory. The advantages of such an establishment did not escape the reflecting mind of an Adams, who, during his presidency, strongly recommended the subject to public sanction; but star-gazing not appearing likely to yield a good profit, the proposal was not acted upon, neither has it met with any encouragement from his successor in office.

The district of Columbia, in which Washington is situated, is, as I have observed, formed out of a section of land ceded by the States of Maryland and Virginia, in both of which slavery is still tolerated; and unfortunately it remains, in this respect, upon a par with its neighbours.

From our arrival in this division of the Union, I was extremely anxious to observe the state and general appearance of the black population, and to discern if there was any very perceptible difference between those who were free, and their more unfortunate brethren. The result of my observations tended to confirm the fact; for although the natural gaiety of the negro race is such, that the slave, if not cruelly treated by his master, may occasionally appear insensible to his degraded situation, yet, compared with even the poorest free black, he bears the stamp of bondage on his forehead. The slaves in this district, as well as in others, when not employed by their owners, are hired out to work at various occupa ions for which they may be qualified ; the owner reaping the profit of their exertions. In conversations with the blacks, I found a great reluctance on their parts to confess that they were not free, each wishing to appear to belong to the envied class; all expressed a great horror at the possibility of their being sold and sent to the south, where slavery flourishes in all its deformity.

The newspapers of the metropolis of free America are regularly disgraced by the insertion of the most revolting advertisements of runaway slaves to be sold by auction ; of gangs of men, women, and children on sale for cash or credit — parents without their off-spring, and brothers and sisters together or separate ; — all which abominations, strange to relate, are countenanced under the very eyes of the champions of the rights of man, and in the presence of the standard of liberty. During the five weeks of our sojourn in Washington, several unfortunate runaways were thus disposed of to pay the expenses of their detention in gaol; all of whom, as I heard, were bought, by the dealers in human flesh, for the southern markets.

It was enough to behold slaves, without voluntarily attending the shocking exhibitions of sales of them; but I did not hesitate to denounce such cruelties, together with the whole system of slavery, as often as opportunities presented themselves. The melancholy reflection, however, that slavery is the crying sin of England, as she still perpetuates it in her colonies, prevented my holding her up as an example to America; and an attempt to show the inconsistency and cruel mockery of the sons of freedom holding their fellow creatures in abject bondage, on one occasion, produced the significant reproof, — " Why beholdest thou the mote that is in thy brother's eye, but considerest not the beam that is in thine own eye?" To turn to the brighter side of the picture, I noticed a few circumstances, which, although perhaps trifling in themselves, may undoubtedly be considered as the commencement of a better state of feeling on the part of the slave proprietors.

One of these was the apparent reluctance in slave owners to make use of the term " slave" in conversation with persons whom they suspected of being hostile to the system; the word "servant" being substituted, as having a less opprobrious sound. Another pleasing fact was the disposition shown to speak well of those who were distinguished for humane treatment of the unfortunate beings dependent upon them.

At Washington we attended two meetings of considerable interest, both of which were held in the great Hall of Representatives.

The first was that of the African Colonisation Society, the object of which is for the promoting the removal of the superabundant slave population from the United States to the coast of Africa, the land of their forefathers. The new settlement, which dates its foundation so lately as the year 1827, is situated about two hundred miles from the British colony of Sierra Leone. The whole of the population, excepting one or two individuals, agents or officers of the Society, are emancipated blacks from the United States. The Report read on the occasion was exceedingly flattering: the settlers were healthy; a regular trade had commenced, and was increasing; a newspaper had been established; places of worship opened; in short, the experiment of self-government on the part of

the blacks had been so far most successful,
and had triumphantly refuted the slave-holders
oft reiterated arguments, that " the negro is
of an inferior race, and incapable of being
civilised!"

The numerous speakers who addressed the
meeting, all concurred in lamenting the evils
of slavery; and one, in particular, who repro-
bated the system in strong language, made
the important assertion, " that experience had
proved, that a slave-holding State could not
long remain neighbour to a State in which the
blacks were free."

The force of this sentiment was evidently
appreciated by the meeting, and was much
applauded. However cheering such language
might be, coupled as it was with the glad
tidings that the germs of civilisation had been
planted in benighted regions, with every
prospect of their bringing forth an abundant
harvest, still the consciousness that the labours of the society must, of necessity, be
limited to the deportation of only such a
portion of the slave population as the planters
find it convenient to emancipate, leaving the
mass in hopeless misery, was a drawback from
the pleasurable anticipations; and this was
heightened by the knowledge that the blacks

themselves would rather remain at home, if in the enjoyment of liberty.

The African Colonisation Society must be looked upon as a well-meant plan, and as one which, in time, may create a moral revolution in the natives of the districts of Africa contiguous to Liberia, and even of those in the interior provinces; but, as regards America, its operations seemed rather calculated *to perpetuate than to extinguish slavery.* The scheme, as far as benefiting Africa, and, perhaps, the individuals removed thither, is a good one; but, viewed as the means of getting rid of the whole black population,—which idea is really entertained by many, although not desired by the owners of slaves,—it is chimerical.

The second public meeting at the Capitol was that of the members of the Columbian Institute, a society formed for the purpose of promoting literature. A most eloquent address was delivered on the occasion by Professor Everett of Boston, in which that distinguished scholar and writer, comparing past ages with the present, and in happy allusion to the wonders of the locomotive engine, and other great and recent discoveries, drew a bright picture of the prospects of mankind, and indulged in the idea of future generations being in the possession of still greater knowledge, and looking back to our triumphs with similar feelings to those with which we recur to the triumphs of our forefathers in the old time before us.

It was our intention to have made a pilgrimage to Mount Vernon, the favourite residence of Washington, and where that great chief, justly styled " Pater Patriæ," retired to repose on his well-earned laurels, after having won and consolidated the liberties of his native country. The distance from Washington is only sixteen miles ; but the river being frozen, and the road for a great part of the way impassable at the time for vehicles, induced us to delay the excursion, until some circumstances occurred, which unfortunately obliged us to abandon it altogether.

The mansion and grounds of Mount Vernon command charming views of the beautiful Potomac, on the banks of which river the domain is situated ; and we were informed that every thing remains much in the state in which it was left at the death of its great possessor. The key of that temple of despotism, the Bastile, is among the curiosities shown to strangers. This trophy of the ever-memorable

14th of July, 1789, was presented to Washington by the city of Paris.

The immortal chief lies entombed in a vault in the grounds, into which honoured receptacle his companion in arms, Lafayette, descended, on that patriot's visit to America in 1824, mingling his tears with the mouldering ashes of his valued friend.

The name of Mount Vernon was given to the estate by General Washington's eldest brother, in honour of the British Admiral Vernon, under whom he served at the taking of Porto Bello. This valuable property is now in the possession of Mr. John Adams Washington, a great nephew of the General. About the middle of February, we bade farewell to Washington and the Potomac, and proceeded to Baltimore. On the eve of our departure, an incident of a ludicrous nature took place at the boarding-house, which caused no little diversion at the time among our agreeable circle, and even now may be worth relating.

Having broken the rule as respects douceurs to servants in favour of a black slave boy, who had performed some extra services, he, not having before been in the possession of money, was determined to spend the

amount to his taste in some of the luxuries
indulged in by white people. The little fellow
had been sent, the day before, to a druggist's,
for an emetic for a lady; and in entire ignorance of its nature, and supposing it must
certainly be something very good, off he flew
to the same shop as soon as he had got his
half-dollar, and asked for more of the same
stuff, *alias* " mixture as before," which he
speedily swallowed. Too soon, alas! he per-
ceived the effects of his mistake; and, after
being the subject of a hearty laugh, he was
admonished to be content for the future without luxuries.

The coach in which we travelled to Baltimore was of a lighter construction than
any we had seen in America, and it was
upon steel springs, which was also a novelty.
The horses were excellent, and the driver
civil without a fee. Our companions were
of different grades as respects fashionable
classification of society, but they were all
sensible, well-informed individuals; and, in
opposition to the taciturnity of English stage-
coach travelling, we beguiled the time with
agreeable conversation.

The principal topics discussed, were the
merits of several of the newest publications,

among which Jefferson's Life and Correspondence, and Captain Basil Hall's Travels
in America, came in for their share of praise
or censure. Nothing in the voluminous pages
of the former appeared to be more highly relished than the celebrated letter, showing up
the reigning sovereigns of Europe, about the
period of the establishment of the French
republic; which production I designated Jefferson's Chapter of Kings.

In this spirited effusion, the philosophical
writer states that one half of the crowned
heads of that period were either imbecile or
actually stark mad; and he attributes this im-
becility of mind, in a great degree, to their
system of intermarrying, and abandoning the
grand principle of nature, which, in the animal
as well as vegetable world, demands constant
change.

The fact, as related by Jefferson, that the
personal accomplishments of George IV., in
early life, had been acquired at the expense
of mental cultivation, was believed the more
readily, because that monarch's pleasures and
habits, even in his maturer years, were almost
entirely those of a voluptuary; and more
than once I heard the cognomen of Sar-

danapalus applied to the sovereign of Great
Britain.

In speaking of Captain Hall's work, our
fellow travellers did not deny that that writer's
descriptions were vivid and faithful, as far as
they went; but they were hurt that, in giving
the truth, he had omitted to give the whole
truth.

The Tory politics of Captain Hall were,
however, as may be imagined, the very anti-
podes of the political creed of the Americans,
who glory in the democratic principles of
their government, which they know full well
are the causes of their national prosperity and
happiness; and the taunts of that gentleman
upon their active and progressive legislation,
which he attributes to a fondness for what he
terms " chopping and changing," rather than
the desire to assimilate the institutions, in all
respects, to the enlightened and improving
spirit of the age, produced some caustic remarks.

Among others, it was observed, that his
assertion that the English people were satisfied to remain as they were, was falsified even
at the very time of its promulgation, first,
in the repeal of the Corporation and Test

Acts; and, secondly, in the emancipation of the Catholics; both which just measures were conceded to loudly expressed public opinion.

The apparently triumphant proof also of the author, as to the satisfaction of the nation with its representative system being expressed by the repeated returns of the same individuals, was justly ridiculed; for it is a matter well known in America, that the people of Great Britain had little share in the choice of the members of the Commons House of Parliament, which the republicans were very well aware they considered a mockery of legislation, and merely a chamber of dependants, and tools of an insolent and grasping oligarchy.

It was a prevailing opinion in the United States, that Captain Hall's volumes were written at the instigation of the Tory government of that period, in order to depreciate republican institutions, and thereby repress the growing spirit of freedom at home. Be this as it may, recent " chopping and changing" proves that, in this respect, such writings have been wholly inoperative; the doctrine of the sovereignty of the people having become so virtually recognised in England, as well as in other countries, as to sanction the probability of our being about to witness great and important revolutions in the art of government, and it is to be hoped, as the result, great and important improvements in the social condition of mankind.

CHAP. XIII.

Baltimore, the fourth city of America, in point of extent and population, has literally sprung up in the memory of man. Eighty years ago it contained not more than twenty or thirty mean tenements, and its shipping was limited to one small square-rigged vessel. The same place now numbers upwards of seventy thousand inhabitants, and its ships trade to every quarter of the habitable globe.

Unlike New York or Philadelphia, the surface of the ground upon which the city stands is irregular. The streets are mostly at right angles, and of a good width ; but they are not kept in neat order, and swine innumerable roam at large. The houses are built of excellent red bricks, quantities of which are exported to New York and other places.

The city contains several handsome public edifices ; the principal of which, in point of extent, is the Exchange. This spacious building contains a noble hall for the accommodation of the merchants and others, who meet shaded from the burning suns of summer, or

s

the cold blasts of winter. A gentleman, to whom I expressed my admiration of the beauty of this hall, remarked, as a singular circumstance, and as one that struck him on his travels, that the ports of Great Britain, the greatest commercial nation in the world, with its humid climate too, should not possess any mercantile places of rendezvous of this description open to the public.

Of the class of edifices dedicated to religion, the Roman Catholic Cathedral stands conspicuously distinguished. Baltimore being, if I may be allowed the expression, the headquarters of Catholicism in the United States, and the residence of an archbishop, a very considerable sum has been expended in the erection of a temple worthy of these honours. The building in question is in the form of the sacred symbol of Christianity, and is about two hundred feet in length. It is surmounted by a dome, after the manner of the Pantheon at Rome ; and contains some paintings, one of which was presented by Louis XVIII. The organ is the largest in the country. On the doors were affixed notices, stating that persons entering the church, and refusing to perform the usual genuflexions, or conform to the ce-

remonies of worship, would be forcibly ex-
pelled.

In the face of this somewhat startling and
questionable mandate of those in authority,
however, we attended mass on the first Sunday
succeeding our arrival ; and although we could
not consistently join in all " the outward and
visible signs," no notice was taken of our
breach of ecclesiastical discipline.

The service was conducted with considerable splendour, aided by most delicious music ;
and the sermon, like almost all I have had
the pleasure of hearing from the pulpits of the
Church of Rome, inculcated good works, and
contained no uncharitable allusions to those
who professed a different creed. The crowded
congregation consisted chiefly of Irish, of
which nation there are great numbers in Baltimore. Among the assembled throng in this
holy place, one individual in particular arrested our attention from the moment of his
entrance. It was the venerable Charles Car-
roll, the last survivor of that patriot band,
who pledged " their lives, their fortunes, and
their sacred honour," to establish the liberties
of their country. This highly respected gentlemen, who is the grandfather of the present
Marchionesses of Wellesley and Carmarthen,—

the former of whom is attached to the court of Queen Adelaide, — was then in his ninety-second year, yet walked along the aisle with a vigorous step.

Contiguous to the Cathedral, but widely opposed as regards the abstract doctrines promulgated by the clergy of these respective places of worship, is the Unitarian Church, a spacious and ornamental structure. The roof, like that of the Cathedral, is a dome. Many of the pews were furnished with small iron boxes, containing heaters, which diffused a most agreeable warmth. The pulpit was upon the same plan as those of the Unitarian churches of New York, although differing in style of ornament.

Amidst the bustle of trade and manufactures, the inhabitants of Baltimore have not been unmindful of the application of the fine arts to commemorate the virtues of the illustrious dead, or to record the triumphs of their fellow-citizens; and two classic monuments, which adorn the city, are the result of their patriotic feeling. One of these, called Washington's monument, is a white marble column, 163 feet in height, upon the summit of which is placed a colossal statue of the General. The choice of situation is good, and the effect imposing. The second work of art, styled the battle monument, was erected to the memory of the officers and soldiers who fell in defence of the city in the year 1814. The design is extremely classical, and is creditable to the artist, whose name I unfortunately omitted to record. A small square erection, supposed to be a mausoleum, is surmounted by the Roman fasces, on the ribands or ties of which are inscribed the names of the individuals slain. In lieu of the axe is a figure of Victory.

This beautiful tribute to patriotism and valour is of white marble, and is about fifty-five feet in height. It is also appropriately ornamented with the national emblems; and at the angles of the iron railing are cannons placed perpendicularly.

The great object of attraction at the period of our visit to Baltimore was the railroad, which, when completed, will communicate with Pittsburgh, on the river Ohio, the Birmingham of America. The distance between the two cities is about three hundred miles; and although eighteen months had scarcely elapsed from the commencement of this magnificent undertaking, the line for the first ten miles was about to be opened.

The rails of this road are constructed of

s 3

timber, the upper edges of which are plated with flat bar-iron, and they are strongly fastened to the sleepers, as the transverse logs upon which the rails rest are technically called. The viaducts already finished are either of freestone or granite.

The labourers employed on this, and all the great works of the kind in progress in America, are natives of Ireland; and I was happy to observe, on looking into their temporary wooden cabins, which are erected at different stations on the road, that, although there appeared a good deal of wild disorder in the domestic arrangements, and the total absence of what an English cottager would term comfort, there was no lack of the means to live; which was the more important, as *philoprogenitiveness* seemed the order of the day.

Every hovel had its swarm of children, its barrel of superfine flour, flitch of bacon, and stone bottle of the " creature," and the interstices were filled up with pigs and poultry.

As if in antithesis to the splendour of the capital from which it derived its name, one of these clusters of habitations was dignified with the title of Dublin; although I could not discern any thing like a window in the place; and the chimneys, if they deserved the appellation, were neither more nor less than old flour-barrels. The country around Baltimore possesses abundant water power or "privileges;" and a number of large flour-mills have been erected in the neighbourhood, together with extensive manufactories in the various branches of iron, copper, lead, glass, paper, cotton, and in fact in almost every department of the useful arts.

One of the towers for the manufacture of shot, situated in the city, is the loftiest erection of the kind I had seen either in America or elsewhere, and the view from the summit is very extensive. To the aged inhabitants, who remember infant Baltimore, the panorama must be particularly striking.

About three miles below the city is Fort M'Henry, the fortification which commands the arm of the Patapsco upon which Baltimore is located. Here we beheld, for the first time, American regular troops, a few of which were on duty. They were in grey uniforms, and looked remarkably well. Several deserters were at work in the area of the fort, with cannon balls chained to their legs, — a mode of punishment substituted for the inhuman and brutalising practice of flogging; which, to the disgrace of the British nation,

s 4

it still permits in its armies and fleets, although abolished in those of every other power. Amongst the ordnance, I noticed a few brass six-pounders bearing the arms of France, and the inscription, " Ultima ratio regum." These guns, which were cast in the reign of Louis XV., were a part of the munitions of war furnished by the French nation to the American colonies during their conflict with the mother country.

Fort M'Henry was bombarded by the British fleet in 1814, simultaneously with the attempt made upon Baltimore by the army under General Ross; but, as I was informed, with so little effect, that the only sufferer was an old woman.

A few miles lower down the river is the field of battle, or rather skirmishing, where the commander of the British forces, General Ross, lost his life; and between Fort M'Henry and the city, several mouldering redoubts serve to remind the traveller of the last unfortunate rupture between the two countries.

The only public place of amusement open during our sojourn in this busy and thriving port was the Circus, which is the largest theatre of that description in America. The principal members of the corps de ballet were French.

The breaking up of the ice, which took place early in the month of March, was the signal for our bidding adieu to the polite and hospitable society of Baltimore; and as soon as the navigation of the rivers again became practicable, we returned to Philadelphia, by the same route as that by which we came, except that in lieu of passing through the new canal, we crossed the peninsula of Maryland and Delaware, by coach, from Frenchtown, on the Elk, to Newcastle, on the Delaware river. The surface of the Chesapeake, as well as of the Elk, on this voyage, were, in many places, literally covered with wild ducks; and we sailed amongst myriads of these birds, who reluctantly quitted the water, even to allow the passage of the steamer.

We arrived at Philadelphia just in time to witness the presentation of the diplomas to the medical students of the University. The ceremony, which took place in the Music Hall, in consequence of the new College not being finished, was conducted with becoming effect, in the presence of a large audience of talent and fashion.

An excellent band, the members of which were all blacks, contributed to enliven the meeting by performing select pieces of music at intervals. The inspiring national air, " Hail, Columbia!" which acts upon the American as " Rule Britannia" does upon the nerves of the Briton, or the "Marsellois" upon those of the sons and daughters of France, was an admirale finale to this intellectual exhibition.

The Medical School of Philadelphia ranks the highest in the United States, and its honours are consequently held in much repute; but in this city, as every where in America, the title of Doctor is assumed by every empiric and petty dealer in poisons, and as freely bestowed by the generality of the people.

During this our second residence in Philadelphia, we had an opportunity of viewing the late President West's celebrated picture of " Christ Rejected," which had recently arrived from London, and was exhibited to admiring crowds in the Hall of Independence. There was something particularly interesting in the contemplation of this chef d'œuvre of the artist in his native city, and in which some of his boyish sketches yet remain; and it must certainly be considered bad taste in the wealthy citizens of Philadelphia, allowing the picture to be returned to England, instead of its being deposited in the Academy of Fine Arts, where it would have been at once an ornament to the city, and an example to youthful talent. In our rambles we also visited a new cemetery, remarkable for its neatness of arrangement. We were shown a kind of iron case for the purpose of protecting bodies from being stolen. This ingenious contrivance was, in form, like a large coffin without a bottom. The lid, sides, and ends, fitted together by bolts, the last of which was secured by a lock. This case, after being allowed to enclose the real coffin in the grave for a few weeks, is removed, and the grave again filled with earth.

Such safeguards will, however, in all probability, ere long, cease to be required, as the practice of the exhumation of bodies for the purpose of dissection will be extinct in America, as soon as the legislatures of the respective States follow the example of that of Massachusetts; which, taking enlightened France as its guide, has lately passed an act authorising the governors of all public charitable institutions to deliver the bodies of those that die therein, which are not claimed in a certain time by their relations or friends, to the anatomical schools.

As we were leaving the quiet precincts of this depository of the dead, we met the funeral procession of a black domestic. The hearse was open at the sides so as to expose the coffin, which was made of dark polished wood, and the lid was roof-shaped. About fifty blacks of both sexes, extremely well dressed, followed, walking two and two, at a slow pace. The effect to Europeans was striking.

Early in April we took leave of the fair city of Philadelphia, where, in the society of some of its chief ornaments, we had spent few indeed but happy days, and returned to New York, by Bordenton. The banks of the Delaware, on our voyage, bespoke the genial influence of spring, and all nature seemed smiling.

At Bordenton, we took the stage to Washington, a village situated on a creek which falls into the Rariton river a little below. About a mile from the former place is the residence of Joseph Bonaparte, Count Survilliers, ex-King of Naples and of Spain. The mansion has nothing in its exterior to attract particular attention, but it contains some fine paintings and other works of art. The woods and grounds are extensive, but the latter are susceptible of much improvement. The Count, who is understood to be exceedingly rich, lives in an easy and hospitable manner, and is highly and very deservedly respected by his farming neighbours, who invariably style him *Mr.* Bonaparte.

That the *ci-devant* sovereign has laid aside state, and all the pomp and circumstance of kingly etiquette, will be credited, when I inform my readers, that on passing his mansion on an excursion in the previous autumn, I saw the ex-monârch standing at his gate, attired as an American farmer, in a rough white hat and a half worn suit. He returned my salute in a friendly and familiar manner, and proceeded to give some directions to a labourer, just as if, as the Americans say, he had been raised on the soil.* In person, Count Survilliers is taller than his late brother Napoleon, stout, and of a hale, ruddy complexion.

At Washington village we again embarked in a steamer ; and, in the evening, landed

---

* Since the above was written, Count Survilliers has returned to Europe.

once more in the ever animated city of New
York.   A few days after our return, the
whole population were agreeably surprised by
the arrival of a fleet of vessels from Europe,
the ports of which they had only left fifteen
or sixteen days.   Such quick passages across
the Atlantic homeward had never before been
performed, the voyages of the fastest sailing
ships being seldom less than thirty days.
Among the vessels which so rapidly ploughed
the main, were the splendid packet Caledonia,
from Liverpool, and the Josephine, from Bel-
fast.

After feasting upon a file of Morning Chro-
nicles wet from the press ; skimming the cream
from the latest Edinburgh Review or Literary
Gazettes ; and turning over the pages of Mur-
ray's, Longman's, or Cadell's " just published"
quartos or octavos, isolated copies of which
look the more tempting in a foreign land ;
we hastened to Boston, proceeding by way of
Providence, the capital of the little state of
Rhode Island.   Our voyage thither, a distance
of one hundred and eighty miles, was made in
a splendid steamer called the President, —
one of the largest and certainly one of the
most elegant vessels on the American waters.
We sailed from New York in the afternoon ;

and rapidly passing the city, and through the channel called the East River, we soon cleared the intricate navigation of the entrance into Long Island Sound,—the Scylla and Charybdis of America. This passage or strait bears the ominous title of Hell Gates,—the name given it by the first settlers, on account of the dangerous nature of the rocks and currents; which, previously to the introduction of steam, could not be passed by large vessels with safety.

A British frigate was wrecked in the attempt, during the revolutionary war; and a few years ago, in a fruitless search for gold, some bottles and other articles were recovered from the wreck by means of a diving-bell. The name of Hell Gate or Gates, by puritanical squeamishness, has lately been metamorphosed into that of Hurl Gate, by which it is now very generally known.

Early the next morning we reached Newport, which possesses one of the finest harbours in the United States.

The new fortifications at this place are upon a scale commensurate with its importance in the event of a war, and the most powerful fleet would not now be able to approach the harbour with impunity. Three hours' sailing up the river brought us to the city of Providence, a flourishing town with nearly twenty thousand inhabitants. Here we took the stage for Boston. The road between Providence and that city, — a distance of forty miles, — is tolerably good, but the country is in general stony and poor.

A few miles from the former place we passed through Pawtucket, situated at the falls of the river of that name. This village is a seat of the cotton manufacture, and contained above a dozen factories in active operation; although, at that period, considerable embarrassment had been experienced in the financial concerns of the proprietors. As we approached Boston, the scenery improved; and after passing a number of pretty country seats, we beheld the cluster of spires rising from the birth-place of Franklin, where we soon after found ourselves agreeably seated.

CHAP. XIV.

Boston, which has been founded two centuries, was originally called Tremont, or Tremountain, from the circumstance of its being situated on three hills. The city is almost surrounded by water; the connection with the main land being formed by a narrow strip called the Neck. The communication, in other directions, is kept up by timber bridges; one of which is no less than 1300 yards in length. The older streets are irregular — indeed, as tortuous as those of the old towns of England; but such as are of later date are laid out at right angles. They are kept in neat order; and, unlike the thoroughfares of all the other cities we had visited, they were not perambulated day and night by swine. Many of the original names have given place to others more congenial to the state of political feeling; thus, Washington has superseded Marlborough, and King and Queen have been metamorphosed into Court and State Street.

The houses are chiefly of brick, and very much in the English style of architecture,

T

many of the better kind having balconies.
Indeed, the general appearance of the place,
the complexion of the inhabitants, and the
absence of black population, except a few
domestics, strongly reminded us of our own
country.

The disinterested and friendly attentions of
the Americans to strangers had been proved to
us in numberless instances, previous to our arrival in this quarter of the Union, but in none
were they displayed more conspicuously than
in the city of Boston, where our reception was
such as to cause us instantly to feel at home.

Availing ourselves of the facilities afforded
by those whose politeness was the more valuable, because voluntary, we proceeded to visit
its numerous public establishments, and its
environs, the theatre of the early glory of the
American republic.

The first object of our curiosity was the
statue of Washington, by the Phidias of the
British school of sculpture, Chantrey.

This grand work of art, which is partially
known to the public through the medium of
engravings, ornaments the new State House,
an edifice of large dimensions, and of handsome architecture. It is judiciously placed in
a recess lighted from above; and is seen as

approached from the grand entrance of the mansion. This greatest of modern heroes is represented standing, enveloped in an ample robe, and holding in one hand a scroll. Those parts of the figure not concealed by drapery display a modification of modern costume. Without presuming to cavil at this deviation from the antique, such is the conception and execution of this beautiful statue, that, independent of the association of ideas, the spectator stands in silent admiration; but indulging in such, the effect is sublime.

It is not in the interior of the State House alone that the eye and mind are gratified. The view from the lofty dome, by which it is surmounted, is as extensive as it is picturesque; and full of historical interest, as regards the commencement of the glorious struggle, which terminated, happily for mankind, in American independence.

At our feet lay the city, with its halls, and its sites, rendered memorable as the places where the intelligence and free spirits of the country discussed their wrongs, or gave vent to their outraged feelings in bold and energetic, yet peaceable remonstrances. Taking a wider range, in one direction the eye rested upon the blood-stained field, where a despotic government was taught, by a severe lesson, to respect the sacred rights of man; while, in another, it gazed upon those eminences, where the military genius of a Washington displayed itself, as if by magic, to the discomfiture of the retiring foe.

Anxious to forget so dark a period of our country's history, and to bury the remembrance of the injustice and madness of our fathers in oblivion, we also beheld the extensive panorama as lovers of nature, and our gratification was extreme.

The wide expanse of the unruffled bay, with its archipelago of islands, the undulated country, sprinkled with smiling villages, and cheerful habitations, together with the bold outline of the distant hills, all combined under an atmosphere as pure as it was mild, produced an enchanting picture, and one which is indelibly impressed on the memory.

In front of the State House is a park, many acres in extent, which, in the colonial times, bore the name of the Common; but having been railed, and ornamented, is now dignified with the title of Mall. Here the British troops were for some time encamped; and near a huge and ancient elm, which still spreads its venerable arms, are the remains of a redoubt, thrown up at that period. Among the number of mansions which form one side of the streets bounding this beautiful verdant enclosure, that of the celebrated patriot, Hancock, is distinguished.

In the edifice appropriated to public meetings of the citizens, called Fanueil Hall, and termed the Cradle of the Revolution, from the preliminary assemblages of the early champions of the people's rights having been held there, we saw an admirable full length portrait of Washington by Steuart, and also a portrait of Hancock by Copley, the father of the ex-Chancellor Lord Lyndhurst. Both these artists were Americans, and both attained a high rank in their profession. The former was, in early life, a pupil of West. A bust of the late John Adams, father of the ex-President, likewise adorns this hallowed temple of liberty.

The Athenæum, which is at the head of the numerous literary institutions of the city, contains a well selected library of nearly 30,000 volumes ; also a collection of casts from many of the finest statues of antiquity, and a cabinet of impressions from rare medals and gems.

I was happy to observe, that these intellectual treasures were all in excellent preserv-

ation. In front of the pedestals of the casts,
neat placards were suspended, bearing the title
or common appellation of the figure or group,
accompanied by a succinct account of the
subject, for the information of such as were
unacquainted with the arts or classic lore.

One of the apartments contained marble
busts of Sir Isaac Coffin, ex-President Adams,
and Dr. Josiah Quincy.

The first of these was by Behmes : the two
latter were the production of a young native
sculptor of the name of Greenough, who has
resided for some years in Italy ; and they not
only interested us as faithful resemblances of
those eminent individuals whose features they
were intended to portray, but acquired an
additional value as able specimens of the talents
of a young artist in a branch hitherto unap-
proached by his countrymen.

The gallant admiral, whose likeness is here
deposited, is an American by birth, but has
served almost all his life in the British navy,
of which he is a distinguished ornament.
He is, nevertheless, exceedingly popular among
his countrymen ; and we heard it humorously
recorded, that whilst on a visit to his native
place, a few years ago, above six hundred persons
of the name claimed the honour of relation-

ship, among whom was a *black man.* Terracotta busts of Washington, Franklin, and
Lafayette, as well as some portraits, likewise
ornamented the chamber. A well supplied
news-room, in which no talking louder than a
whisper is permitted, forms part of this polite
establishment.

Contiguous to the Athenæum is a convenient building, devoted to the advancement of
the arts and sciences. It contains a theatre,
where lectures are periodically delivered, and a
gallery for the exhibition of works of art. The
annual exhibition of pictures was on the eve
of opening when we were about to leave Boston, but, by the politeness of some members of
the committee, we were favoured with a peep
behind the curtain before the completion of
the arrangements. The result of our visit was
gratifying, inasmuch as we saw native talent
existed, which, under the genial warmth and
fostering care of public patronage, will assuredly produce fruit.

Some pictures by the old masters graced the
walls; and we were shown a small portrait in
crayons, by Lawrence when a youth. By the
date of this clever little picture, the artist must
have been only thirteen years of age at the
time of its execution.

Although Boston owes its origin to the emigrant English puritans, a strong tincture of whose rigid observances yet remains among its population, their descendants have so far deviated from the creed of their forefathers, that a temple of Thespis had lately been erected, scarcely inferior in beauty to any in the United States. The façade is of two descriptions of granite—the one gray, the other of a reddish hue—which last has been successfully employed in beautiful Ionic pilasters, which support an entablature and pediment. The interior is finished in a correspondent style of elegance.

Opposite the theatre is an hotel called Tremont House,—one of the largest, and certainly the most elegant building of the kind in America, and, perhaps, not surpassed in Europe. The principal front of this noble mansion is of gray granite, and is ornamented by a chaste and extensive Doric portico of the same material, the whole admirably worked. This fashionable establishment contains nearly two hundred apartments, besides spacious dining and drawing rooms, furnished in the best manner; and yet the charge for board and lodging—in other words, for faring sumptuously every day, and reposing in comfort at night — is only about two guineas per week each person. Wines are not included in the terms of board; but lists of the kinds and prices are furnished by the waiters when asked for, or may be perused in the bar-room, which is a place much frequented in all American hotels.

In the centre of an old and extensive cemetery, contiguous to Tremont House, surrounded by hundreds of the fathers of the country, lie interred the venerable and worthy parents of the illustrious Franklin. It will be recollected by those who are familiar with the life of that truly great man, whose name is no less associated with practical morality than with science, that, visiting the place of his nativity many years after his settlement in Philadelphia, he caused the following simple and beautiful inscription to be placed over the grave of those to whom he owed his birth : —

" HERE LIE

JOSIAS FRANKLIN AND ABIAH HIS WIFE;

They lived together with reciprocal affection for fifty-nine years ; and without private fortune, without lucrative employment, by assiduous labour and honest industry, decently supported a numerous family, and educated, with success, thirteen children, and seven grandchildren. Let this example, reader, encourage thee dili-

gently to discharge the duties of thy calling, and to
rely on the support of Divine Providence.

He was pious and prudent,
She discreet and virtuous.

Their youngest son, from a sentiment of filial duty, con-
secrates this stone to their memory."

The slab containing this inscription having
gone to decay, the inhabitants of Boston have,
with proper feeling and much good taste,
lately erected a massive granite obelisk over
the grave. Upon one side of this lasting
memorial appears the name of Franklin in
raised bronze characters, and underneath is a
tablet with the original inscription.

With equal respect to the memory of Franklin, the printing-press at which the philosopher first worked is carefully preserved in
the city.

Many of the tombs in this and the older
burying grounds of Boston are ornamented
with coats of arms, and bear the names of
colonists of rank. We noticed one to the
memory of Governor Winthrop, who served
the office under the unfortunate but accomplished monarch, Charles I. Several of this
gentleman's descendants are among the principal families of the city at the present day,
to the unremitting kindness of some of whom

we owe much of the pleasurable remembrance of our sojourn in the Athens of America.

In connection with the subject of cemeteries, I may observe, that the horses drawing the hearses at funerals in Boston were led by men walking at their heads, which had a much more solemn effect than when driven by a man seated on a coach-box.

This city being as it were the metropolis of Unitarianism, we naturally expected to find a number of edifices dedicated to public worship according to that faith; but we were not prepared to behold them in all the dignity of the Episcopal and Presbyterian churches, with towering spires and peals of bells. Few, however, of the religious structures of Boston possess particular claims to notice on the score of architecture, but all are commodious; and as the inhabitants are, generally speaking, distinguished for their strict observance of the Sabbath, they are frequented by crowded congregations, who, as every where in America, very properly make it a matter of importance to arrive before the commencement of the service.

We attended public worship at two of the principal Episcopal churches, those of St. Paul and Trinity. The front of the former represents an Ionic temple, and the interior is finished in a correspondently chaste style. Near the altar was a large copy of the celebrated Transfiguration, painted by an Italian artist.

The Bishop of the State of Connecticut officiated on the morning of our visit, and delivered a most impressive discourse. This worthy divine was attired in a simple black gown; he, like his brother bishops of the United States, having wisely rejected those unseemly and ridiculous appendages, wigs, aprons, and lawn sleeves. I observed that, in reading the Liturgy, the Bishop did not bow the head on pronouncing the name of the Saviour in the creeds, — a custom which still prevails in the Established Church of England.

The church dedicated to the Holy Trinity had recently been erected on the site of one built at an early period of the colony. The style is Gothic, but not highly decorated, and the material granite. On the occasion of a wedding, we saw this extensive building nearly filled with females, whom curiosity had attracted to witness the interesting ceremony; and the happy couple had even some difficulty to pass from the church to the hackney coach in waiting, so eager was the multitude to have a near view of the parties.

Old South Church, — so named from its age and situation, — is devoted to the Presbyterian form of worship, and is attended by a large congregation. The building is memorable as having been metamorphosed into a riding-school by the British troops, and used as such for some years prior to the Revolution.

The Gallican feeling to ecclesiastical edifices, if they happened to be possessed by any denomination of Christians save the Church of England, was not uncommon with the British commanders in America, and gave great and just offence to the inhabitants.

The following is a copy of a handbill which was printed at the restoration of the edifice to its legitimate use, and with which I was favoured by one of the members of the congregation : —

ANTHEM.

" This Anthem was sung at the re-opening of the Old South Church, after having been occupied about eight years by the British as a place for training their horses, and was written for that joyful occasion by William Selby, the then Organist of King's Chapel, Boston.

" Behold, God is my salvation ! I will trust and not be afraid ; for the Lord Jehovah is my strength and my song ; he also is become my salvation. He hath raised

up the tabernacle of David that was fallen; he hath closed
up the breaches thereof; he hath raised up the ruins; he
hath built it as in the days of old, and caused his people
to rejoice therein.

" Praise the Lord, call upon his name, declare his
doings among the nations, make mention that his name is
exalted. Sing unto the Lord, for he hath done excellent
things; this is known in all the earth. Cry out and shout,
thou inhabitant of Zion, for great is the Holy One of
Israel, in the midst of thee. Hallelujah, for the Lord
God omnipotent reigneth. Amen."

The congregation of King's Chapel, or, as it
is now styled, the Stone Chapel, from the material of which it is built, as well as from the
hatred of the former title, use a Liturgy peculiar to themselves. This composition appeared
to be framed so as to meet the wishes of those
who dissented from the more disputed doctrines of the Episcopal Church, and yet preferred a written form of prayer. Although
we visited the principal Unitarian places of
worship, we were unfortunately deprived of the
pleasure of hearing the celebrated Dr. Channing, of whose oratory I have already made
mention, and we lamented the circumstance
the more from a knowledge that the delicate
health of that eminent divine contracted the
sphere of his usefulness.

All the public structures of Boston, lately

erected, are of granite, and they are also in an admirable style of architecture.

Among the most conspicuous erections is the market, which measures nearly 550 feet in length, and 50 in width. At each end is a Doric portico, the columns of which are formed of single blocks of granite twenty-three feet high. The interior contains two ranges of shops, in which the different descriptions of provisions are displayed; the variety, however, was less numerous than in the markets of the principal towns of Great Britain. Among the vegetables we noticed the common dandelion, which, cut when young, and boiled, is very palatable, and is much eaten. The prices of most articles were lower than in the markets of New York.

CHAP. XV.

THE country in the neighbourhood of Boston is decidedly picturesque; and the roads are superior to any we had seen in America. They are, in general, made upon the M'Adam principle — if that system can with propriety be referred to any individual in the present day, when it is a well known fact, that the roads in many parts of Italy and Spain have been constructed with broken fragments of stone from time immemorial.

The merit of Mr. M'Adam seems to be in his having improved and extended the method, rather than being the originator of it; and, under this impression, some Americans feel desirous to adopt a new term for the art.

Our first perambulation in the environs was to the celebrated battle field of Breeds, erroneously called Bunker's Hill. Crossing a long timber bridge, we entered Charlestown, which is separated from Boston by the river Charles.

This place, which was originally built of wood, was set on fire by the British, and entirely consumed, during the attack upon the American forces in June, 1775. It has long since risen from its ashes, and is now a cheerful little town, with 7000 inhabitants. In the immediate vicinity is Breeds Hill, the scene of the sanguinary struggle which took place at an early period of the revolutionary war, and in which the Americans showed the most dauntless courage, only retiring when overpowered by numbers, and destitute of ammunition.

To commemorate this important event in American history, the inhabitants of Boston and the neighbourhood are erecting a monument on the blood-stained eminence, as imperishable as the record of the glorious struggle itself. This memorial is a plain granite obelisk, without a pedestal, 220 feet in height, and fifty feet in diameter at the base. A spiral staircase, built within the structure, leads to the summit.

The first block of this colossal memorial, the largest of the kind in the world, was laid, amidst great rejoicings, by Lafayette, on the 15th of June, 1825, the fiftieth anniversary of the battle; but, in consequence of the funds having become exhausted, the progress of the work had been temporarily suspended. Some traces of the redoubt and lines contested on that memorable day are yet visible, and are beheld by every American as consecrated ground.

Adjoining the town of Charlestown, on one side, is the State Prison, a noble building of granite, 200 feet long, and five stories high; and on the other, is the Navy Yard, one of the most complete establishments of that description in the United States.

On visiting this depôt, I was presented with a ticket by one of the marines on duty at the gate, which ticket was demanded on my exit. I saw three vessels ready for launching, one of which was of the largest class of the line. The Columbus of 100 guns, a ship of 80 guns, and a heavy frigate, lay in ordinary at the wharf. A dock sufficiently large to receive a first rate, and entirely constructed of granite, was nearly completed.

This was the fourth naval arsenal I had visited; in all of which, although a foreigner, and alone, I had had full liberty to inspect the ships, the stores, the ordnance, in fact, every thing that attracted my curiosity; and in several instances had received the most particular answers to my interrogatories.

I cannot avoid noticing this extreme liberality to strangers, as opposed to the rules of similar establishments at home, where, to the unintroduced visiter, the gates are hermetically sealed. This system of exclusion is the more to be deprecated, because, in some cases, it proceeds from a narrow jealousy, without a shadow of justification.

I need only mention the refusing admittance to Americans at the dock-yards of Portsmouth or Plymouth; as if that enterprising people could now learn any thing in the beautiful art of ship-building even from Great Britain, when it is notorious, that almost all the great improvements in naval architecture of late years are of American origin.

It was after my visit to the Navy Yard of Boston, that I heard, for the first time in America, any opinions expressed on the subject of the conflict between the British frigate the Shannon, and the United States ship the Chesapeake; the only action on John Bull's own element during the war where the force of the combatants was at all equal. The unfortunate result to the Americans was confidently attributed to the crew of the Chesapeake having been in a state of intoxication. To render this version of the story probable, it is necessary to suppose that the commander

and his brother officers were drunk too : thus
is the problem solved, and the gallant Captain
Broke, and the tars of the Shannon, are
cheated of their laurels.

No triumphs of the Americans caused so
much exultation as the captures of British men
of war; and the walls of half the boarding-
houses in the sea-ports are ornamented with
representations of the taking of the Guerrier
and Macedonian; which vessels, by the by,
are always made to appear as large, or larger
than their opponents, and totally dismasted,
while the latter are in full trim ; but the taking
of the Chesapeake is kept *sub silentio*.

The principal seminary for the education of
youth in the state of Massachusetts is Harvard
College. This alma mater is situated in the
village or town of Cambridge, about three
miles from Boston, on the road to Lexington,
the spot celebrated in history as the scene of
the first martyrdom of the American patriots,
and where the key-note of liberty and resist-
ance to tyrants was sounded. The college
takes its name from its founder, the Rev. J.
Harvard, who was one of the earliest settlers
from the mother-country. The buildings are
more extensive than ornamental, with the exception of a chapel lately erected. The library

contains nearly 25,000 volumes, together with philosophical apparatus, and a museum of natural history.

We were particularly fortunate in making our visit to Harvard College, on what is termed an exhibition day, as it gave us an opportunity of judging, in some degree, of the course of education pursued, and the proficiency of the students. The provost, Dr. J. Quincey, whose bust we had seen at the Athenæum, presided in the theatre, which is commodious, and on this occasion was crowded with beauty and fashion. The recitations, which were in the Greek, Latin, and English languages, were all extremely well delivered; and several compositions in the latter tongue were of a very high character, and exceedingly creditable to the youthful composers.

Whether it was in consequence of the critical acumen displayed by Captain Hall, I know not, but one of the young orators, who had occasion to use the words " chivalry and chicanery," pronounced them both in a style that would have fully satisfied the gallant officer, and made ample amends for the pertinacity of the New York " school madam," who did not conceive that " they that go down to the sea in ships" are the best models in scholastic matters.

The expenses at Harvard College are very moderate ; and particularly so, when compared with those of similar establishments in England. The students are, for the most part, the sons of the wealthier classes ; and although the immediate prospects of many may be the counting-room or the store, they all receive such a course of liberal education as to fit them for higher destinies, should their talents in after-life attract the notice of their countrymen.

In no part of the United States is the subject of education so warmly espoused as in the division of Massachusetts, where that blessing is within the reach of all, free of cost, ample funds being provided for the maintenance of the public schools by the state.

The consequences of this wise liberality are apparent in the state of the population ; which, both as regards the general diffusion of useful knowledge and orderly behaviour, is very apparent.

If, on landing in New York, we were forcibly struck with what I have termed the high character of the working classes, the remark applied in a still greater degree to those of Boston, the population of which city is less adulterated with the poorer class of English and Irish emigrants. The porters, and others, about the wharfs and places of business, with many of whom I purposely entered into conversation, were extremely civil and intelligent, and evidently men capable of exercising the high privileges which their free institutions afford them with sound judgment and discretion.

As a proof of the comparatively comfortable circumstances of the working classes of this city, which contains about 80,000 inhabitants, I was credibly informed that there was only one pawnbroker in the place; and I may add to this happy picture of society, that, in lieu of such melancholy refuges of poverty and crime, booksellers' shops and circulating libraries were more numerous, in proportion to the population, than in any place I had ever visited.

In the neighbourhood of the village of Quincy, and about ten miles in a southerly direction from Boston, are the famous granite quarries which supply the city with that valuable material. As there is no superincumbent stratum, the labour of procuring the granite is considerably lessened, and the blocks are conveyed to the wharf, on the margin of the bay, a distance of three miles, by a rail-road. From the summit of a tower, erected on one of the hills, we enjoyed a most magnificent view of Boston Bay, with its numerous islands, its surface sprinkled with white sails; while, in the distance, the city itself stood proudly conspicuous, with its elevated dome and tapering spires, — the whole presenting a scene of uncommon beauty and interest.

The village of Milton, situated on the stream of that name, and so called from the great republican poet, lies on the road between Quincy and Boston. There was an air of repose and rural simplicity about this nook, which better entitled it to the endearing appellation of village, according to the English signification of the term, than almost any place we had seen in America. Nearer Boston are the eminences called Dorchester Heights, memorable in the revolutionary history as being the spots where Washington caused redoubts to be thrown up in a single night; and which were of so formidable a nature as to cause the evacuation of the city by the British army, which never returned.

These field-works, of which only slight

traces remained, were once more restored on the breaking out of the last war, and are again in a course of dilapidation ; and it is to be hoped no circumstances will ever arise so as to require their reconstruction.

During our stay in Boston, we made an excursion to Salem, a seaport of some note, fourteen miles distant. The road passes through the small town of Lynn, one of the oldest settlements in New England, and now famous for the manufacture of ladies' shoes, of which large quantities are exported to the different southern States, as well as to the West Indies and other places. We learnt, to our surprise, that the price of the necessaries of life were so low in this and several other villages surrounding Boston, that substantial board might be obtained by mechanics at the rate of four shillings and sixpence per week.

After travelling some miles over a poor and naked district, the spires of the churches of Salem suddenly appeared, peeping over the summit of some rocks a short distance before us. The effect was curious.

In a few minutes we beheld the little town and port, where we soon arrived. Salem, by the successful rivalry of New York, and the other great commercial marts of America, has latterly lost much of its mercantile importance ; and, after having numbered its sixty ships, which almost annually sailed round the Cape of Good Hope, or Cape Horn, it now only reckons a tenth part of that number. The town has an air of neatness, and contains a handsome square, and many good buildings, but its chief attraction is its Museum, which had recently been arranged in a capacious hall, erected expressly for its reception.

This extensive depository of the wonders of nature and art owes its existence to the spirit and good taste of the commanders of the vessels belonging to Salem, who engage, on their return from a voyage, to present something rare or curious to the collection. Thus has a valuable Museum been formed, to which additions are continually being made ; and when it is recollected that the donors are neither professed naturalists, artists, antiquarians, or lettered " travelling fellows," but plain nautical " business men," the choice and selection of the specimens and different articles do infinite credit to their discrimination and judgment.

From the extensive trade which Salem has carried on with the Indian Archipelago and China, the catalogue is rich in the productions of that quarter of the globe, whether as regards natural history or ingenious objects of art. The islands of the South Seas have likewise contributed their share of curiosities; and, lastly, the classic shores of the "blue Mediterranean," those inexhaustible mines of ancient art, have not been visited in vain; and the connoisseur may pore over the half-obliterated hieroglyphic, study the bold features of the Cæsars in the corroded medal, or dwell upon the sublime contortions of the Laocoon.

Among the heterogeneous trifles which chance has thrown in the way of the contributors, we observed a note in the hand-writing of the immortal Byron. This little document, which was written during the bard's residence in Genoa, is addressed to a friend, with a request that he will recommend an advocate to him, to defend a paltry suit brought against him by a tailor, who, as he says, in allusion to extravagant charges, " has cut his coat according to his cloth, as his brethren do in every country." In a postscript, the noble writer adds, that he expects some packages to arrive soon; and begs that all may be properly specified at the custom-house, for he will not allow any smuggling. Every relic of the lamented author of " Childe Harold," even the most trifling, is so precious, that we could not peruse this half-angry, half-humorous, and hastily-scribbled note, without painful emotions, accompanied by regret at his untimely, although glorious end.

Shortly before our visit to Salem, the town and neighbourhood had been thrown into great consternation by an event of a nature unparalleled in that quiet and well ordered community. The circumstance I allude to was nothing less than a murder, " most foul, strange, and unnatural," being that of an aged gentleman by his own nephew and some other relatives, who, by the horrid act, thought to anticipate the possession of his property.

As the great poet of nature has expressed it, " murder, though it have no tongue, will speak with most miraculous organ," so in the instance of this at Salem the discovery of the perpetrators of the infernal act was made through unexpected channels, and three of the wretches forfeited their lives ; two by the hands of the executioner ; and the third, conscience-struck, put a period to his existence in prison. The fourth individual having been admitted " state evidence," was allowed to expatriate himself, where it is to be hoped he may lead " a new life unto righteousness," and in some degree make atonement for the horrible crime in which he was an accomplice.

On our return from our trip to Salem, we enjoyed a charming view of the peninsula of Nahant, the Brighton of the Bostonians; and in one part of the road we were agreeably surprised at the appearance of dear hawthorn hedges, the sight of which instantly transported us to Old England.

I have already shown how extremely favourable the American system of boarding is for the easy introduction of strangers into society; indeed, the facilities it affords in forming agreeable acquaintance, and in acquiring local information or anecdotes, can scarcely be imagined by the Englishman who has only been habituated to his own comparatively unsocial mode of existence.

To the evening re-unions of our Boston boarding-house we owe the knowledge of many little facts of by-gone times, which, communicated as they were by eye-witnesses, acquired additional interest.

Numerous were the instances related of the extreme jealousy shown by the New Englanders at the presence of the royal troops, long before the actual commencement of hostilities, even the children saluting the soldiers off duty with vollies of snow-balls; which pastime the little urchins called making war upon King George and the Tories.

The accounts of the detection of smugglers, who thought, notwithstanding non-intercourse proclamations and edicts, that there was no harm in a few pounds of young hyson; the serio-comic descriptions also of unfortunate custom-house officers, tarred and feathered, and their being forced to quaff libations of tea made with salt water, lost nothing in the relating; while the memorable attack upon the vessel laden with tea by a resolute band of patriots disguised as Indians, who discharged the whole into the sea, was pictured by the aged narrators with all that enthusiasm with which we may imagine Goldsmith's "broken soldier" to have been inspired, when he "shoulder'd his crutch, and show'd how fields were won."

From a friend who had been accustomed to meet the great Washington at the social board, we learnt many interesting particulars of the hero as he appeared, when, divested of weightier cares, he mingled with society. To a fine person Washington united the most amiable manners and goodness of heart; and wherever he went he won golden opinions from all sorts of people.

Athough, unfortunately, a slave-holder, it is well known that he treated his negroes with kindness; and the following little anecdote proves that he thought distinction of colour no excuse even for a breach of good manners.

On being observed to return the salute of a negro during one of his rides, the circumstance was repeated by some wealthy but unfeeling individual, accompanied with expressions of regret at such condescension. These remarks happened to reach the ears of the hero himself, who coolly observed, " Does Mr. ——— suppose that General Washington is to be outdone in politeness by a poor negro ?"

Without noticing the slang attributed to the labouring population of what are called the Eastern States of America, and which is greatly exaggerated by travellers, we found some peculiarities in the use and pronunciation of certain words among the best educated inhabitants.

Many persons substituted the verb to admire for that of to like, and spoke of admiring to see such or such a place or thing ; and we heard the word wounds pronounced from the

pulpit as bounds, and not *woonds*, as adopted
in England. Testimony was also sounded with
the *o* long, as in testimonial.

After spending three weeks most agreeably
in Boston, we returned to New York, by way
of Providence and Long Island Sound. The
scenery was most agreeably varied, in consequence of the advanced state of vegetation;
the foliage of the country displaying itself in
all its vernal beauty, and the orchards blushing
in their loveliest hues.

As we approached the islands, which are
scattered about the junction of the Sound and
the East River, all nature seemed smiling;
and the passage of Hell Gate, so formidable
to the early navigators, might have been styled,
with much more propriety, the Gate of Para-
dise. Our steamer, majestically ploughing her
way, and sweeping round the point of the city,
and its beautiful promenades, with a graceful
curve, soon reposed upon the bosom of the
Hudson, and we once again found ourselves
welcomed to the London of the western world.

CHAP. XVI.

A YEAR's residence in New York, from the period of our return from Boston, afforded ample opportunities of studying America and the Americans; not merely under ordinary circumstances, but in consequence of the important and peculiar events of the year 1830, as regarded European affairs, under the excitement also which these produced. A detail of what we saw, and what we heard, together with such desultory information upon various subjects as came within our reach, may help the reader to a better understanding of a country which is, ere long, destined to be as great as she is free, and a few chapters devoted to this object may not prove uninteresting.

As our pious forefathers in the olden time had their festivals, their fairs, and their red letter days, so their emancipated transatlantic descendants have likewise their seasons of rejoicing; the causes of which, with the modes of celebration, I shall proceed to describe in the order of their succession.

The first, then, which occurred after our

arrival, and the most important of the American gala days, was that of the anniversary of the Declaration of Independence, which is kept with the greatest enthusiasm in every city, village, and district in the Union.

As New York is the most populous city, so were the demonstrations of joy proportionably extensive.

No sooner had the rising sun gilded the charming bay, and the verdant promenades of the battery, than the American standard proudly floated on the morning breeze, and a salute was fired by the few remaining veterans of those armies by which the banner of liberty was first unfurled. The thunder of cannon proclaimed the fifty-fourth return of the national jubilee; while the closed stores, and early crowded streets, bespoke that even the " business men " had determined to abandon their " dry goods," and their " counting-rooms," at least for the day.

Although the more intellectual part of the population, as the members of literary and scientific institutions, and the ministers of religion, might be content to celebrate the occasion by delivering patriotic odes and addresses, the joyful feelings of the bulk were expressed in a manner more congenial to their tastes; and a review of some thousand militia, cavalry, infantry, and artillery, with marchings and counter-marchings in close order, open order, and, perchance, disorder, together with a liberal expenditure of gunpowder, formed the grand attraction of the day.

By the term militia, must not be understood the stick and umbrella squads, so humorously described by the inimitable Matthews, and whose military training is limited to a few days in each year; but regular companies, well armed, and handsomely equipped, with all " the pride, pomp, and circumstance of glorious war."

A military command is the acmé of the ambition of an American store-keeper, and a hundred Major Sturgeons forgot their counters in the delights of pie-bald chargers, leopard-skin housings, and gay uniforms; each of whom, either by his apparent knowledge of tactics, or, what seemed to have more influence, his knowledge of holiday display, endeavoured to win a smile from the delighted fair who crowded the windows, or attract the admiration of the countless thousands who filled the streets.

To criticise the moral of an army of shopkeepers, who are not subject to articles of war, and whose services are limited to occasional sunshine musters, or to draw comparisons between such and the mechanical precision of regular troops, would be absurd; suffice it to say, therefore, that a recollection of our own volunteer brigades, at the commencement of the present century, will afford a fair idea of the anti-veteran appearance of those of America. The subject, however, is a delicate one for a foreigner to meddle with; and the danger of an Englishman disparaging even an American awkward squad was soon apparent, by my receiving a rebuke in the dry way so common to that people; for in reply to a remark, not very complimentary to the " brave army," I was reminded, that such were the men, who, in two wars, had either beaten or taken almost all the forces which Great Britain had sent against them.

Feasting, as may be supposed, gave additional éclat to the ceremonies of the occasion; and from the spacious saloons of the City Hall, to the humble dwelling of the artisan, the tables groaned with substantial viands, while the memories of the great father of the republic, and his immortal companions, were drunk in generous claret or sparkling champagne,

the air resounding with the patriotic strains of
" Hail, Columbia, happy land!"

" The moment night with dusky mantle
covered the skies," hundreds of illuminated
booths, skirting the more open quarters of the
city, displayed their attractions to the moving
multitude, in the shape of fringed hams,
pickled oysters, garnished lobsters, and roasted
pigs, with lemons in their mouths, crying,
Come eat me ; all which good things might be
washed down with Philadelphia porter, ginger
beer, foaming mead, or other beverages, more
exhilarating perhaps, but less innocent.

Although these places are the resort of the
working population, a little excess in whom,
at this joyous period, might be forgiven, I
did not, in a perambulation of several hours,
witness a single instance of what could be
termed disorderly conduct.

During the whole of this festival, every
street and alley re-echoed with the reports of
petty fireworks, of which quantities are brought
from China, no less to the profit of the dealers
than to the delight of all the boys, whose little
saving banks are drained upon the occasion.
The anniversary of the Declaration of Independence was immediately followed by another
equally interesting to the philanthropist, —that

of the extinction of black slavery in the State
of New York ; which event took place a few
years ago.

This hallowed act of the legislature, the
first step towards placing the unfortunate
black upon a footing of political equality with
his white brethren, is commemorated on the
5th of July, the day after the National Jubilee.

On this occasion, some hundreds of the
black and coloured population, extremely well
dressed, and wearing sashes and ribands,
paraded the city in martial array, with the
accompaniments of bands of music, colours,
and all the attractive display of an English
election ; while, as a parody upon the shop-
keeper colonels of the previous day, black
committee men, in the national staff uniforms,
blue and buff, and glittering in gold or silver
lace, capered about on their ambling palfreys,
to the great delight of their sombre innamo-
r.tas, who, in all the gossamer of Parisian
modes, crowded the foot walks of the streets
through which this interesting yet half ludicrous procession moved.

As might be supposed, in a community like
that of New York, where but yesterday man
might be bartered and sold by his brother
man, the general feeling towards the blacks

is that of persons to a proscribed caste; and although these unfortunate people are no longer accounted property, and are enabled to stipulate the price of their labour, they are subject to the most degrading treatment.

No persons of colour, whatever may be their characters, abilities, or condition of life, are allowed to sit in any public assembly, even should it be a court of justice, or the house of God itself, except in the particular quarter set apart for them, and this is generally in the most remote and worst situation; and, as if the distinction were to be perpetuated for ever, their very bodies are denied the right of sepulture in the cemeteries of the white men.

On the festival I have described, the insulting behaviour of many of the coachmen and carters was unblushingly displayed in their driving their vehicles so as to interrupt the progress and order of the procession, although we did not witness a single provocation given by any of its members, whose conduct appeared throughout quiet and praiseworthy.

Such were the indignities offered by men who are ready to sacrifice their lives to secure the blessings of liberty for their white brethren — to those whose misfortune is, that Heaven has thought fit to create them of a darker hue ; and so prevalent is the want of Christian feeling in this respect in America, the legacy of the accursed system of slavery, that I but speak the truth when I state, that the majority of the Americans, like the white inhabitants of every country where the evil exists, or has only lately been extinguished, would as readily sit at table or associate with a felon, as with a person of colour.

It will be some consolation to the friends of humanity, however, to be told that, despite of the existing temper, exertions are making by enlightened individuals to raise the character of the coloured population, by the only legitimate means, whether as regards blacks or whites, — the establishment of schools.

The foremost in this work of religion are the members of the sect of Friends, who, in the New as well as in the Old World, whatever may be their peculiarities, are always found in the steps of their great master, going about doing good.

Already hundreds of black children in New York are regularly instructed in the rudiments of knowledge ; and churches, in which black ministers of the Episcopal, Independent, and Methodist persuasions officiate, are attended by crowded congregations of the same colour, whose attention and respectful behaviour afford abundant proof that the lessons of wisdom are not preached in vain.

May we hope, that as this so long neglected family of man rises in the scale of being, so will the antichristian treatment yield to that of philanthropy ; and although physical distinction of race will naturally be a bar to a closer union, may the Americans, as well as others, cease to look upon their darker fellow creatures otherwise than as brethren, and children of the same Almighty Father.

Although the anniversary of the Declaration of American Independence is regularly observed with so much enthusiasm, yet so strong is the feeling of joy in the people at having broken the chain which bound them to Great Britain, that the ebullition of *amor patriæ* on the 4th of July does not suffice, and the day on which the English army evacuated the city and territory of New York is still commemorated. The anniversary of this important era falls on the 25th of November, which is jocosely styled the day for driving the English Tories and sheep-stealers out. The former term was, and still is, used by the Americans, to designate the enemies of civil and religious liberty, as that of Whig is applied in the opposite sense.

The opprobrious epithet of sheep-stealers was bestowed on the British troops in consequence of the licentious system of marauding in which they indulged, and in which they were encouraged by their commanders ; who, as the subservient tools of an obstinate and tyrannical monarch and a besotted nation, subjected the unfortunate colonists, — who, whether active or passive, were alike thrust out of the pale of civil relations, — to almost every outrage and barbarity that could be devised.

The festival of the 25th of November, in the year 1830, was rendered unusually attractive, as it combined the demonstrations of rejoicing on the great events in the politics of France in the same year. It is almost impossible to describe the burst of joyous feeling exhibited by the American people on the arival of the intelligence of the glorious and ever-memorable events of " the Three Days." Nothing but the most lively congratulations met the ear ; the tricolor flag, together with the standard of America, were unfurled in the theatres ; the " Marsellois" was sung nightly by the audience as well as performers, midst deafening applause, and the very costume of the females displayed the popular colours; bonnets, shawls, ribands, every thing, as if by magic art, became *à la mode de Paris ;* whilst the animated countenances of the numerous French residents, proscribed by the Bourbon dynasty, bespoke their inward satisfaction at the prospect of their again returning to " the vine-covered hills and gay regions of France." The perpetuation of regal government, and in the person of a Bourbon too, however the individual might be shorn in state, was not the consummation desired by the Americans, who looked for, and who yet anticipate, as the nucleus of liberty in Europe, the re-establishment of the French republic with their beloved Lafayette at the head.   Still, the triumph of a people to whom they are attached by the ties of gratitude, struggling for the rights of man against a bigoted imbecile and his cold-blooded minions, backed by England and the despots of Europe, was a theme for heartfelt rejoicing ; and it was therefore determined by the inhabitants of New York to celebrate the event by a fête, and that the day should be the same which is set apart to commemorate the overthrow of British domination.

The arrangements for this double festival were upon a most extensive scale ; and by division of labour in the committees, they were completed in a manner which reflected the greatest credit upon every individual concerned.

The month of November, in New York, very much resembles that of September in England; and is consequently better adapted for street parade than the oppressive weather of the summer.

The morning of the appointed day was ushered in by the firing of cannon, and the display of the French and American colours from the ships and public buildings; and soon after, the assembling of the trades and the sounds of inspiring bugles gave note of preparation. A civil procession then took place, which, independent of the associations the occasion created, was in itself one of the most extensive and best organised I had ever witnessed. It consisted of several thousand persons of various occupations, all well dressed, and decorated with tricolor badges. To detail particulars, however, would be superfluous; but I may mention a few of the most remarkable features of this civic and morally grand ovation.

The members of each profession or trade marched together; and before the different branches were drawn cars or locomotive shops, tastefully fitted up, in which persons were beheld at work in their respective descriptions of handicraft.

The butchers, a numerous body, all dressed alike, and well mounted, were preceded by an immense stuffed ox on an elevated platform, which, together with an elegant car containing a black band of musicians in fancy costume, were drawn by teams of oxen decorated with tricolor fillets and wreaths of flowers in a style worthy of ancient Rome. A long line of fire engines, painted and gilt for the occasion, each drawn by four horses in tricolor harness, and the battalion of firemen in uniform, was also peculiarly attractive.

Last in order came the society of printers, having a press of the most approved construction, beautifully ornamented, and surmounted by the sacred motto, " Freedom of the Press," in full operation.

The following ode, which was composed for the occasion by one of their body, and printed during the progress, was gratuitously distributed amongst the moving crowd.

ODE.

O'er regal domes, renown'd in story,
　The trinal banner proudly waves;
And France resumes the march of glory,
　Her gallant sons no longer slaves.
With tyrants vainly had they pleaded —
　But when the Press in thunder spoke,
　It burst their chains with lightning stroke,
And peace and liberty succeeded.

Chorus.

Then swell the choral strain,
　To hail the blest decree;
Rejoice! rejoice! the Press shall reign,
　And all the world be free.

All hail, renown'd chivalric nation!
　Land of the olive and the vine;
Inspired with kindred emulation,
　Our bosoms glow with joy like thine.
Columbia's grateful sons can never
　Forget that, in her darkest hour,
　She owed to Gallic arms the power
To disenthrall her Press for ever.

Chorus.

Then swell the choral strain, &c.

The day which saw the sceptre shiver'd,
　And hail'd Columbia truly free,
From every hireling foe deliver'd,
　We consecrate to joy and thee;
For tyrants tremble now before thee,
　And a free Press, — the beacon-light
　That burst upon oppression's night,—
Has spread eternal glory o'er thee.

CHORUS.

Then swell the choral strain, &c.

Thy charter'd rights, with lawless daring,
    Beneath oppressors' feet were trod,
Till startled despots heard, despairing,
    The people's voice, the voice of GOD !
Their sovereign will was loudly spoken —
    The PRESS proclaim'd it to the world,
    Till freedom's ensign waved unfurl'd,
And Gallia's galling chains were broken.

CHORUS.

Then swell the choral strain, &c.

Thy gallant band of youthful heroes,
    Roused by their bleeding country's prayers,
Undaunted hurl'd on ruthless Neros
    The vengeance due to crimes like theirs.
Too late they see their fatal error —
    Their hireling guards by thousands fall —
    The PRESS resigns its *types* for ball,
And despots fly the scene in terror !

CHORUS.

Then swell the choral strain, &c.

Their deeds shall live in deathless story,
    And song preserve their chaplets green,
Yet still the brightest rays of glory
    Circle one godlike crown serene.
'Tis his, whose youthful valour aided
    Columbia's cause, when hostile bands
    Were laying waste her fairest lands,
And all her blooming hopes had faded.

CHORUS.

Then swell the choral strain, &c.

Immortal La Fayette, we hail thee,
The friend of equal rights on earth ;
Though servile tools of kings assail thee,
Columbia knows and owns thy worth ;
Thou first of heroes, best of sages,
The glorious chaplet thou hast won,
Disciple of our Washington,
Shall bloom like his for endless ages.

CHORUS.

Then swell the choral strain,
To hail the blest decree ;
Rejoice! rejoice! the Press shall reign,
And all the world be free.

The immense line of march was interspersed with banners, pennons, tablets with patriotic inscriptions, and French and American flags, while the whole population vied with each other in the display of tricolor badges and cockades.

Among the individuals of note who assisted in the proceedings, were the late venerable ex-President Munroe, and the veteran Williams, the last survivor of the three militiamen who took Major André prisoner in 1780. These patriots rode in an open barouche, receiving the congratulations of their fellow citizens as they passed along, evidently with all the emotion created by the recollections and associations which the joyous occasion called forth.

After perambulating the principal streets of the city, the marshalled thousands were concentrated in one of the great squares, when, as an appropriate finale and climax to the spectacle, the ode which had been distributed was sung to the air of the Marseillois by the vocal strength of the theatre, accompanied by the orchestra, and assisted in the chorus by the voices of all around.

Public and private dinners and balls closed a day of festivities worthy of the cause to which they were dedicated.

The following laughable apology for hard words was introduced in the speech of a gentleman of New York, at the table to which we were invited : --

" Respected friends, — My oral documents having recently become the subject of your vituperation from their incompatibility with your mental endowments, I hope it will not be deemed an instance of vain eloquence or supererogation if I laconically promulgate, that, avoiding all syllogistical, aristocratical, or peripatetical propositions, all hyperbolical extenuations or exaggerations, my future thesis and hypothesis, whether logical, philosophical, political, or polemical, shall definitively and categorically be assimilated with and rendered

Y

congenial to the cerebums, caputs, and sensoriums of you, my superlatively respectable auditory."

Delivered as this " much ado about nothing" farrago was, by one possessing no small share of *vis comica*, and under the excitement of a brisk fire of champagne, the effect was ludicrous in the highest degree, and will, probably, not be soon forgotten by any of the party.

At one of the convivial clubs of ultra republicans, poetical selections complimentary to France and America, at the expence of old England, were circulated. Only two of these possessed sufficient merit to deserve notice; and although they have before appeared in print, their insertion, in connection with the festivals I have described, may prove acceptable.

AMERICAN INDEPENDENCE.

When pregnant nature strove relief to gain,
Her nurse was Washington, her midwife Paine:
Close by the couch, in holy fillets dress'd,
Franklin and Jefferson stood priests confess'd.
Libation frown'd, when Jefferson the mild
Said, Independence we will name this child;
But infant Independence scarce began
To be, ere she ripened into man.

His potent influence, spread both far and wide,
Across the Atlantic beams with manly pride;
France his god-father, Britain was his rod,
Congress his guardian, and his father GOD.

The following lines were transcribed from a pane of glass at an inn in England in the year 1776 : —

Hail, happy Britain! Freedom's blest abode ;
Great is thy power, thy wealth, thy glory great;
But wealth and power have no immortal day,
For all things only ripen to decay.
And when that time arrives, the lot of all,
When Britain's glory, wealth, and power must fall,
Then shall thy sons, for such is Heaven's decree,
In other worlds another Britain see,
And what thou art, AMERICA shall be.

The successive accounts of the Belgian, Polish, and Italian insurrections, as well as the demonstrations in Spain, were all received with enthusiasm by the Americans, who, devoted to liberty themselves, are no less ardent in their desire that the blessing should be possessed by others.

It was generally believed that the long wished for period had at last arrived when tyranny might receive its death-blow, and that the French armies, obeying the voice of the nation, would march to the deliverance of Europe, and assist in planting the tree of

Y 2

liberty in the capital of every despot, from Lisbon to the confines of Asia. The subsequent truckling, stock-jobbing policy of the citizen king and his cabinet, however, in allowing the heroic but ill-fated Poles to become the victims of a merciless autocrat, and the efforts of the friends of the sacred cause of freedom to be once more paralysed, damped, although it has not extinguished, the pleasing hope.

The fall of the administration of the Duke of Wellington, whose crowning military success the Americans, in common with other nations, attribute to the treachery of Grouchy, and the arrival of the Prussians in the eleventh hour of the contest, and whom they hold in abhorrence for his conduct in permitting the murder of "the bravest of the brave*," caused universal joy; as did the measure of reform proposed by their successors, which was con-

---

* It is painful for an Englishman to reflect that his country's greatest modern heroes, Nelson and Wellington, both st⁔ ᴊd accused of breaches of faith in respect to articles of capitulation, and in both instances in favour of the most unrelenting and tyrannical governments.

The cold-blooded, judicial murders of Naples have left a stain upon the memory of Nelson which all that daring commander's splendid triumphs cannot efface. Vide *Southey's Life of Nelson.*

sidered as one which would inevitably, but peaceably, lead to the emancipation of the people.

Of the individuals composing the new ministry little was known excepting of the more prominent members. It was, however, the " schoolmaster" of England, Henry Brougham, one of the people, on whom all eyes were fixed as the man to lead the " forlorn hope" in the assault. of the citadel of bigotry and corruption; and in spite of the sneers and misgivings of a portion of the press, the opinion of those best acquainted with English politics may be conceived from the following splendid eulogium on this illustrious character, which I extracted from one of the American newspapers of the day. After some well merited compliments to the patrotic and consistent Earl Grey, who has immortalised himself by his devotion to the " old cause," and by the glorious example he has displayed to " his order," the discriminating writer thus proceeds : —

" I cannot call the latter *Lord* Brougham yet; I have too long felt an enthusiasm for his various and extraordinary abilities as a speaker, as a writer, as a statesman, versed in every branch of home affairs, and at home in every branch of foreign affairs; as a lawyer, acquainted with the whole body of the law, and, what is a far higher and more rare entertainment, with its *mind*; as a philanthropist, not in his chamber, but of the most unwearied and buoyant public spirit and exertion; as a practical man, as a philosopher, as a scholar; knowing every thing, and knowing it well; doing every thing, and doing it well; intuitive and laborious; in details a master; a master in general reasoning; as accurate as profound, and of the most persevering, sleepless, efficient activity in every one of his characters; I have too constantly indulged in a boundless admiration of him under them all, to recognise him as yet, under any other than his own simple name. I cannot, on the first instant of the chance, write him down *Baron* Brougham. Who is he? We have never heard of him. It seems like cheating renown of its rights, as Madame de Staël said, when Bonaparte first gave titles to those of his generals who had been winning victories, in numberless campaigns all over Europe, under their own names of birth and parentage."

Although England, when compared with several of the family of European nations, may justly boast of her institutions, and of her enjoyment of civil and religious liberty, every American knows, that it is only by such comparison with the more despotic states that her claims to be considered free can be substantiated. To say nothing on the nature of the executive, the American knows, that where one branch of the legislature, contrary to common sense and justice, is not only independent of.the governed but hereditary, as if talents and judgment could be bequeathed; where another branch, notwithstanding the "large measure of reform," is chosen by a fraction of the nation, and that, too, the monied class, leaving productive labour unrepresented; where the people aie severely taxed for the support of a hierarchy which the majority condemn; where laws exist worthy only of the barbarous age of the Norman conqueror; where a religious test incapacitates the long persecuted Jew, as well as the conscientious sceptic, from holding civil office; where truth is a libel; where the blasphemous and cruel law of primogeniture robs the brother of his natural right; where the estates of a privileged order cannot be made available to the demands of a famishing creditor; and, lastly, where justice is beyond the reach of the poor;—the American, I repeat, well knows that the country subject to these crying wrongs cannot — cannot be called free.

Believing, as the Americans do, that the existence of kings and privileged classes, as such, is incompatible with the happiness of the people, they look forward to the overthrow of their power with eager anticipation; and as they hope, so they confidently predict, that ere a quarter of a century elapses, Europe will have become one comprehensive family of republics.

The extreme horror entertained by the Americans to kings, and all artificial and unnatural elevation of rank, cannot be conceived by those who have not resided in their country. The following anecdote, although trifling in itself, is important, as showing the temper of the people in this respect, and may therefore be interesting : —

A jeweller in New York, with whom I was one day in conversation, showed me a brooch which he stated he had that morning sold to a young mechanic, who selected it, according to his fancy, from a variety in the store. The device, which was executed in garnets, and of French workmanship, was that of a regal crown. The youth, who had never before seen a representation of the emblem of royalty, was informed, on his returning home, no doubt, by some travelled friend, that the subject was nothing less than the hateful insignia. His republican feelings would not permit him to wear the badge of tyranny for a moment, and with breathless haste he hurried back to the jeweller to exchange the bauble for something more congenial to democratic feelings.

CHAP. XVII.

THE month of December is distinguished by a day set apart as a public thanksgiving for the continuance of peace and the bounty of Providence displayed in the general fertility and abundance of the country.

Although every citizen no doubt feels grateful for these blessings, and may inwardly participate in the sentiment " *Deus nobis hæc otia fecit,*" yet so intent are they upon worldly gains and the study of dollars and cents, that not even the recommendation of the authorities, or, what one should suppose would have its influence, the desire of a little relaxation from the fatigues of business, could induce them to make this day really one of rest; and in the main street, which as I have before observed is about two miles and a half in length, and contains hundreds of stores or shops, we did not notice above half a dozen closed, and two of these were kept by Englishmen, who no doubt made their holiday excursions, as they had been wont to do, perchance, to Highgate or Hampstead, in their youthful days; when on

proclaimed solemn fasts the God of tender
mercies was propitiated to nerve the crimsoned
arm of slaughter against the sons of liberty
and the rights of man. Christmas, merry
Christmas, that old English festive season,
which, though no longer the joyously anticipated feast of our ancestors, yet retains much
of its interest in the family grouping and social
recognitions which then enliven the heart and
cheer us on our way, is almost unknown in
America; and the Englishman looks in vain
for these, as well as for the ancient emblems,
the smoking sirloin and plum-pudding:—all
is still business, business; nor is the day at
all observed except by the members of the
Catholic and pseudo-catholic, the episcopalian,
church.

The same remark also applies to Good
Friday, which is considered, like the feast of
Christmas, to be of Popish origin, and not
conducive to true religion.

If, however, the " business men" of New
York have, in their wisdom, abolished some of
the usages of the good old times, they have
made ample amends by the establishment of
a custom at once rational and agreeable, and
which, on the western continent, is peculiar
to themselves.

This substitute for the jollity of Christmas in the "old country" is the gay observance of New Year's Day, when the ladies hold their annual levees, and receive the congratulatory visits of the other sex. Every house is opened on the occasion; and the tables spread with all the variety which the confectioner and the vineyards of France or Madeira can supply.

The visiters, whose female acquaintance are numerous, can afford but a short time to each; and such proceed from house to house in topographical order, an omission of this customary act of politeness without a substantial reason being looked upon as unpardonable neglect. To the great delight of the lovers of punch, gin sling, julip, and the other nectar et ceteras of the bar rooms, the proprietors of the hotels give " free drink" to all comers, a custom which, in a city like New York, is much abused, and is one which the Bonifaces are of opinion would be " more honoured in the breach than the observance."

The evening of New Year's Day is devoted, as in England, to assemblies of the domestie circles, or to more general convivial intercourse. The facilities this delightful arrangement affords of forming new acquaintance, and, as Johnson says, keeping old friendships in re-

pair, are almost inconceivable to the Englishman, who has not entered the parlours and
drawing-rooms of New York on the first of
January levees, where the easy hospitality,
the sprightly and familiar but elegant salut-
ations of the fair, and the perfect freedom but
correct deportment of the men, — in short, the
total absence of that restraint which state im-
poses, — presents a picture of society at once
cheering and satisfactory.   Two other days in
the year remain to be noticed; but they are
distinguishable in a manner essentially different from those already described.   In spite of
the declaration of the venerable Franklin, in
his admirable and useful publication, Poor
Richard's Almanac, that " three removes are
as bad as a fire," the inhabitants of New York
are the most locomotive people on the face of
the earth.   This movable propensity appears
to be partly caused by a progressive state of
prosperity ; for, as the value of property in the
city has always been steadily increasing, the
owners are unwilling to grant leases, hoping
each successive year to add materially to their
rent rolls.

    In consequence of this encouraging state of
things, an annual valuation in fact takes place
of every rented building in the city, and one

day is appropriated to the letting of tenements
and another for removals. These important
seasons are the first of February and the first of
May. On the former, the landlords, which
term, curious enough, is still preserved by the
republicans, visit their tenants; and unless
arrangements have been previously entered
upon, they state the rents they expect to receive for the ensuing.year. If the occupier
of a building assents to the proposals, the affair
is ended; but if the reply is in the negative,
the owner placards the walls with the words
" To Let," to which is sometimes added the
rent demanded ; and on the evening of this
day it is common to see at least one third of
the houses and stores thus ticketed, and these
remain until tenants are found. At last comes
the all-important first of May, which, to a
stranger just arriving, presents the most singular and ludicrous spectable imaginable, —
nothing less than a whole city turned topsy-
turvy, thousands of persons being in the act
of removal, the streets filled with carts laden
with furniture, porters, servants, children, all
carrying their respective movables, from the
candelabra of the drawing-room to the fish-
kettle of the " foolish fat scullion," and the
gingerbread wares of the nursery.

As the operations of entering upon and quitting the houses are simultaneous, the confusion within doors is in perfect keeping with the scene displayed in the streets, the whole affording no bad illustration of chaos.

To an Englishman, with his strong local attachments, this system of change would be an intolerable nuisance ; but the New Yorker, no doubt from habit, not only looks upon it as a matter of course, but seems to feel an elevation of spirits at the anticipation of this agreeable variety in his social existence ; and it is no uncommon circumstance to meet with individuals who have resided in a dozen different houses in as many years ; and yet who speak of their wish to try the advantages of another quarter of the city when the proper season arrives.

The same system is pursued, but not to a great extent, in respect to the larger stores. As a necessary consequence of this annual transplanting of so large a portion of the population, a new directory is as requisite as a new almanac, and such a publication makes its appearance as soon as the tumult has subsided, and the people again find themselves located to their satisfaction.

It being a well known fact that there is

little correspondence in climate between places situated on the same parallels of latitude in Europe and America, we were not surprised to find New York enjoying the sunny skies and genial warmth of an Italian summer, alternated with the piercing cold and driving snows of a Scythian winter. The year of our residence was distinguished by a somewhat longer continuance of the two extremes than usual.

On our return from Boston early in May the weather was delightful, being much like that of the month of June in the south of England; but the atmosphere was infinitely clearer. The temperature of June was considerable, although not at all oppressive; but that of the succeeding months of July and August exceeded what I had experienced in any seaport of Italy or Sicily, except Palermo, during the prevalence of a sirocco. The thermometer of Fahrenheit, which is the one used by the Americans, ranged during several weeks from 90° to 95° in the shade; and what rendered this degree of heat more unpleasant, it was very little reduced in the nights.

The fashionable world at this season flock to the favourite watering places, to hilly resorts, or to their country houses; whilst thousands of

those who are doomed to toil, seek alleviation
of the oppressive warmth in evening excursions
to public gardens and promenades on the
shores of the rivers, or to petite Vauxhalls,
where beauty, music, coloured lamps, and ice-
creams, are the never-failing attractions.

That almost indispensable article in hot
climates, ice, is retailed from covered carts,
on which appears, in conspicuous characters,
the refreshing word ; and perhaps the most
enviable station in the months of July and
August, in New York, is that of a driver of
one of these vehicles.

Through the whole of the summer, thunder
storms are frequent. Several of those we witnessed were of an almost tropical character, the
lightning, both sheet and forked, seeming to
threaten the conflagration of the city, although,
from the very general use of conductors, which
are attached to all lofty edifices, accidents from
the electric fluid are of rare occurrence.

The thunder was awfully grand, and spoke to
the stoutest heart in every intonation from the
distant rumble, to the solemn roll, and the rat-
tling, crashing, angry peal. A most disagreeable accompaniment of the warm season is the
presence of mosquitoes ; and the luxury of
gauze furniture as barriers against the noc-

z

turnal intrusions of these little pests is by no means general.

A still greater nuisance, however, is the multitudes of rats by which the city of New York is infested — scarcely a building being entirely free from them ; and as dogs are almost proscribed animals, these four-footed scavengers roam at pleasure from house to house, just as the larger quadrupeds, the hogs, parade the streets and lanes.

The extraordinary antipathy of the inhabitants to that faithful friend of man, the dog, arises from a foolish dread of the disease styled hydrophobia ; and to such a degree does this anti-canine mania extend, that the cry of mad dog is raised against every unfortunate mongrel that happens to stray from its master.

We found the autumn, or fall, as it is generally designated, a most delightful season ; and even the gloomy month of November, in which Englishmen are said to hang and drown themselves, was almost a continued period of sunshine.

With the exception of an occasional rainy day, the regular never-failing accompaniment of an easterly wind, the weather continued mild and agreeable until early in January, when winter arrived in all its rigour. A snow storm, of two days' and nights' continuance, covered the ground to a considerable depth, to say nothing of the drifts, which, in many situations, formed impassable barriers. No sooner had the fleecy shower descended, than wheel carriages of every description instantly disappeared, and their places were supplied by sledges or sleighs.

These vehicles were to be seen of all dimensions, and in every style, from the dashing and elegantly decorated four-in-hand, with its buffalo robes, or its leopard skins, to the humble sliding frame with its load of wood or coals. For several weeks, no sounds met the ear but the jingle of the hawks' bells, which, for safety, as a sledge makes no noise, are strung round the necks of the horses.

The diversion of sleighing is extremely agreeable, and is one of which the Americans are passionately fond. Not content with excursions by day, they borrow the night, at all hours of which sleighs might be seen skimming along, filled with gay parties, although the thermometer was often much below zero; and scarcely an hotel within ten or a dozen miles of New York was unfrequented by nocturnal visiters.

During the time the snow remains, the

bodies of the mails and stage coaches are placed upon sleigh frames or runners; and as this method is generally adopted, the communications through the country are as rapid as at other seasons.

The funeral processions at this period had a curious effect, the hearses being followed by sleighs in lieu of coaches; and the mourning friends, enveloped in buffalo robes or fur-edged cloaks, had all the appearance of Alpine travellers.

In one of our excursions, we passed a sledge filled with convicts on their way to prison. The party were chained together, but seemed to forget their degraded situation in the delights of a sleigh ride, — an amusement which some of them were not soon again likely to enjoy.

Although the rise and fall of the tide at New York is only about four feet, it was sufficient to prevent the communication with the sea from being interrupted, even while the rivers, a few miles above the city, were passable for the heaviest wagons. Steamers, however, were required to tow the vessels, in consequence of the quantity of floating ice; and even these, at times, were almost powerless from the junction of the masses, which occasionally allowed a passage for hundreds of pedestrians to the opposite shore of Long Island.

The thermometer, from the middle of January to the middle of February, which embraced the coldest period, frequently stood below zero in the day time ; but the average temperature was some degrees higher.

At the latter end of February, the weather grew sensibly warmer, the snow began to melt, the frost broke up, and a few days of heavy rain, with a thunder storm, dissipated every trace of the stern accompaniments of winter. March brought forth the germs of spring ; and the month of April was even more sunny and more cheering than the finest English June.

The winter of which I have made mention, was considered unusually severe, and fuel in consequence rose to an extravagant price. Many hundred loads of wood were gratuitously distributed by the authorities, and by humane individuals, to poor widows, — almost the only description of persons who stood in need of assistance.

Until very lately, wood was the only description of fuel consumed in New York ; but it is now being fast superseded by coal, although the prejudices of the people, in regard to the use of it for culinary purposes, have yet to be overcome.

That these prejudices are somewhat formidable, will appear from the following circumstance, of which I was a witness, a short time before our departure from America.

The use of coal requiring appropriate grates and culinary apparatus in lieu of the andirons or dogs, the ironmongers were anxious to exhibit specimens of their skill in this novel department.

One of these tradesmen had fitted up a kitchen grate and iron oven, which last article was also new to the Americans; and this important innovation upon old modes being advertised, a man was appointed to explain the mystery of their use.

In vain did he assure some of the curious visiters that the famed sirloin might be roasted, a steak broiled, or a pie baked, so as to be palatable, upon such a system; and although this champion of the new régime freely referred to well known individuals in the city, as well as to the commanders of vessels trading to England, who could attest the truth of his assertions, it was evident that his hearers were somewhat dubious upon the subject, and

that nothing less than a knife and fork demon-
stration of a sirloin, steak, and pie, so cooked,
would remove their incredulity. To this
striking instance of the force of long established
custom, I may add, that even among the circle
of our acquaintance, we found it no easy
matter to gain credence to the assertion, that
the flavour of meat roasted before a fire of
coal, was in no respect inferior to that of
meat which had undergone similar treatment
before one of wood.

The Americans, however, are so ready to
adopt whatever is proved to be either nation-
ally or individually advantageous, that the
reluctance I have alluded to cannot long exist;
and as it is probable that a very considerable
saving will be effected by the change in the
description of fuel, the use of coal will, no
doubt, supersede that of wood in those cities
which have greater facilities for obtaining the
former than the latter.

The coal used in New York and Philadelphia
is principally of a hard kind, denominated an-
thracite. It is difficult to ignite, but, when
burning, has the appearance of red-hot stones,
and gives out an intense heat without any
smoke.

This, and other descriptions, are found in

z 4

inexhaustible beds in the State of Pennsylvania; and, being at the surface, are easily
procured.

The coal is sent to New York by a canal
which connects the great rivers Delaware and
Hudson, the traffic by which is increasing
with astonishing rapidity. None of the coal
as yet found is suitable to the purpose of the
steam engine; but a kind adapted for such
had been discovered in the British province
of Nova Scotia, and its introduction on board
the steamers of New York was on the eve of
becoming general at the time of our leaving
that city.

CHAP. XVIII.

To an Englishman of liberal principles, nothing is so interesting in America, as to witness the operation of the machinery of its republican institutions; particularly the system of election to office.

To hear the outcry and horror expressed in England, however, at the bare mention of the terms universal suffrage, annual parliaments, and election by ballot, it might be supposed that where such exist, society must be in a state little removed from anarchy, — yet how different is the fact!

In the city of New York, the elective franchise is almost co-extensive with the adult male population, and the number of those who vote is seldom less than 30,000.

Whether as respects the choice of representatives to the general or state governments, or of the local magistracy, the system of election is the same; every servant of the people being really and truly the choice of that people.

Candidates, if such term is applicable to men, who neither announce themselves as being desirous of office, nor submit to the degradation of a personal canvass, are proposed at preliminary meetings of each political party; and the names of the individuals thus approved, are afterwards printed on small slips of paper called tickets, the backs of which are endorsed with the designation of the offices about to be filled, and to which they relate, as Senators, Congress, State Assembly, Governor, &c.

Every citizen, desirous of exerting the elective privilege, procures a set of tickets from the committee of the parties for whom he intends to vote; and at the appointed time he proceeds to the house of election in the particular ward or district of the city in which he resides.

Here the voter gives his name and residence to the returning officers, who, if they entertain any doubts as to identity or qualificatio., dispute his claim until satisfactory proofs are exhibited that no fraud is intended.

The name and residence of the voter being entered on the books, he deposits the tickets, which are closely folded, in the ballot box, and quits the room.

The period allowed for receiving votes is

three days; and at the election, I witnessed
during our residence in New York, although
upwards of 25,000 citizens polled at each,
there was no confusion or riotous behaviour
in the streets, no bribery or " free drink," nor
parading with colours and ribands, nor exhibitions of the childish mummery called chair-
ing; and notwithstanding party spirit ran
high, and some boisterous oratory might be
heard in those political forums, the ward
houses, a stranger, who had not perused the
newspapers of the day, or noticed the placards
or *ruses de guerre* on the walls, would not
have been aware that any event of importance
was taking place. Extensive as the recent
measure of reform in Great Britain undoubtedly is, and glorious as has been the achieve-
ment of popular opinion over an insolent
faction; still, a closer approximation to the
American system, both in respect to the extension of suffrage and mode of election, will
be found necessary to render the members of
the elected branch of the legislature, what
they ought to be, the representatives of the
whole people.

Justice, then, demands that labour as well
as property should form a part of the basis of
the constituency. Reason and policy require

election by ballot; without which safeguard, bribery and undue influence will most assuredly prevail; and with whatever suspicion the doctrine may at present be viewed, events will too soon prove the necessity of its adoption; and the period is probably not far distant, when election by ballot will be regarded in England, as it is in America, like trial by jury, the palladium of liberty.

The range of American, like that of English, commerce, is only bounded by the limits of the globe; for wherever a ship can sail, there will be seen the American flag. The port of New York, in respect to its foreign trade, may be considered as the London or Liverpool of the United States. The shipping, however, is almost exclusively of that nation; and excepting the arrivals of British vessels on the resumption of the direct communication with the West Indies, I do not recollect to have seen above a score foreign flags in the port.

The branch of trade which most particularly attracted my attention was that, from a participation in which Englishmen in general are yet excluded, the trade to China.

This lucrative commerce is carried on with great success by the Americans, who not only make large and direct shipments of their own manufactures to Canton, but, as is well known, of those of Great Britain also, from the port of Liverpool. The returned cargoes consist of teas, silks, nankeens, shawls, japanned cabinet goods, china, coloured blinds, screens, papers, ivory, and mother of pearl trinkets, fancy stationary, and drawings, fireworks, and an endless catalogue of articles under the class of useful and ornamental bagatelles, which all find a ready sale at a considerable profit as well for the storekeepers as for the importers. The goods are all sold by auction, in packages, immediately upon their arrival, to the retailers, who as quickly display the attractive wares to their customers, the public. The grocers, in particular, vie with each other in exhibiting placards announcing " Fresh Teas;" of which notice the consumers soon avail themselves, well knowing that the flavour of " the beverage that cheers but not inebriates," materially depends upon the freshness of the herb. If any further evidence were wanting to prove, what at length is becoming more generally known, that the Chinese, notwithstanding their peculiarities, are both a people desirous to trade and easily traded with, the American supercargoes and commanders of vessels could supply it. Several of these gentlemen, with whom

I conversed on the subject, assured me that no place afforded greater facilities for the despatch of business than the port of Canton, and no people were more easy to deal with than the Chinese.

A copy of the evidence on the subject of the China trade, taken before the British House of Commons, happening to be in my possession in New York, I took occasion to read it to one of my American friends, who had made several voyages to China. As it cannot be supposed that an individual of that nation can feel any interest in the opening of the trade in England, the opinions of such a one have additional weight, and are, consequently, more valuable. The gentleman alluded to freely designated most of the statements of the witnesses for the East India Company as absurd as they were untrue. He likewise stated that the idea propagated by the servants of that half military and half mercantile company, that they possessed superior influence with the natives, was completely erroneous—any American or even Dutch trader being as promptly attended to, and as much respected, as the most important officer of the British factory; and speaking of the danger to be apprehended from unruly sailors or others,

he quaintly observed, if Englishmen could not
behave as well as his countrymen, who are
uniformly well treated by the Chinese, they
must abide the consequences.

From another friend connected with the
trade, I learnt some particulars relative to an
affair which had recently occurred, and which
tends to prove the commercial ignorance and
mismanagement of the agents of the India
Company both at home and abroad.

A quantity of cotton twist having been
shipped from London to Canton, it was found,
upon its arrival at the latter port, to be of a
description unsuitable to the market. In lieu
of referring to prices current of other countries, and making calculations, as would have
been done by any private merchant, the article
was immediately sold, at a great loss, to the
first buyer who appeared. This individual
happened to be an American, who shipped it
to New York, at which place it was reshipped
to England, where it was ultimately sold to a
very considerable profit.

Among other scraps of information respecting the trade with China, I learnt that large
quantities of tea were sent from the American
ports to Antwerp, Hamburgh, Havre, and
other places contiguous to Great Britain, a

good deal of which, probably, found its way, in an illicit manner, into that country; and I may add, in corroboration of the fact, that the Americans are enabled to sell the best teas considerably below the India Company's prices, that I saw shipments made to Malta, where they are decidedly preferred, on account of the superior flavour as well as cheapness.

As every circumstance tending to remove the film which has for so long a period obscured the vision of the English people upon the subject of China is of importance at the present moment, the following extracts, which I was kindly permitted to take from a letter written at Canton by a young American to his friends at home, will be found valuable as well as highly amusing. This unsophisticated document clearly shows how desirous the natives of China are for increased intercourse with foreigners, and how advantageous a knowledge of the language will be to those who, in the event of the opening of the trade, may choose to settle among that curious people.

The talented young writer thus proceeds : —
" I have been highly honoured lately: not only have several officers of distinction called upon me to converse in Chinese, but this morning two Chinese ladies, also, did me that

honour. One of them was very handsome,
and apparently about twenty-two years of age,
yet her feet were certainly not more than *two
inches and a half long*. She was dressed in
beautifully embroidered silks and satins, and
looked remarkably well. The other lady
might be about four or five years older, but
was good-looking, and was also dressed in the
richest manner. Being both wives of a mandarine of rank in the province of SOOCHOW,
they came in their palanquin, and were attended by quite a numerous retinue of male and
female servants. They also brought five little
children, the youngest of which was about nine
months old. To it I gave a ten cent piece;
which the mother, agreeably to my request,
said she would hang round its neck or arm.
She was highly delighted, as the money came
so far, and was presented by a foreigner.

" The ladies did not talk much, but wan-
dered, or rather *tottered*, all over the house.
I showed them every thing that I thought
would interest them; — father's likeness, which,
they said, did not resemble me much; also, a
letter I had received from mother. This last
surprised them a good deal, having been
written by a female.

" The weather being hot, and the doors

all flung open, I could not keep them out of the rooms; and into my bed-chamber they bolted, accompanied by their whole retinue. Here they examined the looking-glasses, wash-stand, bed, and toilet, and appeared much amazed. Their deportment was very easy and agreeable, and they seated themselves not the least abashed, differing vastly from the females of this province, who are absurdly modest, or rather affect to be exceedingly so.

" After asking me a few questions, which I answered, and staying about an hour and a half, they took their leave.

" I am promised more calls from some of their friends.

" The circumstance of females visiting a foreigner has caused much surprise, *none having ever been allowed to enter the foreign factories before ;* and it would not even now have been permitted, had the ladies not been from a distant province, and the wives of a ' large mandarine.' So soon as they entered, the outside of the gate was crowded with China men, who waited to see them come out.

" This must be set down as one of the most curious incidents in my life so far ; and in consequence of my having so many man-

darines to see me, the Chinese merchants
look upon me in a different light to the other
foreigners; and since the ladies have been,
they know not what to think of it. The fact
is, the mandarines suppose no foreigner understands their language; and consequently,
not being able to converse they never think,
of going to see them; although it shows, since
they have heard of me, that they are anxious
to see them; and when they come I have
nothing but questions put to me from the
moment they enter the house until they leave.
Of course they are mostly about my own
country. They are very eager to obtain information.

" A few days ago I had a visit from a young
literary graduate, named KWEI WAN YAIN,
one of the most learned men of his age, being
only twenty-four, in the empire; so say the
Chinese. He has passed through all the examinations at this place, and next year proceeds to Peking to be finally examined by the
Emperor, which the natives consider as getting ' *great face,*' when he, no doubt, will be
appointed governor of a province, or a minister of state near his Majesty's person.

" One of my other friends is a military
officer, named LE YING, who commands a

fort opposite to the foreign factories. I frequently go to see him; and once went with him on an excursion of pleasure to some gardens, about five miles from the factory, where we spent the day. He often sends me presents of cake and wine. The kindness which all have displayed towards me, shows how pleased they are to come in contact with a foreigner who understands their language; for never being able to have intercourse with them, they really think we are what their government documents represent us to be — barbarians; and they are greatly surprised when they find we actually can behave well, and talk to them too in their own tongue. This effectually removes the barrier, and the more information they get from me, the more they think these barbarians must really be civilised, and are only misrepresented to them."

Perhaps the most interesting event of the present day in America, to the moralist, is the grand effort making to eradicate habits of intemperance among the adult population, and to promote sobriety among the rising generation. The engines more immediately employed to effect this laudable purpose, are those denominated Temperance Societies, the main injunction of which is, the complete abandonment of the use of ardent spirits, except when required medicinally.

So convinced are the Americans, from the success of local experiments, of the advantages likely to arise from these institutions, that they are now formed in almost every city and district of the Union, in some of which they enumerate as members a considerable portion of the population.

That the habitual drunkard, or even tippler, should be at once reclaimed by their operation, would be little less than a miracle; nevertheless, the progress of reformation has advanced with a degree of celerity almost unparalleled. Spirits, in whole communities, have disappeared; the poison is no longer required or given to the labouring husbandman, even in the cities. Brandy, which, until lately, always appeared on the tables of the boarding-houses, and was taken *ad libitum*, being included in the charge for board, is seldom seen; proprietors of those hot-beds of vice — dram-shops — have, in some instances, abandoned their residences, and removed to situations where the system of reform has made less progress; clerks and others in search of employment in offices or stores, find it advantageous to enter the Temperance Societies; and, lastly, the shipping interest, encouraged by intelligent commanders, who well know that sobriety is an invaluable quality in the sailor, and that a vessel will be better navigated by men who prefer a cup of cocoa to a glass of liquid fire, have also joined the " Holy Alliance."

As a specimen of the description of moral tools with which the members work, I may subjoin a copy of one of the small hand-bills, which are most extensively circulated, and which, there is good reason to believe, produce a powerful effect. At the head of this little collection of aphorisms are two vignettes, one of which represents a family in apparently comfortable circumstances ; but the husband, having returned home in a state of intoxication, has thrown over the table, and, in a fit of brutal rage, threatens the person of his wife with violent usage, The other affords but too faithful a picture of the result of yielding to the degrading vice of drunkenness. On the floor of a wretched hovel, devoid of the simplest article of furniture, is depicted the corpse of the infatuated subject of the first plate, surrounded by his afflicted widow and helpless children, who, naked and hungry, bewail their miserable lot.

" THE WONDERFUL ADVANTAGES OF DRUNKENNESS.

If you are determined to be poor, be a *Drunkard ;* and you will soon be ragged and pennyless.

If you would wish to starve your family, be a *Drunkard ;* for that will consume the means of their support.

If you would be imposed upon by knaves, be a *Drunkard ;* for that will make their task easy.

If you would become a fool, be a *Drunkard ;* and you will soon lose your understanding.

If you are determined to expel all comfort from your house, be a *Drunkard ;* and you will do it effectually.

If you would expose both your folly and secrets, be a *Drunkard ;* and they will soon run out as the liquor runs in.

If you think you are too strong, be a *Drunkard ;* and you will soon be subdued by so powerful an enemy.

If you would get rid of your money without knowing how, be a *Drunkard ;* and it will vanish insensibly.

If you would be a dead weight on the community, and ' cumber the ground,' be a *Drunkard ;* for that will render you useless, helpless, burthensome, and expensive.

If you would be a nuisance, be a *Drunkard ;* for the approach of a drunkard is like that of a dunghill.

If you would be hated by your family and friends, be a *Drunkard ;* and you will soon be more than disagreeable.

Finally, if you are determined to be utterly destroyed in estate, body, and soul, be a *Drunkard ;* and you will soon know that it is impossible to adopt a more effectual means to accomplish your end."

As all institutions, however valuable, are liable to suffer from the indiscreet zeal of their friends, so the Temperance Societies have not escaped ridicule. Forgetting that it is the abuse, and not the use, which constitutes the crime, some enthusiastic persons have denied themselves even those liquors, which, taken, as all things should be, in moderation, contribute to nourish the body and exhilarate the spirits; in short, to innocent gratification, mental as well as bodily: and we witnessed, in several instances, the tables of these " righteous overmuch" groaning under every eatable luxury, but on which no liquid but that of the crystal fountain was allowed to be seen.

A ridiculous instance of scrupulosity as to the use of ardent spirits occurred a few months previous to our leaving New York. The circumstances are as follows: — As port wine is little drunk by Americans, that people, from custom, have recourse to the wine of Madeira in the ordinance of the Sacrament. Now, the Madeira, being adulterated for the American as for the English market with a considerable portion of brandy, was denounced by the more rigid members of the Temperance fraternity as an abomination, and a substitute was immediately thought upon. Such was opportunely found in the wines of fine France, which are not subjected to any admixture; and an advertisement soon after appeared from an eminently zealous individual, recommending the use of Burgundy, of which some friend had received a good supply. What rendered the matter still more ridiculous, the advertisement was accompanied by a chemical certificate of the total absence of brandy in its composition. The effect of this solemn farce was the immediate re-stocking of the vestry wine bins, and of course the easing of many tender consciences, who had periodically polluted their lips with wine in which there might have been a portion of brandy.

During our residence in New York we enjoyed several opportunities of viewing the ingenious American operation of removing houses; but as this mechanical process has been so minutely and faithfully described by Captain Basil Hall, in that officer's Travels, it would be superfluous to dwell upon the subject. A few months previous to our departure from America, however, we witnessed the still more curious and delicate one of raising a house.

The building in question was of brick, three stories high, to which the owner decided to add a fourth. The addition was not made, as it would have been in England, by taking

off the roof, and erecting a superstructure ;
but the whole building was raised to a sufficient
height to allow of a substruction. The means
employed to effect this were simple, but powerful. A series of oblong holes or spaces were
opened in the walls round the edifice ; and by
the introduction of screws and blocks, all of
which were equally and simultaneously employed, the weighty mass was elevated.

The operation occupied several days; and
on passing the spot, a week or two afterwards,
I beheld the enlarged mansion furnished and
occupied ; the whole of the brick-work, even
the heavy and lofty chimneys, being quite
sound and uninjured, and those parts of the
gable ends exposed above the roofs of the
adjoining tenements only requiring the slight
process technically called pointing.

CHAP. XIX.

Even at the commencement of the present century, the journey from New York to Montreal, a distance of only 380 miles, was the labour of several weeks, and was likewise attended with considerable fatigue. Now the same is accomplished in three days and nights; the latter being passed in excellent beds, in the steamers and canal packet boats.

Having decided to return to England by way of Quebec, we prepared for our departure as soon as we ascertained that the navigation of the northern canal and Lake Champlain was opened for the season, which, in the year 1831, took place about the middle of the month of April.

The last day of that month is spent by the busy New Yorkers in packing up their household goods and chattels, preparatory to the grand remove of the 1st of May, which I have already attempted to describe; and, amidst the general bustle occasioned by this topsy-turvy system, we also found ourselves occupied in the arrangement of the contents of trunks, portmanteaus, and, as a lady was in the case, band-boxes.

On Sunday morning, the 1st of May, 1831, we shook hands with some of the kindest-hearted people in the world, and once again embarked in one of the magnificent steamers which grace the Hudson. The weather was delightful; and it being what is termed a packet day, several of those splendid ships, destined for London, Liverpool, and Havre, were majestically sailing down the bay; the mails and passengers having been put on board by the attendant steamer, which, upon the vessel's entering the blue ocean, brings back the company or the individuals who may have taken the trip to repeat the last adieu, and to drink prosperous gales in claret or champagne, which, with other good cheer, is provided in the most liberal manner by the generous owners and commanders. The animated scene, however, with the gay spired city of New York, soon disappeared; and long before evening we had passed West Point, and the bold bluffs and precipices of the Narrows.

At one of the villages on the river we took on board above 100 passengers. They were all farmers, with their families, household furniture, and effects; and were emigrating from the comparatively populous shores of the Hudson to the fertile and almost boundless prairies of the west; where, for a few shillings per acre, they could each select their lots; commence, as is the delight of the American, improvements,— and lay the foundations of the future greatness of the district.

Among the numerous passengers from New York were some woollen manufacturers, several wool growers from the interior, and also some importers of foreign goods.

An interesting discussion was started by some of the mingled company upon the subject of the manufacturing interests of America; and as I felt anxious to elicit their opinions upon the policy or impolicy of the protective system, I did my best to agitate and keep alive the topic. As I anticipated would be the case, the manufacturers and wool-growers were decided friends of the high tariff: first, as a measure of retaliation, because Great Britain refused to receive American flour or grain, — the staple articles of produce, — upon a favourable footing; and, secondly, because, as the manufacturing interest had been created by the help of the tariff, and, in spite of many discouragements in the onset, was then flourishing under its protection, it would be, as they alleged, worse than madness to abandon a system which was rapidly enriching their country, and rendering it completely independent in the event of foreign war.

The importers argued upon the Huskissonian theory, that if wool or any raw material could be imported at a cheaper rate than it could be produced at home, it was sound policy to avail themselves of such importation; and further, that if any particular branch of business could not be carried on by them as successfully as by foreigners, it was folly to think of protecting or forcing such by premiums: in short, the maxim, — buy at the cheapest market and sell at the dearest, — seemed to have made a proper impression on the minds of the debaters on the anti-tariff side of the question.

These wise arguments, however, were not relished by the manufacturers; nor did the listening throng, several of whom joined in the course of the discussion, applaud them. The general impression appeared to be, that with cheap government, and consequently cheap food, they should, if the protective scheme was continued, eventually triumph over every obstacle, and render their great country not only the most powerful, but the richest and most independent, of any in the world.

Politics and political economy, slavery and prison discipline, were successively discussed, until the preparations for turning in, as the nautical phrase for going to bed expresses it, put an end to the debates.

As there were at least 500 passengers to be accommodated, and not half that number of beds, it required no little activity on the part of the stewards to make arrangements for the overplus. This was done, however, with all the alertness of men accustomed to the business, by drawing out the sliding tables, and placing rows of mattresses and bedding upon them; thus creating very fair substitutes for the regular berths. On popping my head out in the night, the cabin presented the appearance of a long ward in a public hospital, with all the beds occupied.

As the ladies' cabin was also crowded to an overflow, a trespass had been made upon that of the gentlemen; the division being formed by a crimson curtain. From the situation of the lights in that part of the cabin, the shadows of its inmates were thrown upon the curtain, in the manner of the exhibitions styled *les ombres Chinois,* or the Chinese shades.

Unfortunately, the fair passengers commenced the operation of unrobing with such
rapidity, that no little mirth was created in our
cabin before the information of the awkward
affair could reach the ears of those whose
business it was to rectify the mistake.

Darkness succeeded this ludicrous exhibition, and the vessel ploughed her way until
near midnight, when, from the great weight
and quantity of heavy goods and baggage on
board, it grounded, and remained, until the
flow of the tide in our favour, immoveable.

The sudden stoppage of the machinery
caused some apprehension and alarm among
the females; one of the most anxious of
whom, I heard exclaim, in no very subdued
tone, " What is the matter?—what is the
matter? say, right away, what is the matter;
do tell me the worst!" After a short pause,
a deep voice from the deck dryly replied
to these repeated interrogatories, " Nothing,
madam, nothing; only the bottom of the
vessel and the top of the earth are stuck together;"—a pretty quaint definition of a ship
being aground. On being awoke by the ringing of the bell at six o'clock in the morning,
I found we were alongside of the wharf at
Albany. Here a scene was exhibited, which,
although provoking to the sufferers on such

occasions, is productive of much mirth to the cautious or more fortunate traveller.

It is the custom of the servants of the steamers to collect and clean all the boots of the passengers. These are claimed by their respective owners at the general boot-room; but, as may be supposed, when the vessel is crowded, it becomes no easy matter for an individual immediately to recognise his own among so many pairs; and mistakes, and, in some instances, exchanges too, no doubt occur. The consequence was, some beaux, who commenced their travels with the latest and most fashionable cut, were seen marching about with the brogues of a back-woodsman; young gentlemen, and those who had " their toes unplagued with corns," perhaps figured in the easy shoes of an invalid; while such unfortunate disciples of Morpheus, who had snored an hour too long, had to make the best of boots which had long since seen their best days, and to repair which would have been as useless as the blunderbuss which stood in need of a new stock, lock, and barrel.

The steamers which ply between Albany and Troy—a distance of six miles—not sailing on the morning of our arrival at the former place, we proceeded in one of the stages which run hourly between these two cities. The road follows the course of the Hudson, and is tolerably good. Near Troy, we passed the United States' arsenal for the district, where many thousand stand of arms, and a train of artillery, are kept in order for service. A few of the brass field-pieces, preserved as trophies, were taken at the surrender of the British army under General Burgoyne, in the year 1777.

Passing the river on a ferry raft, on which the stage was driven, we alighted at the principal hotel in Troy.

Troy is a thriving, cheerful little town; and, although a recent settlement, already contains above 13,000 inhabitants, and is celebrated for an extensive and excellent seminary for young ladies.

As we arrived too late for the public breakfast, we partook of this meal in a private room, and were attended by the daughters of the proprietor of the hotel. The persons and manners of these young females were interesting; and, during breakfast, they occasionally seated themselves by the table, and freely entered into conversation.

I found they had been educated at the seminary alluded to; and, among other branches of useful learning, had made some progress in the exact sciences. A copy of Euclid's Elements, in which appeared the elder sister's name, lay on a side-table. The beautiful daughters of an independent landlord, serving tea and coffee, eggs and rolls, and conversing with the guests upon courses of education and problems of Euclid, was an exhibition peculiar to America; and one which illustrated the state of society in that " happy land" in a most striking manner.

The country in the rear and vicinity of Troy is hilly; and one of the beautiful eminences is distinguished by the classical title of Mount Ida.

Taking leave of our intelligent Trojans, we crossed the Hudson, which is here about a quarter of a mile in width, and embarked in the packet-boat on the great western canal, which we pursued as far as the junction with the northern line—a distance of about two miles. Here, by a series of well finished locks, we entered the latter; and soon afterwards crossed the river Mohawk, just below the grand falls called the Cohoes. The torrent is precipitated over a precipice nearly fifty feet in height; and the volume of water being very considerable, the effect, when viewed from the rapids below, and in connection with the surrounding scenery, is exceedingly fine. The towing path is carried across the stream on a timber bridge of great strength.

In the evening we passed Bemus Heights, the scene of the memorable contest between the British under General Burgoyne, and the Americans under General Gates, in the year 1777. The old farm-house, in which General Fraser breathed his last, is still shown, although *it has been removed* a short distance from the place where it originally stood.

General Fraser was interred, at his own request, in a redoubt on the field of battle; and a monument was ordered to be erected on the spot some years ago by the British government; but it is said the agent employed the money to his own use, and the grave of this brave warrior still remains unmarked by the slightest memorial.

A few miles further, we saw the ground where the army of Burgoyne surrendered themselves prisoners of war to their more fortunate antagonists.

These historical and interesting sites are all within an easy ride from the celebrated Saratoga springs, the Harrowgate or Cheltenham of America, and at which hundreds of the fashionables of the southern States spend their summer months.

Near Fort Edward, which we passed in the night, is the spot rendered tragically memorable by the murder of the lovely Miss M'Rea, by the Indians, in the revolutionary war. This unfortunate young lady, who is reported to have been extremely beautiful, was the daughter of a clergyman, and engaged to be united in marriage to an officer in the army of Burgoyne.

Her lover, anxious for the celebration of the nuptials, engaged a party of Indians to convey the damsel to the camp.

Contrary to the wishes of her friends, the fond girl committed herself to their care, and was escorted by them to a certain spring on the road, where they were met by another band, who likewise claimed the privilege of being her body-guard. It is supposed an altercation ensued between the parties about their charge, during which they were attacked by the whites. Melancholy to relate, on the termination of the conflict, Miss M'Rea was found tomahawked and scalped.

Her lover, on hearing the horrible intelligence, died of grief. Her name is still inscribed on the tree, under which the murder was perpetrated, and where her maimed body was originally interred. The remains have since been removed to the churchyard of the village of Sandy Hill.

The country through which we passed, during the evening after our leaving Troy, exhibited the appearance of high civilisation, in well cultivated farms, smiling villages, and a numerous well fed, happy population; but on looking out of the cabin in the morning the scene was completely changed.

In lieu of gliding on a canal between fertile fields, we found ourselves sailing in a creek, with which the former communicates, bordered by sterile rocks and inhospitable shores, covered with pine woods, and almost without inhabitants.

The air, too, was both " nipping and eager;" very different from that of the valley of the Hudson, to which noble stream, after coursing it above 200 miles, we had bidden adieu.

The towing path in this wilderness serves a double purpose, being also the mail coach road; if an ill-defined causeway, where the traveller is either drawn axle-deep in mud, or jolted over transverse logs, deserves that appellation.

After travelling most comfortably the whole

length of the canal—sixty-five miles, enjoying the company of agreeable fellow passengers, and receiving every possible attention and hospitality, from the captain of the packet and his assistants, we reached the village or port of Whitehall.

In a short time after, the steamer arrived from St. John's; and the united passengers at the hotel, to the number of nearly a hundred, were summoned to breakfast. Although I have already had occasion to allude to the abundance displayed at this meal in America, I must be allowed to notice this breakfast at Whitehall in a special manner; such bountiful doings being unknown in any other country.

My readers may, then, imagine, a table nearly long enough for a city feast, well covered with steaks, cutlets, eggs, ham, sausages chickens fricasseed and barbacued; stewed and fried eels, with delicious trout; add to these good things, rolls, cakes, and an inexhaustible supply of excellent coffee; and some idea may be formed of the substantial repast; which, to hungry travellers, was indeed, as Dominie Sampson would have had it, " prodigious." Some idea of the cheapness of provisions may be formed, when I state, that the charge for this meal was only about eighteen pence sterling each person.

The waiters, who performed their duties in a style fit for the best hotels in England, received nothing from the guests.

As soon as the company had risen, and a portion of the *matériel* had been removed, they sat down in their turn, and followed up the attack with vigour.

The village of Whitehall has latterly become a place of importance, in consequence of the opening of the northern canal, and the increased traffic between New York and the towns bordering on Lake Champlain, as well as Lower Canada, to which province it is in the direct line. The streets are laid out sufficiently wide, but they were not paved or even Macadamised. The canal, which branches from the creek, where it ceases to be navigable, on account of rapids and falls, communicates with the head of the lake by a series of locks.

As the steamer did not sail until noon, we beguiled the interval by strolling up the hill in the rear of the village, from which there is an extensive prospect. The surface of the ground is rocky, but much wooded, and so infested with snakes, as to require the pedestrian to carry a stick, and keep on his guard against these reptiles ; although they will not molest the intruder on their domain, if they can effect their escape.

We saw at least half a dozen, of various sizes and species, in the distance of a few hundred yards. One of these, a young copper head, with a most brilliant pair of eyes, viewed us with such innocent surprise, that I allowed it to make its way to its nest. We did not hear the sound of rattle-snakes, but we were told that the hill was covered with these venomous creatures. About one o'clock, we embarked with a number of other passengers in the steam-packet Franklin, for St. John's.

This vessel was of large dimensions, the machinery powerful, and the cabins fitted up in a style of elegance, almost equalling, if not exceeding, any we had previously seen.

The captain or pilot instructed the engineer in regard to speed or stoppages by a bell, the number of strokes on which designating the particular command.

Lake Champlain, in the vicinity of White-hall, is narrow and tortuous, having the appearance of a river flowing between lofty hills ; although it soon widens and pursues a more direct course, it is not until Crown Point is reached—a distance of forty miles—that the lake opens to a considerable extent. This formerly important post, with its companion Ticonderoga, situated at the outlet of the beautiful Lake George, exhibit extensive remains of the fortifications erected in the French Canadian war; and in the former place, a number of guineas were lately discovered, which had been buried for security.

In the course of the afternoon, we passed a rocky promontory, the end of which had been separated by some convulsion of nature to a distance of thirty feet from the main land ; the opposite surfaces of the fracture exactly corresponding.

Twelve miles further, on the east side of the lake, is Burlington, a flourishing village, near to which, on an eminence commanding an extensive and beautiful prospect, is the University of the State of Vermont.

At Burlington we landed several passengers, the operation being conducted with the same degree of rapidity as on the Hudson river.

Pursuing an oblique course on the now expanded lake, we had a charming view of the woods, and lofty range of mountains of Vermont, gilded by the rays of the setting sun ; and after a most agreeably spent evening, enlivened by " the feast of reason and the flow of soul," midnight found us entering the bay of Plattsburgh,—a name recalling no very agreeable associations to English ears. At the pier of this lake port, where several large trading sloops were lying, we had again the disagreeable task of bidding farewell to passengers, for whom even a short intimacy had sufficed to win our good opinion.

Although I have more than once had the pleasure to record the polite attentions of the Americans, I cannot omit to mention an instance of the most disinterested kindness shown to us by some of our fellow travellers, who landed at this place.

The party had come several hundred miles on a visit to some of their friends, near Plattsburgh, with whom they purposed to remain a few weeks.

Without the slightest acquaintance with either myself or my wife, beyond that which travellers of congenial sentiments form while journeying together, these friendly individuals invited us, in the most pressing manner, to accompany them, and to remain as long as we could make it convenient; assuring us of a most hospitable reception, and of their desire to render our stay agreeable. It was with

great regret that we were obliged to decline
the proffered civilities; and with more than
ordinary feelings of sorrow that we parted, in
all probability never to meet again.

In the churchyard of Plattsburgh lie interred, side by side, the British and American
officers who fell in the military and naval conflicts near this place, in the year 1814.

Among the British are the gallant Commodore Downie, and Lieutenant-Colonel Wellington. A monumental slab has been placed
to the memory of the former gentleman, which
bears the following inscription : —

" Sacred to the memory of GEORGE DOWNIE,
ESQ., a Post-Captain in the British Royal
Navy, who gloriously fell on board His British
Majesty's Ship, the Confiance, whilst leading the vessel under his command to the attack of the American flotilla, at anchor in
Cumberland Bay, off Plattsburgh, on the 11th
of September, 1814. To mark the spot where
the remains of a gallant officer and sincere
friend were honourably interred, this stone
has been erected by his affectionate sister-in-
law, Mary Downie."

The permitting this complimentary epitaph
to be inscribed in the public cemetery, must
be regarded as honourable to American feel-

ing. The unfortunate killed of the rank and
file were all buried on a small island opposite
the village.

The deathlike stillness of night, combined
with the recollections that both the water we
were sailing over, as well as the shore which
it laves, had been crimsoned with the blood
of so many of one's fellow creatures, produced
a powerful sensation on the mind; and I only
awoke from the reverie into which I was
thrown, on passing the promontory called
Cumberland Head, which forms the northern
boundary of the Bay of Plattsburgh. From
all I could learn respecting the actions, the
simultaneous disastrous issues of which to the
British forces is too well known, it appears
that the success of the Americans on land was
principally owing to the deadly fire of their
numerous riflemen, who in no instance miss
their aim ; and that the circumstance of their
flotilla carrying heavy carronades rendered
the bravery of the British, who had only long
guns, of less avail at close quarters.

Who was to blame in respect to this and
other oversights, it is now useless to enquire ;
but I may remark, that much of the cause of
failure, in all the actions between the British
and the Americans, from that of Saratoga in

the first war, when Burgoyne and his bat-
talions were taken prisoners, to the horrible
butchery of New Orleans in the last, when
the Americans killed 1500 brave veterans, with
scarcely any loss themselves, or of their own
force, may be found, partly in the aristocratic
constitution of our army, in which the accident
of birth or fortune, not military service or
talent, procures command; and partly in the
contempt in which the Americans were held
by the British officers generally; a contempt
eagerly fostered by a nation which had so
often been flushed with victory when com-
bating people less imbued with the love of
liberty, and who were not, like the Americans,
fighting "*pro aris et focis*," for God and their
country.

Soon after daylight we passed Rouse Point,
situated at the entrance of the narrow channel, at the northern end of the lake, the borders of which are here low and marshy.

Under the impression that this important
post fell within the boundary line of the
United States, the American government had
proceeded to fortify it in a most efficient manner; but the commissioners appointed to settle
the frontier, deciding that it pertained to

Canada, the works were immediately dismantled and rendered useless.

The recent arbitration of the King of the Netherlands would seem to reverse the matter; and it is probable that the Americans have acted somewhat precipitately, and not with their wonted cool deliberation, in thus destroying the work of their hands.

At this imaginary line of separation, we bade adieu to the United States of America, —a country in which we had sojourned two years, in which we had found many friends, formed many sincere friendships, in which we had spent some of the happiest hours in our lives, and which we could not leave without a sigh. Ten miles from the frontier is the celebrated Isle aux Noix, the Portsmouth of Lake Champlain, at which, in nautical language, we touched. The frames of a number of sloops and gun-boats lay rotting on the stocks, or had already fallen to pieces; but the fortifications appeared in excellent order, as well as the extensive barracks and store-houses.

A solitary British serjeant was the only living being we beheld; yet the sight of this individual, together with the bas-reliefs of the royal arms in the pediments of the buildings, were not only novelties, after two years' acquaintance with eagles and caps of liberty, but were striking preludes to the scenes about to open.

The view of the arsenal having given rise to a conversation on ship-building, I asked an American passenger, whether it was true that, during the last war, his countrymen had converted growing trees into vessels of war in the short space of a month. The answer was in the affirmative, and that one of these hastily constructed floating batteries mounted 100 guns. On my remarking that ships so quickly built could not last, my friend replied, with a dry smile, that they lasted long enough : they lasted until they took all yours. Unfortunately for my national credit, this was true to the letter.

An uninteresting sail of fourteen miles brought us to the village of St. John's, the port of entry at the British end of the lake.

The distance between Whitehall and this place is about 140 miles ; which we had accomplished in sixteen hours, including various stoppages to land passengers.

An officer of the Custom-house came on board to pass the baggage, which service was performed in the most gentlemanly manner ;

and having taken leave of the star-spangled
banner, and the commander of the steamer,
who, to a thorough knowledge of, and strict
attention to, his professional duties, united
urbanity of manner the most engaging, we re-
paired to the best hotel in the place, and
joined the *table d'hôte*, with all the keenness of
appetite created by scenting the morning air.
The poverty of the meal, however, and the
tout ensemble of the house, compared with
Whitehall, or indeed with any village of the
same class in the United States, which we
had seen, was particularly observable, and
did not give us a favourable opinion of the
prosperity of the settlement.

The scanty population seemed to consist of
English, Irish, and Scotch; and here and
there an idle soldier might be seen. Breakfast being over, we took our seats in the stage
for La Prairie, on the St. Lawrence, a distance
of eighteen miles.

By the word " stage" must not be understood
any thing like the gay-panelled and well-
finished vehicles of England, nor yet the
ruder but commodious ones of America; but
only a light waggon, in which, on two cross
benches sat the passengers with their trunks
and baggage behind them.

For a short way the road ran parallel with the river Richelieu, the outlet of Lake Champlain into the St. Lawrence ; and although very far from being what would be tolerated by our commissioners of turnpikes, was still carriageable at a moderate pace.

What succeeded it is not easy to describe, — even Moody's " waggon-rut lane" falling short of the realities of this route.

Now driving over heaps of half-broken stones, — now through mud axletree deep, sometimes of the colour and consistency of printers' ink, — then through morass so soft as to leave us in some doubt whether we were to go a yard farther or bivouac on the spot, — and if, by dint of whip and voice, the hardy ponies proceeded, it was only that we might be rattled over a series of transverse logs, not unaptly termed corduroy road; or, lastly, be see-sawed over springing fascines sunk in the mire.

In this delightful manner we journeyed to the village of La Prairie, where we arrived much in the condition of the poet who thus describes his feelings after similar miseries : —

> " Though every bone is aching
> After the shaking
> I've had this week over ruts and ridges
> And bridges," &c.

and we at length began to think that the American's advice, to travel with a supply of cotton to stuff between the jaws, was not altogether a joke.

This part of Canada is flat, and to the eye of the artist uninteresting; but it is cleared of wood, and well cultivated, and contains numerous substantial frame-houses, with churches at regular intervals. The roofs of the latter are formed of tin, and in some of the yards we saw large crucifixes, to which were attached the implements used at the crucifixion, as the hammer, pincers, spear, sponge, &c., just as are commonly seen in some of the states of Italy.

We met a priest in his cassock, whom, according to the custom of Catholic countries, I saluted, which mark of respect was very politely acknowledged.

The appearance of such a personage in the habit of his order, the sight of the peasantry at work in their red or grey woollen caps, their gay manner, the sound of the French language, together with the Catholic emblems, were strongly contrasted with the country we had so lately left, and at every step the distinction seemed even more and more apparent.

Our fellow travellers, or, perhaps, as correctly speaking, fellow sufferers, from St. John's, were, a New Englander or Yankee, and a Canadian : the former, a middle-aged man, shrewd and observant; the latter, young, volatile, and extremely opinionated ; in short, one of those happy individuals who are upon excellent terms with themselves.

As is generally the case, when Americans and Canadians meet, it is not long before the merits of their respective countries are the topic of conversation ; so the batteries of disputation opened between our two companions soon after we started from St. John's; and, whether the assertion of travellers, that national egotism is a distinguishing feature in the American character, be true or false, the quantum possessed by our Canadian certainly exceeded any thing we had previously witnessed.

With this happy mortal, Canada was nothing less than the modern garden of Eden : its frame-houses were the most delightful places of residence on the earth; the diet of the Canadian farmers was fit for kings ; the dialect was one which the Parisians themselves might study with advantage ; the religious establishment was a model for all other nations ; the productions of the soil were the envy of the neighbouring territory; and even the highway over which we were jolting, at any other season of the year was superb!

Making full allowance for this exuberance of *amor patriæ*, which, after all, is pretty much the same with the unread and untravelled of every country, we did not venture to weaken it by comparisons, to which our friend would probably have been unwilling to listen.

To a jocose suggestion, however, which he made, on our remarking some peculiarity in a sheep which we passed, that we should present it to the British Museum; my wife laughingly replied, " that half a mile of his road would be a greater curiosity." His subsequent silence, showed that the sally was not received in the same spirit with which it was made.

At La Prairie, the magnificent St. Lawrence first burst upon our sight. The poverty of the place, which only afforded a few dry biscuits and vile spirituous compounds, which latter we of course rejected, was entirely forgotten in the splendour of the view.

The great breadth of the majestic river, the white breakers of the rapids of La Chine, a few miles above; and in the distance below, on

c c 3

the opposite bank, the city of Montreal, with its glittering spires, backed by the wooded eminence which gives name to the island itself, formed a picture of absorbing interest.

In the midst of our enjoyment of this sublime prospect, we were hurried into the bateau which was to convey us with other passengers to the city.

The bateaux navigating the St. Lawrence are very large flat-bottomed boats, with the head and stern alike, both rising in the galley style.

That in which we embarked contained a cargo of ashes in barrels, together with about twenty persons, including the boatmen, two of whom were old Canadian voyageurs, and had been on the inhospitable shores of the northern lakes.

Montreal is situated nine miles below the village of La Prairie; but the current runs with such rapidity, that considerable exertion was requisite to prevent us being carried too far. The passage was free from danger, notwithstanding occasional eddies and waves excited alarm among the timid.

What gave a peculiar charm to this little

voyage was the chant of the rowers, which was exceedingly plaintive and beautiful ; and, although the air did not resemble that of the Canadian boat song so deservedly popular with us, the exquisite melody of the latter was naturally associated with the scene.

CHAP. XX.

STRIKING as is the contrast to the stranger who is transported from Dover to Calais, it is certainly not greater than that between the American cities and those of Canada; and in no part of my travels do I remember to have witnessed, in the course of a few days, a greater falling off in the general appearance of national prosperity, than in our being transferred from even the third or fourth class cities of Albany or Troy, to the rising entrepôt of Montreal.

In lieu of a clean and commodious landing pier, like those of the United States, on which elegant hackney coaches and cars await the passenger's arrival, to convey him to a well-supplied hotel, our bateau was rowed, or rather hauled, upon a muddy beach, amidst a crowd of shipping, at the foot of one of the meanest and dirtiest little streets or alleys that can be conceived. How we were to get on shore at all was not instantly apparent. But our suspense was not of long continuance; for in a few minutes a number of small carts, each of which was drawn by a hardy pony, were

backed into the water to the side of the boat;
and trunks, band-boxes, and all, were as
speedily stowed in them by the officious and
loquacious drivers, in their *bonnets rouges*,
and the owners of the baggage, ladies as well
as gentlemen, were requested to take their
seats upon their movables.

In this way, like so many camp followers, we
were driven up the muddy bank, and into the
crowded market-place; where, nothing loth,
we descended from our elevated stations, and,
wading through mire possessing the quality of
birdlime, proceeded to a boarding-house,
which was politely recommended by the
superintendent of the news-room, who had
visited our bateau in quest of the latest intelligence from the great capital, New York.

I have said that my first impressions, on
landing in America, were the high character
and independent bearing of the labouring population, and the absence of rabble : those on
landing in Canada were the suavity and politeness of the natives, whose air and manners
were as perfectly those of their parent country
as was their language ; and it required no
stretch of imagination to fancy ourselves in
one of the smaller and poorer cities of France,
remote from its fascinating metropolis.

The boatmen, carters, and porters all touched or raised their caps when addressing well-dressed persons; and on receiving their demands for any services rendered, they did not fail to return a *Merci, monsieur*,— a piece of courtesy unknown, in any instance where the obligation is mutual, among the independent and sturdy republicans of the United States.

The company in the boarding-house were likewise of the French school; and the meals, both as to the description of cookery and the time devoted to them, bore a closer resemblance to the custom of France than America; whilst the smiling *femmes de chambre* might have just arrived from the " gay, sprightly land of mirth and social ease."

The city of Montreal, which contains rising, as the Americans would express it, 30,000 inhabitants, is about two miles in length, and half a mile in width. It consists of two long streets, the upper and the lower, the latter of which is extremely narrow and dirty; and these are intersected by others of the poorest character.

The buildings are all of stone, but in general not more than two stories high; and the window shutters and outer doors being of sheet-iron, they have something of a prison air. The roofs are all constructed of tin, which, I was surprised to learn, was extremely durable, the lustre remaining even at the expiration of half a century. I observed the sheets of tin were so doubled at the edges that the nails with which they are fastened were invisible, and of course protected from the weather.

Permanent ladders are placed on all the roofs, as means of escape in case of fire. The stores or shops are principally kept by English or Scotsmen; but they have not the least pretensions to elegance; and as the goods are wholly of British manufacture, they do not comprise the tempting variety exhibited in the marts of America. I only saw two or three booksellers' establishments; and only one of these, which was kept by an American, possessed an extensive, or even useful, collection of works. The proprietor of this store received the English reprinted publications from New York and Philadelphia almost as soon as issued in those places, thereby anticipating the arrivals from London. Among the books of this class which had just been received, was the description of that magnificent labour, the Manchester and Liverpool railroad, — a topic of intense interest in the United States, in which the locomotive steam-engine is about to be so extensively introduced.

Among the public edifices, the new Catholic Church stands eminently conspicuous. This immense building, which, though not yet completed, has cost as much money as would have sufficed to construct a railroad from La Prairie to St. John's, and which is capable of holding above 10,000 persons, is constructed of bluish-grey stone, in a plain style of Gothic architecture. The grand entrance is under a lofty portico, between two noble towers. The interior, which has extensive galleries, is divided into pews ; and as the floor is inclined towards the high altar, the whole of the congregation have a good view of the officiating priests.

This spacious house of God, like all the great temples of the Catholic religion in countries where that faith is generally professed, is open at all hours ; and the humble penitent may be seen pouring out his inmost thoughts to his ghostly confessor, and receiving words of comfort ; or, in silent contrition before the sacred image of his Saviour, vowing to lead a new life unto righteousness.

On the Sunday I beheld every part of the

building crowded to excess. The sermon was delivered in the French language. One third of the congregation appeared to be natives of the Emerald Isle, and all looked well fed and well clothed. The beadles, who attended about the entrances to preserve order, wore liveries of blue faced with red; and their staves of office were ornamented with the royal arms of England. The union of these outward and visible signs of Protestant ascendency with the emblems of the Catholic faith could not fail to be noticed by every English stranger; for although the circumstance was trifling in itself, the effect was momentarily confusing.

The English Episcopal Church is a spacious edifice, with a lofty tinned spire. Over the altar is a copy of that splendid relic of art, the Last Supper, by Leonardo da Vinci. As is customary in British garrisoned towns abroad, there are two morning services on the Sunday; the first of which is for the military, the second for the *bourgeois*.

The majority of the pews on the morning of our visit were empty; and from the dusty state of that into which we were shown by the sexton or pew-opener, it apparently had not been occupied for many months. The duty was performed by missionary clergymen, sent out by the Society for the Propagation of the Gospel in Foreign Parts. A collection was made, or, as the Americans have it, was taken up, after the sermon; and it was with no small degree of vexation that we subsequently learned the receipts were for the purpose of keeping the church clean,—a duty, as our soiled apparel had borne witness, wholly neglected.

The *Hôtel Dieu*, or Hospital for the Sick, the Seminary for the Education of Youth devoted to the Priesthood, and the several nunneries, appeared to be well-regulated establishments. I noticed, in the first mentioned, portraits of that weak monarch, Louis XVI., and his profligate queen, as well as some other relics of France under the old *régime*, for which there still lingers an attachment.

The barracks and other Government buildings of Montreal are large, and handsomely finished; and an extensive *place d'armes* affords the inhabitants opportunities of witnessing military parade, and enjoying eloquent music, — both which are provided at the expense of John Bull.

In the market-place is a handsome monument to the memory of Nelson, erected some years ago by the British residents in Montreal. The design of this work of art is a Roman Doric column, upon the summit of which is a statue of the hero. The column itself is of the same description of stone as that used in the erection of the great Catholic Church; but the figure, as well as the ornaments of the capital, the base, and the bas-reliefs on the pedestal, representing the principal victories, are executed in terracotta, or artificial stone, and appeared to bear the frost pretty well.

At Montreal commences the grand chain of canal and river navigation, the object of which is to facilitate the communication between the provinces of Upper and Lower Canada.

The canal which forms the first link, and which communicates with Lake St. Louis, at the mouth of the Ottawa river, is about seven miles in length. The locks, at its junction with the St. Lawrence, are of the most approved construction, and the bridges connected with them combine durability with taste in design.

The great work called the Rideau Canal, which, after the expenditure of many hundred thousand pounds, is at length opened, commences at Kingston on Lake Ontario, and ends at the rising little settlement of Bytown, on the Ottawa river. Whether, in the execution of this project, a proper regard has been paid to economy in the expenditure is questionable ; but as the requisite funds were supplied by Old England, I did not find the Canadians deeply interested in that part of the subject, more particularly as they would reap the advantages.

Having devoted a day or two to the inspection of the iron founderies, the ship-building yards, and other establishments connected with the trade of this growing port, and taken a farewell view of the magnificent scene presented from the eminence in the rear of the city, the slopes of which are studded with the villas of the wealthy inhabitants, we embarked in one of the steamers for Quebec. The dimensions of these vessels are much the same as those on the waters of the United States ; but, as they are intended more for the conveyance of produce and general cargoes than for passengers, the part allotted for the latter is on a smaller scale, but not less elegant, the tables not less bountifully supplied, nor are the attentions to comfort in any degree inferior.

We left the wharf at Montreal about noon, and rapidly passed the small fortified island

of St. Hélène, on which is the arsenal and
the barracks for the artillery. Much as we
had heard from the Canadians in praise of
the scenery of the St. Lawrence, we did not
find their descriptions in the least degree
exaggerated.

From Montreal to Lake St. Peter, a distance of fifty miles, which we passed before
night, the margin of the river exhibited a
succession of picturesque villages, in each of
which the glittering spire of the parish church
was a conspicuous object. The style of the
cottages, shaded as they were by lofty trees,
and backed by their little orchards and gardens, strongly reminded me of some parts of
the " wide and winding Rhine ;" although the
illusion was occasionally weakened by the
sight of canoes skimming across the stream,
the navigators of these frail barks wearing
woollen caps, sashes round the waist, and
rough leather mocassins, or Indian shoes.

At Berthier, one of the most interesting
and populous of the settlements, we stopped
to take on board a supply of wood, while
some of the deck passengers, unfortunately
for the comfort of others, availed themselves
of the opportunity to procure a supply of
whisky.

Among the individuals upon whom this spirituous stimulant operated with most effect, was a poor schoolmaster, who, with the loquacity and gifts of Caleb Quotem himself, so mingled, or mangled, his Latin, French, and English, that had he been a disciple of the Irving school he could not have spoken in terms more unintelligible.

While this facetious pedagogue was *compos mentis*, I had entered into conversation with him as with one from whom something might be learnt relative to Canadian affairs; and in this idea I was not disappointed. He corroborated the statement I had heard from other quarters, of the reluctance shown by the Catholic clergy to the diffusion of the English language; and to such an extent did my informant represent this anti-English feeling to prevail, that even his offers to teach it gratis to his poorer scholars were rejected by those under whose guidance they placed themselves. However we may lament the ignorance displayed in regard to the refusal of the means of knowledge, we may certainly attribute some part of the repugnance to the officious spirit of religious proselytism which distinguishes so many well-meaning but over-zealous Protestants, and which, in some communities, operates as a bar to a more perfect union of the population.

We passed Lake St. Peter, which is formed by a considerable expansion of the river, and also the old settlement of Trois Rivières, in the night. The captain, a Canadian, was indefatigable in his attentions to his passengers, ever studying their comfort and their tastes; and chess, backgammon, and cards were in requisition to a late hour. My evening, however, was devoted to explaining to a circle of enquirers, by the assistance of pencil diagrams, such matters in the construction of railroads as could not be so well understood by general newspaper descriptions; and it was a source of considerable pleasure that I found myself enabled to satisfy the curiosity of my fellow travellers.

Morning found us sailing rapidly between banks of considerable elevation, upon which were seen the white snug cottages of the native peasantry, and occasionally the more extensive mansion of the seigneur, or the neat parish church.

As we approached Quebec the river expanded, assuming the appearance of a lake, and the distant scenery became more mountainous. Passing the spot rendered memor-

able as the winter-quarters of the discoverer of
the country, the enterprising Cartier, about
noon, a bend of the river suddenly brought
us in sight of the lofty promontory of Cape
Diamond, and soon after the eye beheld the
cove where the gallant Wolfe, like the stan-
dard-bearer of Cæsar on the strand of Albion,
leaped from his crowded barge to head his
brave comrades against their ancient and
inveterate foe.

Steering our way midst ships at anchor, and
tortuous rafts of timber destined for old England, we soon reached the point of debarkation
at Quebec.

No sooner had we come in contact with the
wharf, than a crowd of mercantile emissaries
rushed on board, and divided the contents of
the letter-bag, which was emptied on a table
for their accommodation.

On landing, we immediately proceeded to
the city, or what is termed the Upper Town,
in contradistinction to the Lower, which skirts
the base of the lofty hill, and is, in fact, the
Wapping of the place. A very steep zigzag
street, appropriately named Mountain Street,
conducted us to the gate; soon after passing
which, we found ourselves in a large, irregular,
open market-place, on one side of which was

the Cathedral, and on another the barracks, formerly the convent of the Jesuits.

It being the feast of the Ascension, or Holy Thursday, the shops were closed, the citizens were in their best attire, and every thing bore the quiet aspect of a Sunday in England. Having located ourselves as agreeably as the paucity in the choice of comfortable boarding-houses admitted, we commenced our perambulation of this semi-English, semi-French city:

Before I proceed to a description of this Gibraltar of the west, I may mention, that its distance from New York is about 550 miles, which we performed by rivers, lake, and canal, except the trifling portage between St. John's and La Prairie; and that the total expense of travelling this route, unattended as it is by fatigue, except in the portage alluded to, was only eight pounds, exclusive of wine, the taking which is optional.

The city and fortifications of Quebec cover the extremity of a bold promontory, the side of which, toward the St. Lawrence, is almost one continued rocky precipice, whilst that to the river St. Charles is, comparatively speak-ing, of little elevation.

The boundary to the land side is chiefly on a level with the adjacent country.

The hill called Cape Diamond, from the circumstance of crystals being found embedded in the rock, is covered by the magnificent citadel. Scarcely a vestige of the original plan now remains, the present extensive works, which are hastening to completion, being entirely new. They are constructed upon the most approved system of modern fortification, and embrace a very considerable area, in which, besides a noble structure for the officers, are bomb-proof barracks for several thousand troops, as well as magazines for provisions and munitions of war.

The granite which is used in the buildings is brought down the St. Lawrence to the foot of the mountain, and then drawn up an inclined plane, to the height of 450 feet, by a steam engine. The bricks are all imported from London; and I need scarcely remark, that it is on the treasury of honest but extravagant John Bull that the bills are drawn for the millions thus squandered for the defence of a country, which has never yet, nor, in all probability, ever will, remunerate its protector.

On the highest pinnacle of the fortification

is a small tower on which is a telegraph, and also a gun, which, as is usual in fortresses, is fired at the periods of sunrise, noon, and sunset.

It is the *coup d'œil* from this eminence which has been so eulogised by travellers; and although our expectations were raised to a high pitch, they were on our visit to the tower in question even more than realised. Standing on the verge of a rocky precipice, between four and five hundred feet in height, we looked down on the city, and on the glassy surface of the majestic St. Lawrence, as on a lake, on which lay, with sails unfurled, and with sleepy banners, many a freighted bark; while here and there glided the barge with glittering oars, or skimmed some frail canoe.

Extending the field of vision, the eye embraced the slopes of Point Levi, the picturesque Isle d'Orléans, and the cultivated districts of Montmorenci and Lorette, studded with white cottages innumerable, while the more distant woody hills spoke the line of demarcation between the abodes of civilisation and the mountain range whose bleak and inhospitable sides repel the efforts of industrious man, and appear to say, " Hither shalt thou come, but no farther." The city itself is completely walled ; every commanding situation or angle is planted with heavy cannon and mortars, backed by pyramids of shot and shells; and its five gates are also appropriately and strongly fortified. Dismounted guns, decayed carriages and platforms, bespoke piping times of peace, although the strong guards at the gates, and the number of sentinels which met the eye at every turn, would seem to denote a state of active warfare.

The streets of Quebec are narrow, and several of them very steep, but they are macadamised, and kept in neat order.

The houses, like those of Montreal, are seldom more than two stories high, and are also roofed with tin. Many of the better kind have double windows, to exclude the winter's cold, which is exceedingly severe.

The shops, although their signs announced the occupants to be from London, are, in general, poor, and possessed few attractions, even less than those of Montreal ; and if the literary character of the place is to be judged by the number of booksellers' establishments, that of Quebec is low indeed, for I only found two, and the catalogues of these were made up of Catholic prayer-books, school-books, and religious tracts.

An opposition, however, may, ere this, have started into existence, as I saw in the window of a son of Figaro some attempts at introducing a different description of literature; cheap editions of Shakspeare, Byron, and Moore being conspicuously displayed among periwigs, razor-strops, and Windsor soap. Any thing in the shape of an engraving or work of art is as unknown as in the wilds of Labrador ; and a recent attempt to introduce such was attended with considerable loss to the spirited but unfortunate speculator. The château or castle of St. Louis, the residence of the governor, is commodious, and from the terrace or gallery overhanging the lower town there is a charming view of the St. Lawrence.

In the immediate neighbourhood are the two principal religious edifices, the Catholic and English Protestant cathedrals. The former is spacious, but, as regards the exterior, is totally devoid of ornament.

The high altar is splendidly enriched with gilding, and the walls are decorated with paintings, one of which was almost miraculously preserved in the ruins of the church, when it was set on fire by the bombs of the British army, during the siege of 1759.

The English church is a plain stone building, with a lofty tinned spire. The congregation, on the morning of our attendance, was not numerous. The service, as regards the officiating ministers, was well performed; but the musical department exhibited much weakness, the burden of the song falling upon half a dozen little urchins, in white surplices, whose small voices were wholly unequal to the task imposed upon them, unassisted as they were by more powerful lungs. Near the altar is a handsome marble monument to the late bishop of the diocese, Dr. Mountain.

The governor of the Canadas, Lieutenant-General Lord Aylmer, with his lady and suite, were present. The former was received at the gate of his mansion with all the pomp of military parade. I could not help contrasting this circumstance with the unpretending appearance of General Jackson, at Washington, who, although chief magistrate of an immense and powerful country, had not a single sentinel at his door, nor, when he appeared in public, was he attended by a servant.

Besides the two principal places of worship described, the methodists have also their Zion, and the Calvinistic Scotch their kirk; unopposed, as far as I could learn, by those theological reformers, the Unitarians.

As at Montreal, there is an extensive seminary attached to the cathedral, and a convent of nuns, at which places the children of the principal inhabitants receive their education.

Various were the novelties which we met with in Quebec; among others, the dog-carts particularly attracted our attention. These little vehicles, of which there are a number, are used for the conveyance of milk. Each cart contains two large tin vessels, and is generally drawn by one dog properly harnessed, and driven by a boy; who, when he has supplied his customers, takes his seat on the cart; and if perchance the road should be down a hill home, he drives at as quick a pace as his faithful companion can carry him; and, after a few hours' respite, poor Cæsar or Hector recommences his laborious round.

We found the markets very indifferently supplied with provisions, and the prices higher than in the cities of the United States. The same remark applies likewise to those essential articles, groceries, particularly to the teas, of which no fresh supply had been received for a long period. Of the produce of the country we met with maple sugar and syrup, both of which are much used by the Canadians.

The taste of the former, which is manufactured into hard cakes, is less agreeable to the English palate than the produce of the sugar cane, and, like Indian meal, would require time to reconcile one to the use of it.

The peasantry appeared a cheerful, healthy race. The men all wore woollen caps, either scarlet or grey, and capots, or coats with pointed hoods, like those worn by the Italian mariners, and on their feet a species of mocassin made of uncoloured leather.

On my expressing my doubts to a vender of these last-mentioned articles as to their durability, the irritated Canadian immediately seized a mocassin with his teeth, and, although he gnawed for some time with almost savage fury, sparing neither his grinders nor canines, he failed to penetrate the tough and well-stitched material, proving thereby the excellence of his wares. The most attractive of the inhabitants were the Indians, whom we saw in considerable numbers. The men had little to distinguish them from the tribes we had seen on the borders of Lake Erie, but the expressive features of the females were decidedly more prepossessing.

Their dress exhibited a compound of that of both sexes. Blue cloth pantaloons or trousers, a blanket folded round the body under the arms ; a beaver hat, with a broad band of silver lace; the ears, which are pierced round the edges, amply decorated with pendent glitter, and thick black hair hanging over their shoulders, seemed to be the *ne plus ultra* of fashion.

Some of these damsels, fairer than the rest, were pointed out to us, as being the daughters of Canadians who had intermarried with Indian women; and such occurrences are common.

These descendants of the aborigines possess villages and lands of their own, and receive large sums annually, in the shape of presents from the British government, to ensure, as it is said, their attachment.

The men are addicted to drinking spirits ; a vice rather encouraged than discountenanced in all British colonies, in order to promote, as it is called, the interests of our West India possessions.

Both sexes, but particularly the females, show much ingenuity in the fabrication of various articles of Indian dress, as well as models of canoes ; snow-shoes, and a hundred arctic bagatelles, which are bought by the British, and also by the numerous American strangers who visit the Canadas in the summer months.

CHAP. XXI.

THE environs of Quebec abound in picturesque and romantic scenery; but to a Briton,
the great interest is in the celebrated Plains of
Abraham, which, associated as they are with
our school reading, have already become classic ground.

These plains, where the forces of Britain,
under the gallant Wolfe, measured their
strength with those of France, under the
brave Montcalm, are a little more than a mile
from the city; and we embraced an early day
after our arrival to visit so famed a site.

Passing through St. John's Gate and its
winding outworks, we entered the populous
suburb of the same name, in which we saw
the Protestant burial-ground, I am sorry to
say, in a most disorderly state; and soon
after, reached the detached fortifications or
martello towers, which stand elevated above
the surrounding country. We here entered
upon the blood-stained field, much of which
is yet uninclosed, and is used for reviews of
the troops, and also as a race-course.

The identical spot where England's youthful

general expired in the arms of victory was pointed out to us. The day was clear, the sun shone bright, all nature wore a lively aspect; and the wild strawberry blossomed in beautiful simplicity where once had been the tug of war.

The woody cliffs to the St. Lawrence remain in the state in which they were at the period of the memorable battle; but a narrow winding road has been made by the Government from the cove, called after the intrepid commander, and where the army landed, to the plains.

On the beach, near this interesting spot, we saw several large ships on the stocks, and on passing a small snug public house, we were no less pleased than surprised to behold the well-known effigies of Tam O'Shanter and Souter Johnny, which were placed as ornaments in an upper window, no doubt oft-times recalling to the inmates, who were from the " land o' cakes," pleasing recollections of home and friends. The sight of these little mementos of the old country, amidst the unpruned forest in other lands, awoke sensations of a mixed and melancholy nature, only known to those who have been placed in similar situations.

Returning to the city by a route through a wood of firs, which had been recently tapped,

and whose wounds were still oozing, we passed
the site of the redoubt to which the troops of
Wolfe found themselves opposed at daybreak,
and also the ground over which the French
commander marched to the contest.

The glorious success of Wolfe has been a
favourite theme for the English historian to
the present day; but, without a wish to pluck
a leaf from the well-earned laurels of the hero,
whose plan of operations exhibited the highest
order of talent, and whose courage in the field
led him to jest at scars, it must be allowed,
that the difficulty of ascending the precipice
has been much exaggerated, it having been
performed in the night, without meeting with
any opposition from the enemy; and in regard
to the decisive action on the plains, although
the numerical forces of both parties were equal,
the British army was composed wholly of regulars, while half of that of the French consisted
of militia and Indians, who did not support
their general. The French regulars, however,
made amends for the want of courage in their
comrades, and the loss on both sides was considerable; the commanders in chief, as well as
their respective seconds, having all fallen.

A handsome obelisk, sixty-five feet in height,
has lately been erected, on an elevation near

the garden of the Governor's residence, to the memories of Wolfe and Montcalm. So French is the feeling, however, of the population, even at this day, that the memorial, although uniting, as it does, a compliment to the defeated party, has given offence; and this tribute to valour is viewed as a trophy of British prowess at the expense of France and her descendants, and a sentinel is posted at the base, to protect it from mutilation.

A more humble but interesting memorial of Wolfe exists in the town, in the shape of a carved wooden figure, which is placed in a niche in the front of a small tavern.

This humble work of art, which is about four feet in height, represents the youthful General dressed in his regimentals, the colours of which are red faced with yellow, with a white belt, and wearing, as the officers did at that period, what are called side-arms. The cuffs of the coat are of the true Justice Woodcock dimensions, as well as the three cornered hat. On the pedestal, in old fashioned letters, is the inscription, JAMES WOLFE. As this effigy was executed soon after the death of the gallant commander, there is no doubt that it presents us with a fac-simile of the man; and although one should not wish to see it embellishing a

E E

public square, or a classical hall, yet should it be most religiously preserved in its present situation, as long as the country remains under British rule.

The lower, or mercantile town of Quebec, as it may be called, being the seat of the commerce of the port, skirts the base of the mountain. Near its southern extremity, which is the hive of the labouring classes, under Cape Diamond, is the spot where the brave Montgomery gloriously fell, in the daring but unsuccessful attack on Quebec, on the 31st of December, 1775. At the period in question, the passage between the mountain and the river was extremely narrow and rugged, and although the construction of wharfs and stores has altered its appearance, the exact situation of the battery from which he and his aids-de-camp received the fatal discharge, may be readily understood.

The whole of the lower town, during our short residence at Quebec, exhibited considerable bustle, from the number of vessels daily arriving from Great Britain, not only with general cargoes, but with emigrants, who were landing by thousands. The great majority were of the poorest description from Ireland; but some were English farmers, who had brought their families, and such small sums of money as they could raise, to try their fortunes in the New World. All were proceeding towards the borders of Lake Ontario; where, as Franklin expressed himself, when speaking of the emigrants in his day to Philadelphia, the question is not, Who are you? but, What can you do? and where, as in the United States, high wages and cheap food await the industrious labourer or artisan, although he may not as there enjoy the great privilege of a freeman, — a voice in the affairs of the country.

In my rambles, I witnessed the humiliating spectacle of a fellow creature standing in the pillory. The offence for which the unfortunate individual was thus punished, was enticing soldiers to desert. I was also several times present at auction sales; at which, as many of the buyers did not understand French, the auctioneer also used the English language; and the rapid transition from one to the other, in expatiating on the excellence of the articles, or in the advance of the biddings, produced a singular effect.

The shortness of our stay in Canada precluded the possibility of my acquiring such an insight into the character and habits of the

people, as our long residence in the United
States had afforded in regard to the Americans; it was, however, sufficient to enable
me to view the most striking features, as well
as to make some observations upon things as
we found them in this favourite but expensive
colony. The Canadians of all ranks are strict
Catholics; observing the different fasts and
ordinances, and making their reverences to
the clergy, who wear their cassocks in the
streets, with all the scrupulosity of the natives
of Spain or Portugal. Theatrical performances are wholly forbidden, as well as the
study of the works of those luminaries of
French literature, Voltaire, Rousseau, and
others of the galaxy of talent, whose labours
are to be found on the book-shelves of almost
every individual in France.

However rigid the ecclesiastical rule may be,
it is but just to observe, that the Catholic
clergy of Canada, like their fellow labourers
of the same faith in every clime, are distinguished by their attentions to the spiritual
wants of their flocks; and by day or by night,
in summer's heat or winter's cold, the priest
as cheerfully obeys the call of the poor, and
them that have none to help them, as that of

the rich man who is clothed in purple and fine linen.*

* Since the above was written, the author has been favoured by his friend Dr. Harlan, of Philadelphia, with a copy of the very interesting Report of the Medical Deputation, of which Dr. H. was a member, from the Sanitary Board of that city to Canada, during the prevalence of the late awful and mysterious epidemic.

The devoted attentions of the clergy to the sick and dying, are stated to have been most praiseworthy, but he cannot resist extracting a passage from the pamphlet in question, which displays the exemplary conduct of one individual in particular, and affords an example of genuine practical Christianity, as delightful to contemplate as it is worthy of imitation.

Speaking of the Indian settlement called Caughnawaga, the inhabitants of which suffered severely by the pestilence, Dr. Harlan thus expresses himself: —

" This village, an ancient settlement of the Indians of the same name, a band of the Iroquois, is situated on the right bank of the St. Lawrence, eleven miles west of Montreal. It is located on an elevated plane of secondary limestone, covered with gravel and clay, and contains 1000 Christian Indians, under the fatherly and spiritual direction of Mr. Mann, a Catholic priest, highly respected for his devotion, love of truth, and eminent Christian virtues. During the fatal pestilence, which laid waste this remnant of the Aborigines, he exercised towards these children the offices of father, friend, physician, nurse, and spiritual comforter and guide."

It is impossible to peruse this simple eulogium, without being reminded of the Divine declaration touching good works, — " *Verily, I say unto you, Inasmuch as ye have done it unto one of the least of these my brethren, ye have done it unto me.*"

As to the newspapers of Quebec, they are merely apologies for such publications, and reminded me strongly of those precious specimens in this department of literature, — the Gazettes of Milan or Naples. Whether any degree of censorship is exerted by the ecclesiastical or civil governors, I did not ascertain : be this as it may, however, the limited diffusion of political knowledge in Lower Canada, compared with the wholesome agitation of such subjects in the United States, was strikingly apparent, and impressed me with very unfavourable ideas of the state of Canadian government.

Independent of the excessive severity of the climate, and the almost general use of the French language, the nature of the tenures of lands, and the antiquated system of jurisprudence, are also serious obstacles to the English settler in this quarter; where such is the power of the aristocracy and the superior clergy, fostered as it has been for political purposes by the British government, that if we may credit the words of an intelligent native with whom I conversed, " it is quite useless to go to law with a seigneur or a priest." The middle classes are, however, gradually gaining strength ; and, taking a leaf from their neighbours' book, are beginning boldly to assert their rights.

The conciliatory behaviour of the Canadian executive, who, in addition to the fairest promises of attention to the public wish, had actually began to fulfil such, by dismissing the King's Attorney-General at the desire of the people, proves that their voice is heard.

That the policy of the British government will henceforth be more in unison with the voice of the colonists, and that measures worthy of an enlightened ministry, which numbers amongst its members the greatest man of the age, will be pursued, is certain; still it must not be concealed that we hold the Canadas, not by any attachment of the inhabitants, who have nothing in common with us; but by the numerous army dispersed in all the populous places, where a sentinel is visible at every turn; and by the influence of the immense sums granted for the making of canals and for other public works. Whenever these are withdrawn, it requires little of the spirit of prophecy to foretell the result, which would unquestionably be the establishment of two independent republics,—a consummation equally beneficial to the Canadas as to Great Britain.

Being anxious to reach England, we did not

prolong our stay in Quebec to the extent desired either by our friends or ourselves.

Having selected a ship of good repute, bound to Liverpool, we reluctantly took leave of our Canadian acquaintance, and embarked on the 21st of May, 1831, amidst a crowd of miserable Irish emigrants, who had just landed in rags and filth from their fertile but much oppressed country.

Loosing every sheet, we soon felt the influence of a delightful breeze, which, together with the current, carried us swiftly but smoothly along, affording us varied and charming views of Quebec, Point Levi, and the stupendous falls of Montmorenci, until the Isle of Orleans shut out the magnificent scene from the sight.

The St. Lawrence, immediately below this fine island, is no less than fifteen miles in width; and it gradually expands, until it merges into the gulf of that name, where it reaches ninety miles.

The right bank, for nearly 150 miles, is, like the district above Quebec, studded with villages, among which that of Camourasca is noted for the beauty of its situation. In the background rise the lofty mountains, which until lately were the supposed boundary of the United States in this direction; but which, by the decision of the King of the Netherlands, fall in the British territories.

At Green Island, opposite the great river Saguenay, our pilot bade us farewell. Here the water was brackish ; and soon after, the appearance of floating sea-weed, bespoke our approach to the great ocean.

The shores of the territory of Gaspee are bold and precipitous, and covered with eternal forests. A too near approach to these inhospitable regions, occasioned by the force of the current during a calm, afforded us more than a hasty view of one point, where frowning pine-crowned bluffs, in the gloomy recesses of which lay the winter's snow, presented no very cheering spectacle in the event of our being driven upon this savage coast.

Passing the long, low, uninhabited island of Anticosti, which lies in the middle of the Gulf of St. Lawrence, and famed, by the accounts of shipwrecked mariners, for its numerous bears, we got a glimpse of the dangerous cluster of rocks called the Bird Islands, from the quantities of sea-fowl which hover about them.

After fifteen days' sailing in the intricate and often tempestuous approach to the St. Lawrence, during which we had enjoyed all the variety that such a cruise affords, in the sight of whales, seals, and porpoises, gulls and petrels, we descried the misty mountains of Newfoundland, and occasionally spoke some of the small coasting sloops belonging to that country of fogs and storms. A smart and favourable gale springing up, carried us briskly to the great bank, on which we passed through a fleet of fishing vessels at anchor. It being night, they had lights at the mast-heads; a precaution necessary to escape being run down by larger vessels sailing in this track.

These comfortless barks are constructed internally so that the body of the fish, the livers, and the offal, may be kept apart. The fish is dried on shore; the liver is converted into oil, and the offal is thrown into the sea at a distance from the fishing grounds. The cod-fish are caught by lines; the bait being lowered to the bottom, which, in the usual resorts of the fishermen, is about thirty fathoms.

One could not behold this little fleet tossing on the boisterous ocean, so far from land, without increased admiration of the philosophical daring of Columbus, who, with vessels scarcely larger than those employed in the fisheries, undertook his glorious enterprise on the then unknown waste of waters, and gave a new world to civilised Europe.

The wind sat in the shoulder of our sail ; and after fourteen days' ploughing the deep, and occasionally spying a vessel in the horizon, but looking in vain for the three chimneys, or any other of the thousand dangers displayed in the older charts, — all which sources of alarm and anxiety to the mariner have probably been nothing more than dead whales, or water-logged wrecks,—we obtained soundings ; and, as the mists of morning dispersed, we discerned Cape Clear, the most westerly point of the Emerald Isle.

In the course of the day, we were hailed by the crews of several fishing-boats from Baltimore, — the insignificant port which gave the title to the settler of Maryland, and which is perpetuated in the name of its chief city. These hardy and industrious individuals brought us fresh fish, vegetables, and eggs ; but the shortness of our passage rendered such luxuries less welcome than they would have been to the more distant voyager. Nevertheless we regaled these good-hearted fellows, whose wildness of manner and attire exceeded any thing I had ever witnessed, with a few bottles of rum, with which they appeared much delighted.

Our sail up the Irish Channel was rendered particularly agreeable by the union of a fair wind and charming weather; and we, with our agreeable fellow-passengers, Major K——— and lady, were again enabled to enjoy the smoking board, which the unbounded hospitality of our skilful and generous captain displayed.

In our conviviality we did not forget the well-known old song, —

" Ye gentlemen of England, who live at home at ease,
Ah, little do ye think upon the dangers of the seas ;"

the true feeling for the excellences of which can only be properly understood by those who have rode o'er the foaming billows,

" When the stormy winds do blow."

Having taken on board a pilot, the very antipode of the one under whose guidance we entered the harbour of New York, and the breeze continuing fair, the bleak bold coasts of Anglesea and North Wales were soon passed ; and at sunset, on the 21st of June, 1831, we anchored in old Mersey's tide, and the next morning landed in the *portus omnium gen-*

tium, Liverpool, after an absence of two years and six weeks.

The facilities shown in the inspection and passing of the baggage were highly creditable to the Custom-house establishment of the port, as well as to the Government; the most gentlemanly behaviour on the part of the officers being combined with a proper regard to the protection of the revenue.

Once more at home, we enjoyed its pleasures among those we loved, not a little heightened by the resumption of some of those national habits which the traveller in foreign climes is for a season obliged to abandon.

As an Englishman, deeply imbued with *amor patriæ,* and mixing again with Englishmen, I hailed the increased diffusion of information and liberal opinions in politics and political economy with pleasure.

The mass of the population seemed to have turned over a new leaf, and to have at last found out the philosophers' stone, — " that magistrates were set up for the good of nations, not nations for the honour or glory of magistrates."

Amidst so much to cheer and delight, however, the aristocratic bearing and purse-inflated display of the higher classes, contrasted with

the cringing servility, the abject poverty, and
the squalid wretchedness of the lower, were
strikingly apparent to us, who had been resid-
ing in a land where, generally speaking, there
is neither poverty nor riches; but where all
are fed, as a wise and beneficent Creator intended, with food convenient for them.

THE END.

LONDON :
Printed by A. & R. Spottiswoode,
New-Street-Square.

Foreign Travelers in America
1810–1935

AN ARNO PRESS COLLECTION

Archer, William. **America To-Day**: Observations and Reflections. 1899.

Belloc, Hilaire. **The Contrast.** 1924.

[Boardman, James]. **America, and the Americans.** By a Citizen of the World. 1833.

Bose, Sudhindra. **Fifteen Years in America.** 1920.

Bretherton, C. H. **Midas, Or, The United States and the Future.** 1926.

Bridge, James Howard (Harold Brydges). **Uncle Sam at Home.** 1888.

Brown, Elijah (Alan Raleigh). **The Real America.** 1913.

Combe, George. **Notes on the United States Of North America During a Phrenological Visit in 1838-9-40.** 1841. 2 volumes in one.

D'Estournelles de Constant, Paul H. B. **America and Her Problems.** 1915.

Duhamel, Georges. **America the Menace:** Scenes from the Life of the Future. Translated by Charles Miner Thompson. 1931.

Feiler, Arthur. **America Seen Through German Eyes.** Translated by Margaret Leland Goldsmith. 1928.

Fidler, Isaac. **Observations on Professions, Literature, Manners, and Emigration, in the United States and Canada, Made During a Residence There in 1832.** 1833.

Fitzgerald, William G. (Ignatius Phayre). **Can America Last?** A Survey of the Emigrant Empire from the Wilderness to World-Power Together With Its Claim to "Sovereignty" in the Western Hemisphere from Pole to Pole. 1933.

Gibbs, Philip. **People of Destiny:** Americans As I Saw Them at Home and Abroad. 1920.

Graham, Stephen. **With Poor Immigrants to America.** 1914.

Griffin, Lepel Henry. **The Great Republic.** 1884.

Hall, Basil. **Travels in North America in the Years 1827 and 1828.** 1829. 3 volumes in one.

Hannay, James Owen (George A. Birmingham). **From Dublin to Chicago:** Some Notes on a Tour in America. 1914.

Hardy, Mary (McDowell) Duffus. **Through Cities and Prairie Lands:** Sketches of an American Tour. 1881.

Holmes, Isaac. **An Account of the United States of America,** Derived from Actual Observation, During a Residence of Four Years in That Républic, Including Original Communications. [1823].

Ilf, Ilya and Eugene Petrov. **Little Golden America:** Two Famous Soviet Humorists Survey These United States. Translated by Charles Malamuth. 1937.

Kerr, Lennox. **Back Door Guest.** 1930.

Kipling, Rudyard. **American Notes.** 1899.

Leng, John. **America in 1876:** Pencillings During a Tour in the Centennial Year, With a Chapter on the Aspects of American Life. 1877.

Longworth, Maria Theresa (Yelverton). **Teresina in America.** 1875. 2 volumes in one.

Low, A[lfred] Maurice. **America at Home.** [1908].

Marshall, W[alter] G[ore]. **Through America:** Or, Nine Months in the United States. 1881.

Mitchell, Ronald Elwy. **America:** A Practical Handbook. 1935.

Moehring, Eugene P. **Urban America and the Foreign Traveler, 1815-1855.** With Selected Documents on 19th-Century American Cities. 1974.

Muir, Ramsay. **America the Golden:** An Englishman's Notes and Comparisons. 1927.

Price, M[organ] Philips. **America After Sixty Years:** The Travel Diaries of Two Generations of Englishmen. 1936.

Sala, George Augustus. **America Revisited:** From the Bay of New York to the Gulf of Mexico and from Lake Michigan to the Pacific. 1883. 3rd edition. 2 volumes in one.

Saunders, William. **Through the Light Continent;** Or, the United States in 1877-8. 1879. 2nd edition.

Smith, Frederick [Edwin] (Lord Birkenhead). **My American Visit.** 1918.

Stuart, James. **Three Years in North America.** 1833. 2 volumes in one.

Teeling, William. **American Stew.** 1933.

Vivian, H. Hussey. **Notes of a Tour in America from August 7th to November 17th, 1877.** 1878.

Wagner, Charles. **My Impressions of America.** Translated by Mary Louise Hendee. 1906.

Wells, H. G. **The Future in America:** A Search After Realities. 1906.